Black Intimacies

THE GENDER LENS SERIES

Series Editors

Judith A. Howard
University of Washington

Barbara Risman
North Carolina State University

Joey Sprague
University of Kansas

The Gender Lens Series has been conceptualized as a way of encouraging the development of a sociological understanding of gender. A "gender lens" means working to make gender visible in social phenomena; asking if, how, and why social processes, standards, and opportunities differ systematically for women and men. It also means recognizing that gender inequality is inextricably braided with other systems of inequality. The Gender Lens series is committed to social change directed toward eradicating these inequalities. Originally published by Sage Publications and Pine Forge Press, all Gender Lens books are now available from AltaMira Press.

BOOKS IN THE SERIES

Yen Le Espiritu, *Asian American Women and Men: Labor, Laws, and Love*

Judith A. Howard and Jocelyn A. Hollander, *Gendered Situations, Gendered Selves: A Gender Lens on Social Psychology*

Michael A. Messner, *Politics of Masculinities: Men in Movements*

Scott Coltrane, *Gender and Families*

Myra Marx Ferree, Judith Lorber, and Beth B. Hess, editors, *Revisioning Gender*

Pepper Schwartz and Virginia Rutter, *The Gender of Sexuality: Exploring Sexual Possibilities*

Francesca M. Cancian and Stacey J. Oliker, *Caring and Gender*

M. Bahati Kuumba, *Gender and Social Movements*

Toni M. Calasanti and Kathleen F. Slevin, *Gender, Social Inequalities, and Aging*

Judith Lorber and Lisa Jean Moore, *Gender and the Social Construction of Illness, Second Edition*

Shirley A. Hill, *Black Intimacies: A Gender Perspective on Families and Relationships*

Black Intimacies

A Gender Perspective on Families and Relationships

Shirley A. Hill

ALTAMIRA
PRESS

A Division of
ROWMAN & LITTLEFIELD PUBLISHERS, INC.
Walnut Creek • Lanham • New York • Toronto • Oxford

ALTAMIRA PRESS
A division of Rowman & Littlefield Publishers, Inc.
1630 North Main Street, #367
Walnut Creek, California 94596
www.altamirapress.com

Rowman & Littlefield Publishers, Inc.
A wholly owned subsidiary of The Rowman & Littlefield Publishing Group, Inc.
4501 Forbes Boulevard, Suite 200
Lanham, Maryland 20706

PO Box 317
Oxford
OX2 9RU, UK

British Library Cataloguing in Publication Information Available

Library of Congress Cataloging-in-Publication Data

Hill, Shirley A. (Shirley Ann), 1947–
    Black intimacies : a gender perspective on families and relationships / Shirley A. Hill.
    p. cm. — (Gender lens series)
    Includes bibliographical references and index.
    ISBN 0-7591-0151-5 (hbk : alk. paper) —ISBN 0-7591-0152-3 (pbk : alk. paper)
    1. African American families. I. Title. II. Series.

E185.86.H666 2004
306.8'089'96073—dc22
                                                                2004013259

Printed in the United States of America

♾™ The paper used in this publication meets the minimum requirements of American
National Standard for Information Sciences—Permanence of Paper for Printed Library
Materials, ANSI/NISO Z39.48-1992.

CONTENTS

Confronting the Challenge of Voluntary and
    Equitable Motherhood
Summary

ACKNOWLEDGMENTS

I owe a tremendous debt of gratitude to Barbara Risman for her championing and support of this book. She heaped praise on my earliest drafts, offered encouragement and insightful comments, and is incredibly fast with feedback—especially for someone who at any point might be practically anywhere on the globe. Thanks so much, Barbara! I would also like to thank Judy Aulette and Donna Franklin for reviewing the manuscript and making some very helpful observations. I thank my son, Edwin Jr., for his feedback on some early drafts and also my husband, Edwin Sr., for patiently proofreading every chapter, often several times. Finally and foremost, I thank God for constantly bringing new opportunities into my life that stretch me intellectually and spiritually.

CHAPTER 1

Postmodern Chasms
The Politics of Inequality

Indeed, there is no major area of American life these days, from education to politics to religion, where society is not coming to terms with a
new black leadership class–one whose credentials, in many cases, have
very little to do with their color, and one whose very existence raises
questions about the continuing viability of the "black leadership"
mode of old.

—Ellis Cose[1]

Progress by African Americans during the latter half of the twentieth century was nothing short of astounding. As the legitimacy of racial segregation and exclusion began to crumble under the weight of a vibrant,
well-organized social protest movement, African Americans moved rapidly to take advantage of expanding educational and economic opportunities. The rate of high school completion among blacks quadrupled
between 1960 and the 1990s, and the number attaining a college degree
more than doubled. By 2001, more than 16 percent of black people over
the age of twenty-five had completed four or more years of college (compared to 3.5 percent in 1960),[2] and nearly 23 percent held managerial/
professional positions.[3] Between 1967 and 1997, the median household income for African Americans grew faster than it did for white households,
the rate of black poverty fell to a historic low of less than 25 percent,[4] and
Ellis Cose, long a critic of how racism had marred the lives of even successful blacks, heralded what he described as a startling ascension of
black males to the "universe of the corporate gods."[5]

This economic and educational progress has been mirrored in other
important arenas, such as literature, politics, and the media. Scholarship

1

on African Americans has proliferated, with black people playing key roles in articulating and analyzing their own historic and current experiences. Media representations capture much of their class and lifestyle diversity in television shows like *Family Matters*, the *Cosbys*, and *Living Single*, whose contents imply that race is fairly irrelevant in the lives of black people. Gains on the political front have also been remarkable: In its January/February 2004 edition, *The Crisis* reported that the number of black elected officials increased from 1,469 to 9,101 between 1970 and 2001. The century also witnessed innumerable black firsts, including the establishment of the country's first national holiday honoring a black American, Martin Luther King.

Acknowledging the great advances of the twentieth century suggests neither that racism is dead nor that African Americans have gained parity with whites. Racist ideologies, policies, and practices, upheld by law, custom, and organized violence, were used to justify more than 250 years of slavery, followed by another century of racial segregation, and race remains a key factor in shaping the life chances of black people. Much of the struggle for racial justice has revolved around refuting ubiquitous stereotypes and myths about black people that impugned virtually every aspect of their lives and culture (e.g., their intelligence, morality, sexuality, attractiveness, family organization). Ideologies of blacks as inferior, subhuman, and threatening sanctioned slavery, segregation, and oppression and yielded immense benefits to capitalism by allowing it to fully exploit the economic and reproductive labor of African Americans.

Yet black people have fought consistently to expand their position, power, and participation in American society, whether through outright rebellion, organized protests, the courts, or the quiet encouragement of parents who insisted that their children could transcend racial barriers. Growing up in a city distinguished by its support for racial segregation—Birmingham, Alabama—National Security Adviser Condoleezza Rice said her parents "couldn't sit at the Woolworth counter, but they believed I could be president."[6] They invested heavily in Rice's educational and social development, their aspirations reinforced by a supportive community determined to prepare their children for a better life. Indeed, it was multiple forms of personal and public resistance to racism, discrimination, and political disenfranchisement that culminated in the civil rights movement of the 1960s and forged black unity around the issue of ending racist laws and practices.

Civil rights activists called on America to live up to its ideology of equality and, especially through nonviolent protest, touched the conscience of the nation. Vital to the project of ending racial oppression was a redefinition of blackness that countered hegemonic notions of race and insisted that black people were "human" and thus entitled to liberty, integrity, and opportunity. The historic and pervasive denigration of African Americans in virtually every aspect of the dominant culture made redefining blackness a massive project: Overt and subtle expressions of racism were challenged; patterns of institutionalized racism were uncovered; and media portrayals linking blacks with crime, welfare, and deviance were increasingly criticized as racist. Civil rights leaders constructed a poignant yet ultimately simplistic portrait of the African American population that rejected theories of innate black inferiority, shifted the focus from biological to social and legal definitions of race, and demanded the racial integration of public facilities and equal access to education, housing, and employment. Black people coalesced around support for racial liberation, and, despite sharp differences in strategies for achieving that goal, perceptions of solidarity enhanced their political clout and elevated the importance of their mission on the nation's agenda.

The saliency of race, however, frequently suppressed the reality of intraracial divisions among blacks by creating carefully cultivated Rosa Parks–like images of valiant black respectability that was ever demeaned by senseless racism. Mainstream civil rights activism embodied Gunnar Myrdal's comforting claim that "the Negro is only an American and nothing else,"[7] and it implicitly promised that blacks, freed from segregation and oppression, would conform to dominant societal values. Yet, despite immense progress, African Americans have remained overrepresented among those who are poor and unemployed.

Images of black solidarity and unity provided a solid basis in arguing for civil rights and an end to racial segregation; indeed, the simple black/white dichotomy of race and racial privilege promulgated by the civil rights movement, along with its sanitized portrait of African Americans, effectively politicized the issue of racial inequality. It generated a wealth of scholarship documenting the history of black people, fostered new images and definitions of blackness, and supported policies of racial justice. The emphasis on abolishing socially and legally sanctioned racial segregation demanded a singular external focus on the debilitating consequences of racism, a focus that of necessity trumped any investigation of intraracial divisions among African Americans. But now, more than forty years after the civil rights movement's historic March on Washington, achieving racial equity remains an elusive goal. Moreover, notions of racial pride and unity have faltered as it became clear that chanting pride in blackness could never completely erase the psychological damage of internalized racism, that the appeal for racial solidarity could not dispense with crucial class and cultural differences among black people, and that revolutionary calls for racial liberation that ignored or even endorsed gender oppression could not silence the voices of black women.

I contend that the very success of the civil rights movement has exacerbated and brought to the fore class, race, and gender divisions among African Americans, rendering the image of a monolithic black population impossible to sustain in the postmodern era. That image has been permanently fractured by the demand of black women that gender oppression be addressed, the sharpening of class polarization, the rise of a new generation of artists and writers creating and glorifying black cultural expressions once deemed unacceptable by the old guard, and a surge in the number of interracial people and black immigrant groups—all of whom challenge the very meaning of blackness. The growing diversity of black people has resulted in disenchantment with the political leaders and organizations of the civil rights era, as well as more dissension over the definition, consequences, and solutions to racism.

Although virtually no one contends that racism is dead, it has clearly lost much of its privileged position in explaining racial inequality and the persistent problems plaguing black America. In a sharp break with the civil rights logic of white racism as the formidable barrier, scholars today are beginning to expand their focus to a broader range of institutionalized inequities. Within this evolving framework, the study of gender among black people, often subordinated to the research on racial inequality, has contributed to the development of intersectionality theory—an interdisciplinary perspective that addresses the multiple, intersecting systems of oppression especially experienced by women of color.

The Evolution of Intersectionality Theory

In a curious twist of fate, we find ourselves marginal to both the movements for women's liberation and black liberation, irrespective of our victimization under the dual discriminations of racism and sexism.

—Deborah K. King[8]

Gender is intricately implicated in virtually every aspect of African American life, yet, despite the work of some nineteenth-century feminists of color, the full significance of gender inequality and its relationship to class and race was not systematically explored until the civil rights era. During the 1960s, Frances Beale described being black and female as "double jeopardy,"[9] and scholars have since argued that inequalities based gender, race, and social class intersect and act synergistically to construct the social location of women of color within multiple systems of domination.[10] Multicultural and multiracial feminism evolved from this theorizing, which, as Rose Brewer has noted, recognizes that for African American women, "gender takes on meaning and is embedded institutionally in context of the racial and class order: productive and social reproductive relations of the economy."[11] The central role of racial domination has been underscored by Bonnie Thornton Dill and Maxine Baca Zinn in their preference for the concept of multiracial rather than multicultural feminism. They argue that while multicultural may simply denote different backgrounds and histories, "multiracial feminism" recognizes race as a power system and as the fundamental organizing principle of social relationships. Intersectionality theory embraces and even broadens these tenets by including inequalities that transcend the class, race, and gender dynamic. Patricia Hill Collins describes intersectionality theory this way:

> The construct of intersectionality references two types of relationships: the interconnectedness of ideas and the social structures in which they occur, and the intersecting hierarchies of gender, race, economic class, sexuality, and ethnicity. Viewing gender within the logic of intersectionality redefines it as a constellation of ideas and social practices that are historically situated within and that mutually construct multiple systems of oppression.[12]

The matrix of domination approach, or intersectionality theory, was prefigured in the early social activism and writings of black feminist pioneers such as Sojourner Truth, Anna Julia Cooper, Ida B. Wells, and Fannie Lou Hamer, all of whom understood that black women were penalized by the inequalities of race, gender, and poverty yet found themselves more or less ignored by liberation movements led by black men or white women. Even before slavery ended, African American men were lobbying for patriarchal privileges, especially in their families, and saw the subjugation and control of black women as essential to their mission.[13] Black and white women occasionally joined forces in their quest for gender justice during the nineteenth century, yet racism undermined the strength of such coalitions. For the most part, African American women were left to establish their own organizations, and in doing so they tackled an array of issues impinging on the welfare of African Americans. The historic social activism of black women and their remarkable record of self-help and community work in dealing with the health, education, housing, and economic needs of their people is now widely documented. For example, the National Association of Colored Women, formed in 1896, called on women to engage in race work specifically because they were wives and mothers, and Mary McLeod Bethune's National Council of Negro Women intended to "harness woman power to fight oppressive and demoralizing poverty, unemployment and racism, hunger and malnutrition, unfair housing and unresponsive social services."[14]

This legacy of activism somehow seemed lost or trivialized during the 1960s, when black women found themselves excluded from full participation in both the civil rights and the feminist movement. Myra Marx Ferree and Beth B. Hess describe the civil rights movement as essentially a continuation and expansion of a more than century-long struggle against racial injustice that originated among southern blacks.[15] Rather than including the challenges of class and gender inequality in their activism, however, most civil rights activists sought racial integration, political participation, and equal opportunity for blacks within the existing framework. By 1970, the civil disobedience and nonviolent protest of the early movement had taken a decidedly militant and masculinist stance. Black males were seen as the central victims of racial oppression, and leaders of the movement shied away from addressing issues such as welfare and poverty among black women and children.[16]

In a radical critique of white racism, black power advocates began to demand, as Leith Mullings points out, an "autonomous geographic, institutional, or cultural space that allows [blacks] to participate as equals, either within the parameters of the state or in an altered political relationship with Euro-American civil society."[17] Yet their vision of freedom focused on the liberation of black men and the relegation of women to secondary roles. Indeed, the subordination of women was often seen as a critical step to the empowerment of black men, and black women who resisted found themselves harshly castigated and even ostracized. In her book *Too Heavy a Load*, historian Deborah Gray White quotes a black female activist who described the role of women in the black power movement this way: "[A woman] was considered, at best, irrelevant. A woman asserting herself was a pariah. A woman attempting the role of leadership was . . . making an alliance with the counterrevolutionary, man-hating, lesbian, feminist white bitches."[18]

The blatant sexism experienced by black women made their acknowledgment of gender oppression inevitable, yet few were able to find a comfortable niche in the mostly white, middle-class feminist movement. Ferree and Hess point out that while the leadership of the women's movement has always included some women of color, the majority of black women saw feminism as failing to meet their specific needs and, at worst, simply racist. All too often, black women faced "indifference to their concerns, disregard of their contributions, patronizing efforts to "recruit" and "educate" them to support goals and priorities established by white women."[19] In addition to the sexism of the male-dominated civil rights movement and the racism of white feminism that made it difficult for black women to articulate their own experiences, there was a central conflict in the goals of the civil rights and feminist movements: One sought to institute and the other to undermine patriarchy. As Ferree and Hess note:

> Much of the African-American male leadership, and virtually all of their white male sympathizers, believed that the costs of racism were borne primarily by black men, "emasculated" by their lack of economic power. They claimed that without the power that comes from earnings, black men "lost" control over their families, and without the ability to dominate their wives and children they lost self-respect. The ideal that men should be sole providers for their families was accepted uncritically, so that poverty was seen as a blow to the male ego, the only ego that counted.[20]

Support for patriarchy by black men generated ambivalence for black female activists by placing the gender issue squarely on the agenda. Yet, I have often maintained that the study of gender entered African American scholarship through the back door, making its first rather subtle entrance in reaction to the "black matriarch thesis," and then more overtly as literature by black women exploring their own experiences led to a revolutionary expansion of African American studies and feminist thinking. As early as the 1920s, scholars like E. Franklin Frazier were describing black families as matriarchal, yet the issue of female-headed families did not become politically charged until it was implied during the civil rights era that women reigned over and/or dispensed with men in black families, thus laying a foundation for weak families that impeded racial progress. Revisionist family scholars of the mid–twentieth century rejected the notion of black single-mother families as a legacy of slavery or as inherently pathological. Rather, they recast them as products of persistent racism, yet as strong, viable units. The focus on the viability of female-headed families brought the roles of black women to the fore, yet it fell considerably short of a gender analysis. Indeed, as I argue (chapter 3), this work introduced a masculinist bias to the study of the history of black families, which I challenge with a postmodern analysis of black women's family decision making after the abolition of slavery.

By the 1980s, a proliferation of scholarship by women such as Darlene Clark Hine, Paula Giddings, Jacquelyn Jones, Bonnie Thornton Dill, and Deborah Gray White provided a rich historic context for understanding how race had shaped the gender experiences of black women. Like revisionist scholars, they rejected derogatory descriptions of black women as the matriarchal heads of dysfunctional families by capturing their strengths, sacrifices, and social activism, but they also noted the oppression they endured based on gender, class, and race. The central claim to emerge has been that, as a result of their specific social location, the experiences of African American women differed from those of both black men and white women. White feminists, for example, claim that while patriarchy is ancient in origin, the gendering of family work unfolded most prominently during the industrial transition of the 1800s, when the home and the labor market became separate spheres. Men were sanctioned as breadwinners, and women were stripped of their economic roles, relegated to the private sphere of the home and idealized as innately domestic and submissive. These historic experiences were, of course, at odds with those of African American women, most of whom were still enslaved when the cult of domesticity became the ideological norm for white women.

Slavery undermined the provider role for black men, whose position in the family was tenuous and often not even acknowledged, and forced black women to prioritize their work roles. Even after slavery ended, the sharecropping system, racial exclusion, poverty, and the need to survive kept most black women engaged in labor market work. The images used to control African Americans were also race- and gender-specific, although themes of sexual deviance and suitability for menial labor was implied in all of them. While depictions of black women as mammies, Jezebels, and matriarchs[21] justified their economic and sexual exploitations, images of black men as Sambos (docile, childlike), Jacks (stealthy, untrustworthy), and Nats (dangerous, rapists)[22] legitimized black male servitude and social control. Thus, racial subjugation was shaped by a gendered racism that degraded and demeaned the lives of black people, but it also exempted African Americans from the emerging ideology that relegated women to the home and from the restrictive boundaries of the new femininity. As a result, black women combined employment, family life, and social activism, thus fortifying images of themselves as strong, independent, and capable and garnering at least a modicum of equality with black men in their family lives.

In exploring the unique history of black women, a rich legacy of scholarship has now begun to reveal what P. H. Collins calls the subjugated knowledge about subordination of black women, a move necessary in the effort to "reconceptualize all dimensions of the dialectic of oppression and activism as it applies to African-American women."[23] Drawing on Nancy Hartsock's articulation of standpoint theory, which understands knowledge and ideology as shaped by social position, Collins points out that the interdependence between consciousness and experience has given rise to a unique self-defined black feminist standpoint on oppression. "Black women's ability to forge these individual, unarticulated, yet potentially powerful expressions of everyday consciousness into an articulated, self-defined, collective standpoint," according to Collins, "is key to Black women's survival."[24] This book expands the work that seeks to uncover and articulate the experiences of black women and thus the interactive nature of race, class, and gender oppression.

Focus and Framework of the Book

The current book brings a gender lens to the multiple systems of oppression that have shaped the lives of African American women and men. I focus on how gender is defined, enacted, performed, and perpetuated among black people, their attitudes and perceptions about the role of gender in their lives, and the broad implications of it in their experiences. Gender is so-cially constructed by broader societal forces but also is continually revised and revived by socioeconomic and political forces, and thus is an emergent category for understanding social life. With this in mind, I interrogate static social constructions of black cultural norms and even of black womanhood and bring fresh insights to the study of how gender, both at the structural and interactional levels, shapes the intimate and family lives of African Americans. I see this book as a "postmodern" analysis of the African American experience because it builds on and critiques revisionist and historical research of the civil rights era, challenges the idea of a universal black experience, highlights the diversity of African Americans, and brings a gender focus to areas rarely studied, such as how gender affects intraracial intimacy and child socialization. I use the word *chasm* to emphasis that the work explores the ever-evolving dynamic and divergent experiences of black people, especially based on gender, social class position, and political perspective.

The data used in this book are drawn from diverse literatures and sources—mostly academic research, but also the media, novels, biographies, and my own personal experiences. Key in shaping this analysis of gender is my own research, which has consisted primarily of ethnographic explorations and interviews (mostly with black women) in three specific areas: (1) family caregiving for children who are chronically ill; (2) the race, class, and gender socialization of children; and (3) genealogical interviews with family members.[25] Throughout the book, I use observations and quotes from more than seventy interviews I have conducted in conjunction with these projects. I also occasionally use interview data from other research projects, recontextualizing it for the purpose of this study. I see these diverse sources of literature and knowledge as critical in discussing the experiences and consciousness of African American people.

In this work, I hope to make three contributions to emerging literature on black people and the theoretical tools that are being used to produce it. My first and most general goal is to bring a "gender lens" to the exploration of how the identities and experiences of African Americans have been shaped by dominant societal norms about patriarchy or, perhaps more specifically, their lack of ideological commitment and/or economic resources necessary to conform to such norms. I contend that the key gender issues facing black people are tied to the fact that race and class oppression has left most of them at odds with dominant societal ideals about the appropriate roles of men and women and the proper formation of families, yet it has also penalized their cultural and structural adaptations to this oppression. In exploring these topics, I move beyond the static view of gender that draws more on the historic than the contemporary experiences of African Americans and analyses that fall short by failing to integrate the experiences of black men and women. I rethink cultural representations that implicitly depict black women as emerging valiantly from racial oppression and black men as perpetually crippled by it and explore how these images often become prescriptive in nature, perpetuating patterns of behavior that are inimical to the health and well-being of black people. Overall, I build on black feminist scholarship while also addressing its limitations with a more class-based, cultural, and intraracial look at how gender affects the intimate and family experiences of contemporary African Americans.

Second, I see this book as contributing to the development of intersectionality theory by integrating it into new areas of study and also by highlighting some of its limitations. The idea of recognizing the significance and interacting nature of race, class, gender, and sexual oppression is theoretically appealing, yet efforts to do so can yield a bewildering array of demographic categories (e.g., black/poor/female, wealthy/Hispanic/lesbian) that may ultimately mask the diverse experiences of the people within each category. Uniform populations rarely reside within categories that lump people together based on these variables; research like that of Elijah Anderson, for example, shows us that among poor black people there are multiple realities and adaptations to poverty, even though they ostensibly occupy the same race and class location. Moreover, despite the widespread criticism of processes such as "othering," the creation of irreconcilable categories may prove overly racialized (or gendered or classed) and run the risk of encouraging a focus on difference, while ignoring experiences common among women and undermining the viability of interracial coalitions. Race and class undoubtedly shape the lives and gender experiences of women, yet issues such as male domination, gender discrimination and occupational segregation at work, and the struggle to balance the demands of work and family affect all women.

Intersectionality theory also correctly identifies class as a dimension of domination, yet it often tacitly implies that it is a "jeopardy" faced by black women, thus ignoring class privilege and diversity among African

Americans. Race and class status are often conflated in ways that inadvertently construct images of "the black woman" on the experiences of those who are poor, and these images are then compared to middle-class white women to illustrate difference. The majority of African American women, however, are not poor, and throughout this book, I highlight the significance of class diversity and even class advantage in shaping political attitudes, marital prospects, and child-rearing work.

Race also falters as a unifying category of analysis in twenty-first-century postmodern America. Although now widely recognized as a social rather than biological construct, the social significance of race varies based on colorism (e.g., the intraracial status hierarchy based on skin tone) and has been further complicated by the growing number of interracial people who insist on claiming multiple ethnic heritages and by black immigrant groups who do not share the African American experience. As discussed in more detail in the next chapter, skin color has been historically linked to privilege, class position, and mobility among blacks, and the increasing number of blacks who identify as multiracial is likely to intensify these distinctions. The federal census for 2000 was the first to officially acknowledge the multiracial heritage of Americans by allowing the selection of more than one racial group. More than 7 million Americans identified themselves as multiracial, leaving nearly 13 percent of Americans (36.4 million people) indicating that they either were black or had black heritage.

Nonnative black immigrants from the Caribbean or Africa are also redefining the meaning of being black. At a predominantly white cosmetology school where I euphemistically ask for a black stylist (e.g., someone who can "work with ethnic hair"), I often am assigned to a black immigrant student for whom the African American experience is fairly meaningless. One Ethiopian student who came to the United States as a refugee, for example, shrugs off any discussion of racial politics and can scarcely say enough about the opportunity to work, get an education, and move ahead in American society. Indeed, the progress of black immigrants is now exceeding that of native-born black people, as evidenced by the recent observation that West Indian and African immigrants are significantly overrepresented among black undergraduate students at Harvard University.[26]

Finally, I hope this book contributes to a rethinking of the notion of culture, which I believe must be acknowledged and reintegrated with the dominant structural analyses of the African American experience. The culture of poverty thesis that originated in the 1950s described the seemingly self-defeating behaviors and attitudes of poor people as initially stemming from their exclusion from mainstream society but over time taking on a life of their own as a set of intergenerationally transmitted cultural values. Despite the recognition that structural forces of inequality (e.g., racial discrimination, poverty) shape people's behaviors, the culture of poverty thesis was used by a handful of early social scientists to explain the "pathological" behaviors of the poor racial minorities and these behaviors were often seen as causing the social problems that beset them. Such cultural analyses fell from grace during the civil rights era, when reiterated by D. Patrick Moynihan in his now-infamous study of black families. His implication that the lack of socioeconomic progress by blacks was linked to weak, dysfunctional female-headed families sparked a more than thirty-year controversy over the nature and viability of African American families. Revisionist scholars of the 1960s and 1970s worked hard (and rightly so) to shift the emphasis to the impact that structural forces such as racism, segregation, and racial exclusion had on black families and to see their adaptations to these forces as contributing to the strength of black families. The structural perspective was reactive in nature, fueled by efforts to dispel the seeming relentless criticism of blacks for failing to conform to the marital, family, and gender norms of the dominant society. It led to a critical rejection of the culture of poverty thesis, and, further fortified by William Ryan's potent argument against "blaming the victim," it has left many scholars highly skeptical of cultural analyses of African Americans.

While the emergence of the structural perspective challenged the hurtful legacy of erroneously attributing racial and class inequality to the cultural values of disadvantaged people, the dismissal of culture proves problematic in several important ways. Neglecting culture makes it difficult to understand how people adapt to poverty and oppression, masks human agency, and diminishes the credibility of scholarly work. Failing to consider culture can further victimize "the victims" by ignoring how oppressed people actively mediate structural forces and by inadvertently portraying them as puppets in the hands of an intractable social system. Yet those disadvantaged by class and racial inequalities have created multiple, inventive strategies for coping and actively participating in their own survival. Rose Brewer has argued that "a challenge to Black feminist theory is explicating the interplay between agency and social structure,"[27] yet neglecting culture tends to camouflage human agency rather than revealing the fact that poor African Americans can and do make effective, empowering individual choices. Black community organizations and churches have sought to end institutional and legal barriers to racial inequality, but they also tirelessly invest in self-help efforts designed to improve the quality of life for blacks—often with much success. Focusing solely on structural forces often (at least ideologically) places solutions and power outside the province of those who work hard to curb teenage pregnancy, drug abuse, and crime by suggesting that only changes in white racism and societal level forces can make a difference. Denied any responsibility for the adversities that they face or any power to effect change, marginalized populations are also logically deprived of credit for their own successes.

Beyond the theoretical merit of culture, the structural perspective, unhinged from culture, flies in the face of people's ordinary, everyday observations, leaving teachers and scholars with the uphill battle of proving that unseen social forces explain most human behavior. Although I see the structural perspective and the sociological imagination concept as key contributions to the study of human behavior and work hard to convey them to my undergraduate students, I am often disappointed with the results of essays where they are asked to explain their class, race, or gender biography in structural terms: Most simply do not quite get it and, worse yet, probably think that voicing any skepticism will mark them as ignorant and/or racist. While one can handily show the systematic nature of the outcomes of social inequality (e.g., lower wages for women, more crime and teenage pregnancy among the poor), explaining the success of many people despite these obstacles is difficult without discussing the interconnection among structure, culture, and human agency. Scholars *should* bring a broader analytical perspective to discussion of social issues, but it is often the case that our praxis distances us from the very people we claim to understand and speak for. Extolling the strengths of single-mother families, for example, may write out of the story their isolation and despair, and even avid support for generous welfare policies can ignore how welfare dependency devastates the self-esteem and psychological well-being of many poor women.[28]

Analytically, structural forces do deserve primacy in understanding oppression, as they create myriad policies and practices that naturalize, institutionalize, and perpetuate inequality. Yet structural and cultural forces interact in shaping behaviors, making it important to understand the multifaceted nature of culture and its consequences, although doing so is not always easy. There is no single, dominant, unifying culture among African Americans; indeed, A. Wade Boykin and Forrest Toms[29] have sought to bring some clarity to the issue by explaining that blacks are influenced by three intersecting cultures—the mainstream, black, and minority cultures. Ideologically, studies overwhelmingly show that black Americans support the values of the mainstream culture—those based on white, middle-class norms—although those who are disadvantaged by poverty often find that they are unable and/or unwilling to bring their behaviors into conformity with those norms. Black people in favorable economic circumstances do the best job of adhering to behaviors sanctioned by the dominant culture, but they also share with their less privileged counterparts unifying black cultural themes that have emerged from their African and American experiences. Afrocentric scholars, for example, argue that the African culture continues to shape the values of black people. They note that extended families, the value of motherhood, the productive labor roles of women, and the privileging of consanguinity over conjugal relations are all essentially retentions of African values, although their perpetuation has been a result of blacks' exclusion from the dominant society.[30] Although Afrocentrism presents a rather stagnant and unsatisfying view of black cultural norms as wedged in precolonial African values, the case remains that many African Americans do claim to cultivate and enact these cultural patterns of behavior.

The minority culture remains most controversial, generating arguments over whether the behaviors of poor black people are adaptations to poverty and racial exclusion or reflective of firmly entrenched yet distorted cultural values that impede their economic progress, perpetuate inequality, and contribute to a burdensome welfare system. Robin Jarrett points out that the "deviant cultural values" perspective has been pro-mulgated primarily by journalists and politicians, who seek to blame and punish poor people rather than by social scientists, most of whom see the minority culture as an adaptation to oppressive structural forces. Challenging the deviant cultural values thesis, for example, Ann Swidler explains that a culture "is not a unified system that pushes action in a consistent direction" but rather a "tool box" from which courses of action are devised to deal with everyday experiences.[31] Behaviors are even less tied to cultural values among those who have "unsettled lives" characterized by change and un-certainty. Swidler contends that "[a]ction is not determined by one's val-ues. Rather action *and* values are organized to take advantage of cultural competences."[32] Minority cultures clearly fit Swidler's insightful analysis, and the "tool boxes" they draw from contain behaviors that are conducive to survival as well as some that are destructive. Jarrett's research invokes culture to show how single black mothers cope with poverty, welfare, and social stigma, and she highlights their human agency and survival strate-gies. Yet it is also fair to acknowledge that race and class disadvantage can alter attitudes and behaviors in ways that perpetuate racial stereotypes and impede economic advancement. William J. Wilson, for example, argues that the economic transition of the 1970s, which left many young black men unemployed, undermined the sense of efficacy for many people in the in-ner-city black neighborhoods and led to a focus on dangerous expressions of masculinity (e.g., gang violence) and a growing tendency for men to denigrate women. While these behaviors are a response to racial oppres-sion and in some cases even an expression of resistance to it, whether seen as cultural "values" or "tools," they are deliberately cultivated for the pur-pose of achieving status and are pathological in that they promote violence and misogyny.

Another example of how poor people sometimes resort to behaviors that perpetuate their poverty is found in Sharon Hays's research on wel-fare reform. While her study substantiates the view that most poor women hold mainstream cultural values and are optimistic that job train-ing and employment will improve their lives, she also found that a sig-nificant minority—as many as one-third—did fit the stereotypes associated with the culture of poverty. Thus, a thorough analysis of race and class oppression must acknowledge that it promotes adaptive as well as maladaptive cultural behaviors.[33]

Overview of the Book

The key topic in chapter 2 is the historic and contemporary diversity among African Americans, especially based on class, color, race, and gen-der. I examine the historic social construction of race and its centrality in defining the black experience and the struggle to redefine the meaning of blackness during the civil rights era. I argue that a monolithic portrait of the black population emerged during the civil rights movement but that the movement's very success is now shattering black unity and solidarity. I document the emergence of class, color, and gender divisions that were obfuscated prior to the civil rights era but that have now been exacerbated, not only leading to a splintering of political unity among African Americans but also challenging the very meaning of being black. I discuss the racial disparities that continue to exist between blacks and whites based on income, wealth, health, and life satisfaction and the debate between those who see these disparities as a product of continuing racism and those who contend that racism is being overemphasized by those who insist on denying black progress and fail to consider how the behaviors of black people contribute to racial inequality.

Families, the topic of chapter 3, are pivotal in constructing, organizing, and perpetuating depictions of gender. Moreover, since American ideology defines the family narrowly and holds it responsible for the values, welfare, and socioeconomic success of its members, studies of black families have often been political and contentious. At the center of the dominant ideology is the contention that families should be composed of two-married parents; thus, most black family research has been fueled by efforts to either refute hegemonic depictions of the family or explain why so many black families have not conformed to that norm. In this chapter, I provide a critical overview of two genres of black family scholarship: the mostly pre–civil rights era work that claimed slavery had destroyed the black family and revisionist era work that, among other things, strongly contended that two-parent families were the norm during and after slavery. In contrast, I offer a postmodernist account of how gender shaped black families after slavery, highlighting black women's frequent resistance to the campaign to force them to marry after slavery. I contend that the extent to which African Americans complied with the marriage mandate has been overstated, as has the resiliency of those unions that were formed, and that black women often insisted on forming families according to cultural traditions that dated back to precolonial Africa and that were reinforced by slavery. Many working-class, poor, and even wealthy black women did not find patriarchal marriage and domestic life particularly appealing, a fact now being underscored by scholars such as Angela Davis in her research on legendary black female blues singers. Davis finds that their songs were remarkably devoid of themes of "children, domestic life, husbands, and marriage";[34] rather, they depicted women as free of domestic orthodoxy, both reclaiming their sexuality and resisting the objectification of it.

Chapter 3 concludes with a look at the economic and family declines experienced by poor blacks in the late twentieth century, noting that revisionist themes of resiliency in black families and the valorization of the single women who headed them were challenged as marriage rates plummeted and drugs, homicide, violence, teenage pregnancy, and welfare dependency reached epidemic levels in black neighborhoods. The experiences of African Americans living in poor, urban areas became the focus of countless studies and theories of the underclass during the 1980s, as it was scarcely possible to avoid paying attention to the behavioral aspects of the new poverty. I argue that racial integration, class polarization, the loss of traditional family resources, and diminished respect for black women all contributed to the changing nature of families, and I also look at the efforts to discipline poor black mothers through the promotion of work ("workfare") and marriage ("wedfare") policies.

Chapter 4 is devoted to intimate relationships among African Americans. Here I argue that ideological support for hegemonic gender ideologies remains strong among many black women and men, thus creating considerable gender tensions in their relationships. The dominant tradition of "marrying up" is difficult for black women, whose education and occupations often give them a status advantage over black men. Marriage has also always been problematic, as the history and race/class position of most blacks are fundamentally at odds with ideology and logic of the traditional marriage contract. Their experiences almost demand greater gender equity and flexibility in relationships, yet research provides contradictory findings on the extent to which they have achieved this. For example, despite their high levels of employment, most studies show that black women perform most of the housework and child care in their families. Even African American men and women who live nontraditional lives—lives that do not line up with mainstream gender ideologies—often still idealize outmoded Eurocentric versions of intimacy that advocate male dominance and female subordination in relationships. The gap between their ideology and lived experience, and the failure to effectively challenge mainstream notions of masculinity and femininity, has created a gender dilemma for black men and women. Many find themselves blaming each other for their fragile relationships: Black women criticize black men for their dismal economic performance and meager contributions to families, while black men see black women as failing to be supportive and submissive.

Motherhood, the focus of chapter 5, has been described as one of the most divisive issues among black and white feminists: While some white feminists claim that motherhood is oppressive to women, black feminists note that it can also be a source of pride and satisfaction. Both the African and American experiences of black women historically have placed a premium on their fertility, reproductive abilities, and child-rearing skills. This motherhood tradition also stems from their long history of effectively raising white children, a theme that continues to be prominent in the media. I argue that a black cultural ethos of motherhood has evolved that reinforces the idea that black women "naturally" value the work of having and rearing children and that depicts them as having an almost innate capacity for mothering. I examine the historical significance of motherhood among black women and the social construction of the "good mother" during modernization in ways that excluded black women, and I look at the consequences of the motherhood ethos that suggests they prioritize mothering work and are perpetually available as "other mothers." Such an ethos may displace the necessity of fathering and inadvertently promote and romanticize childbearing, especially among those who have few other opportunities for fulfillment. In demystifying the motherhood ethos, I examine the perils of motherhood and the overlooked historic support for reproductive rights.

Chapter 6 explores how the social class status of African American parents affect the race and gender socialization messages they convey to their children. Many studies have pointed out that black parents racially socialize their children, but rarely have they examined how parental perceptions of racism in their children's lives and their race socialization strategies vary by class. In terms of gender, most scholars have contended that it plays at best a minimal role in the socialization of black children, yet these contentions were rarely if ever based on systematic research. My research, starting with a study of how mothers provided care for their chronically ill children, led me to doubt the notion of gender neutrality in the socialization of black children. I eventually conducted a broader study on a race- and class-diverse sample of parents, and the data shared here focus largely on the findings of that research. There is significant support for gender equality in socializing black children if one looks at the educational and career aspirations parents have for their children, but beyond that, class status shapes their views on gender. I argue that those who are securely middle class—or in second-generation middle-class families—evince the strongest support for teaching their children gender equality, and they are also the most proactive in their racial socialization of children. Support for teaching gender equality, especially in the family, wanes as class position declines, with working-class and poor black women expressing the strongest support for adhering to conventional gender ideologies. As a prelude to chapter 7, I conclude the chapter by discussing the perils of growing up in poor families, especially the exposure of poor children to violence in their families, schools, and neighborhoods.

Domestic violence became a common theme in family research during the latter decades of the twentieth century, with scholars generating a proliferation of research on the abuse of spouses, children, and intimate partners. Research suggests that such violence is and has always been higher among African Americans, yet little attention has been given to the link between racial oppression and intimate partner violence. Between 1960 and 1990, rates of black male homicide nearly tripled,[35] but despite concern over black men as a "vanishing species," very few researchers looked at how this violence affected women and children. Rather, there has been a significant "deracialization" of studies on family violence, perhaps in an attempt to prevent racial stereotypes of black people as inherently violent. In chapter 7, I look at gendered violence in the lives of African Americans, especially that directed against African American women by men, including their male partners. I argue that beyond the usual explanations for domestic abuse—the cultural pervasiveness of violence, learned helplessness, patriarchy, and poverty—other distinctively racial factors shape violence and responses to it among African Americans. For example, the theme of black male victimology, the idea that black men are the primary victims of racism, is often seen as justifying their violence against women. African American women are reluctant to call on legal authorities to control black men, as such intervention has often been more punitive than helpful, and those who do publicize their abuse find themselves described as pawns being used by whites to entrap black men.[36]

Chapter 8, entitled "Resolutions," redresses the issues discussed in this book and makes a few suggestions for social change. For example, I argue that while accepting gender equity is the optimal strategy for solving the gender dilemma that has historically faced black women and men, most solutions currently being offered are patriarchal in nature. Stemming from religious organizations such as the Promise Keepers, they often insist that black people conform to the two-parent, male-headed model of family—a perspective that violates the sensitivities of most feminists. Yet such families are often appealing to African American women who have grown weary of running families alone with insufficient resources. I also return to the issue of race, noting the importance of new theories on race and arguing for strengthening enforcement of civil rights and equal opportunity laws, but also of forming interracial coalitions where open, honest dialogues about race can transpire. Racism operates differently in the lives of poor and middle-income African Americans, and it is important to form policies and responses that address those differences. If racial equality is to be achieved, crucial structural and cultural changes will need to occur.

Notes

1. E. Cose (2002:42).
2. U.S. Bureau of the Census (2003); http://nces.edu.gov/programs/digest/do2/tables/PDF/tables8.pdf.
3. U.S. Bureau of the Census (2003); www.bls.gov/cps/cpsaat12.pdf.
4. U.S. Bureau of the Census data, cited in H. R. Kerbo (2003:337).
5. E. Cose (2002).
6. O. Winfrey (2002).
7. Quoted in B. Blauner (2001:89).
8. Quoted in B. Guy-Sheftall (1995:299).
9. F. Beale (1970).
10. J. Lorber (1998 :134).
11. R. Brewer (1993:17).
12. P. H. Collins (1999:263).
13. See, for example, D. Franklin (1997); E. Higginbotham (1993); C. B. Booker (2000).
14. Quoted in D. Franklin (1997:16).
15. M. M. Ferree and B. B. Hess (1994).
16. D. Franklin (1997); D. G. White (1999).
17. L. Mullings (1997:134).
18. D. G. White (1999:220).
19. M. M. Ferree and B. B. Hess (1994:123).
20. M. M. Ferree and B. B. Hess (1994:55).

21. P. H. Collins (1990).
22. C. B. Booker (2000).
23. P. H. Collins (1990:13).
24. P. H. Collins (1990:26).
25. See appendix.
26. C. Page (2004:B9).
27. R. Brewer (1993:15).
28. M. E. Ensminger (1995).
29. A. W. Boykin and F. D. Toms (1985).
30. M. K. Asante (1987); W. W. Nobles (1974, 1985).
31. A. Swidler (1986:277).
32. A. Swidler (1986:275).
33. S. Hays (2003).
34. A. Davis (1999:13).
35. D. Massey (2001).
36. A. M. White (1999).

CHAPTER 2

Theorizing Race

The Challenges of Black Progress, Diversity, and Decline

The American Negro exhibit is a group of two. Both of these mechanical toys are built so that their feet eternally shuffle, and their eyes pop and roll. Shuffling feet and those popping, rolling eyes denote the Negro and no characterization is genuine without this monotony. One is seated on a stump picking away on his banjo and singing and laughing. The other is a most amoral character before a share-cropper's shack mumbling about injustice. Doing this makes him out to be a Negro "intellectual." It is as simple as all that.

—Zora Neale Hurston[1]

What are Negroes to do when they are continually painted at their worst and judged by the public as they are painted?

—W. E. B. Du Bois[2]

Institutionalized racism and the pernicious laws and customs that it generated to subjugate black people elevated race as the dominant discourse in articulating the oppression of African Americans. Regardless of class or gender position, black skin was equated with intellectual and moral inferiority and was the basis for segregation, economic exclusion, and the denial of civil rights. After slavery and Reconstruction ended, the legalization of racial segregation and a host of Jim Crow customs and black codes solidified African Americans' position at the bottom tier of the racial hierarchy. Still, historic strands of resistance to racial oppression gained momentum as African Americans struggled for racial uplift and survival—whether through owning land, helping their communities, promoting education, working through the courts, or taking

23

their protest to the streets. Threatening a March on Washington by thousands, a coalition headed by A. Phillip Randolph persuaded the government in 1941 to bar discrimination in the defense industries and, a few years later, to desegregate the armed forces. The 1954 *Brown* decision banning legal segregation in schools was another watershed event; it captured the attention of the nation by striking down the separate but equal doctrine and paved the way for new boldness in the struggle for civil rights.

Out of necessity, African Americans from diverse backgrounds forged a fragile coalition around the goal of fighting for racial liberation, although those who were educated, male, and middle class garnered most of the accolades for being stridently and visibly engaged in the civil rights movement. Racial oppression had significantly curtailed whatever privileges might have accrued to African Americans based on their class or gender position, and this made it easier to create a monolithic portrait of black people as equally oppressed. Reversing the historic view that greater freedom could be attained by deemphasizing race, the civil rights movement constructed race as the master status and key factor shaping the lives of African Americans.

This racialization of the black experience became most evident to me in interviewing my family members who came of age in rural Arkansas during the early 1900s. Many displayed a remarkable determination to escape the crippling sharecropping system and improve their lives through hard work and education, but there was often a striking absence of any race discourse in their stories of family life, work, and survival. Although they lived under strict rules of racial segregation and endured personal insults and inequities at the hands of whites, they somehow never really seemed to grasp the broader picture of how race and racial oppression had so thoroughly structured their lives. Racism seemed, oddly, both omnipresent and invisible.

The civil rights era's emphasis on the primacy of race in shaping life chances resonated with the evolving consciousness of most African Americans, providing them with the vocabulary needed to articulate their plight and demand their freedom. This unification under the banner of race, however, often obscured historic intraracial differences and tensions among black people. While fighting racial oppression politicized African Americans, the rhetoric of racial liberation often tacitly called for male domination, ignored the implications of class diversity, and accepted hegemonic definitions of race. Not surprisingly, the unity formed around race waned as black feminists expressed concern over gender equity, class and political polarization among black people grew, and new definitions of race emerged. For example, the nascent vision of early black female activists that race work must include ameliorating a broad range of social injustices came into full articulation as African American women were marginalized in both black protest and feminist organizations of the 1960s, leading them to conceptualize race, gender, and class as intersecting inequalities. Yet the intersectionality perspective's implication of social class as one of the "jeopardies" faced by African American women ignored growing intraracial economic diversity and failed to interrogate the meaning of race. As early as the 1960s, for example, Andrew Billingsley had classified 40 percent of black families as middle class, although he noted that their exclusion from mainstream society made race more salient than class in their lives. Now, even the meaning of being black has become more contested with a surge in interracial people claiming multiple and fluid racial identities and an increase in black immigrants who do not share the historic experiences or political agenda of African Americans.

The central argument of this chapter is that the portrayal of African Americans during the civil rights movement as a unified, homogeneous group obfuscated significant class, color, and gender distinctions among them and that the very success of the movement has now exacerbated those distinctions. I begin by examining the concept of race and its saliency in the lives of black people, noting that race and racial categories are not only socially constructed and the basis for oppression but that they also belie the significance of intraracial divisions. After discussing the historically created intraracial differences, I look at how African Americans coalesced around the issue of race during the civil rights movement, effectively paving the way for significant social and economic gains over the past four decades. Virtually every study of racial attitudes reveals a dramatic decline in white support for racial segregation, and, based on a poll conducted by the *New York Times* in 2000, a majority of African Americans believe that racial progress has been achieved (58 percent) and that race relations are generally good (51 percent), while only 7 percent say that racism is the most important problem facing black people.[3]

Yet significant racial disparities between blacks and whites in wealth, health, income, and well-being remain, and much evidence can be marshaled to show that racism and discrimination have not vanished. The waning biological significance of race clearly has not altered the fact that race is, as economist Glenn Loury has pointed out, "embodied social signification" that has "profound, enduring, and all-too-real consequences."[4] Still, the evidence of racial gaps and gains has polarized those who say racism is as potent as ever in producing seemingly intractable racial disparities and a growing group of scholars who say its impact is being overemphasized. While the dominant racial discourse claims that racism is a permanent feature of American society and/or that it has simply morphed into new forms, new racial theorists such as John McWhorter contend that blaming the oppressor has become a "seductive drug" used to allay fears that "at the end of the day, black people are inferior to whites."[5] Unfortunately, neither those who see racism as still powerfully shaping black lives nor those who claim it is overstated do much to foster a critically needed intraracial discourse. I conclude the chapter with a look at emerging postmodern diversities among African Americans—based on age, race, social class, gender, and political allegiance—that are now challenging the very meaning of being black.

The Historic Diversity of African Americans

Based on skin color, my mother might easily have "passed" for white, yet given the legal definition of race and her cultural upbringing, she never doubted that she was "black" or—perhaps more fitting for someone born in 1909—a "Negro." Historically, racial designations of black or white were made with regularity and ease based on rules such as hypodescent (or the "one drop rule") or, even more practically, on physical features. The racial classification system in the United States equated skin color with race, assumed racial purity by forcing people to identify with only one racial group, and created panethnic racial groups that subsume distinct ethnicities and ignore their differences.[6] Dark skin automatically marked one as a racial minority, and, should the skin color test fail, an interracial person with a white and a racial minority parent was legally classified as belonging to the race of the nonwhite parent. The centrality of skin color in racial designations is most evident in the fact that African Americans—along with people from Africa, Jamaica, Haiti, the West Indies, and other places with black populations—are classified as "Black or Negro" despite their multiracial heritage or diverse ethnic and national origins. After much debate among policymakers, the 1850 census veered from the "one-drop" definition of blackness by including the category "mulatto" to describe persons born of black/white interracial unions— but only in an effort to prove the dangers of miscegenation.[7] Not surprisingly, scientists later found mulattoes to be physiologically inferior to "pure"-blooded persons and subject to premature death.

The rules of racial classification exemplify the importance of the black/white distinction in America and reveal the arbitrary, socially constructed nature of race. The quest for racial justice challenged biology as the basis for race, exposing it as a social construct used historically to justify racial oppression and privilege. Europeans traveling to Africa during the 1500s often commented on the color and customs of Africans, but as Kathleen M. Brown has noted, the "emphasis on blackness and inferiority did not begin in earnest until the late seventeenth century, after the English were themselves solidly committed to the slave trade."[8] Notions of race as a scientific biological category and black people as innately inferior legitimized their enslavement and oppression and held sway over many scholars and public officials, who drew on genetic/biological theories to explain the plight of black people. These ideologies gave race a primacy in the experiences of black people, yet status differences between them existed even in precolonial Africa based on tribal affiliation, skills, and work, and they were reconstructed in America. In addition, the legal imposition of a black/white racial dichotomy belied a status stratification system among blacks based on color and physical features (e.g., light skin, straight and/or long hair, and sharp facial features).

The Politics of Status, Class, and Color

In early American society, the most notable status distinction that existed among black people was based on whether they were enslaved or free. Prior to the 1865 Emancipation Proclamation Act, freedom came to African Americans sporadically and often in problematic ways. The 1799 Gradual Manumission Act passed in New York, for example, freed children born to enslaved women after July 4, 1799, enslaved males and females at the ages of twenty-eight and twenty-five, respectively, and all slaves by 1827,[9] thus sometimes placing even those in the same family in divergent statuses. Free blacks often went to great lengths to distance themselves from their enslaved counterparts, despite the fact that both were routinely denied citizenship rights, and with the *Dred Scott* decision blurring the distinction between free and slave, they had good reason to do so. Among enslaved Africans, the clearest distinction was between slaves who worked in the house and those who worked in the field. In his classic work on the history of black families, E. Franklin Frazier quoted a former slave who spoke of the distinction between "aristocratic" house servants, "dressed in the cast-off finery of their masters and mistress, swelling out and putting on airs of imitation," and the lot of those who worked in the fields and looked to house servants as "a pattern of politeness and gentility."[10] The exposure of the so-called aristocratic house servants to white households accelerated their assimilation into values and customs of the dominant culture, creating a notable class and status divide among black people.

While most slaves worked in the field, the division between slaves who worked in the house and the fields often fell along gender lines, making gender an important dimension of the class divide. Black women were often enmeshed in the day-to-day family lives of white slave owners and gained status from these positions. Sexual liaisons between female house servants and their white slave owners—whether based on coercion or consent—produced children who legally inherited the slave status of their mothers but also some social advantages of white ancestry. Being fathered by white men often meant lighter skin, a greater likelihood of learning to read, better occupations, and even emancipation. Marie Therese Coincoin, an enslaved house servant in Natchitoches, Louisiana, was the twenty-five-year-old mother of four children when Frenchman Claude Thomas Pierre Metoyer became enamored with her in 1767.[11] He arranged to take Coincoin as his mistress; he lived with her in a nineteen-year union that produced ten additional children, and he eventually emancipated her and gave her sixty-eight acres of land. Through determination and hard work, Coincoin managed to purchase all of her children out of slavery, and, by the time of her death in 1817, they had amassed nearly twelve thousand acres of plantation land and about ninety-nine slaves. Her descendants became the wealthiest family of free blacks in the country, the nucleus of the black elite class. Achieving such wealth, however, was far from the experience of most enslaved black women. Despite some variations in privilege, for most slavery simply deprived them of the right to marry, reap the rewards of their own labor, control their own bodies, rely on black men for provision or protection, or exercise maternal rights over their children.

Although race often easily overrode any privileges based on class, there was significant occupational diversity among black people during slavery, based on region and labor demands (see chapter 3). The social class diversity initiated by slavery grew in the succeeding generations, although the class system of blacks differed from that of whites. The central class distinction among blacks was between those who had steady jobs, intact families, and clung to middle-class values of respectability and those who did not. In the *Black Bourgeoisie*, E. F. Frazier evoked outrage among black and white Americans by his highly controversial and sad portrayal of black middle-class Americans. Disrupting the notion that black people had emerged from slavery unscathed and were steadily advancing into the economic mainstream, Frazier's work exposed the economic marginality of the black middle class and their persistent feelings of inferiority and status anxiety. Although they trumpeted their cultural achievements, refused to identify with the black masses, boasted of their light skin and white heritage, and believed in the myth of racial salvation through economic development, they were not accepted by white society and lived in what Frazier called a world of illusion and make-believe. Moreover, awareness of their fragile grasp on middle-class life often created intense and public intraracial class conflict, as when poor, rural, southern blacks flooded urban northern areas. Their migration created a moral panic among more assimilated and affluent northern blacks who, as Donna Franklin notes, saw their own status jeopardized by the "floating, shiftless, and depraved element" of their race.[12]

In *Our Kind of People*, heralded as the first truly penetrating analysis of the black elite, Lawrence Otis Graham describes growing up among privileged, wealthy, professional African Americans, where family name was paramount, marriage among equals was arranged, summers were spent in Martha's Vineyard, and social calendars were filled with balls, cruises, debutante cotillions, art auctions, and formal parties. He writes of learning early in life that there were two kinds of black people: those who passed the "brown paper bag and ruler test" and those who did not. The social value of light skin and straight hair, often indicative of white ancestry, has never been lost on African Americans, whose obsession with color is seen in the extraordinary number of terms devoted to its description (e.g., *high yellow, caramel-colored, bright skinned, café au lait*).

Skin color also has been inexorably tied to social class. In 1987 Bart Landry, for example, describes the oldest black middle class to evolve from slavery as an occupationally diverse group of mulattoes born mostly of slave women and their owners who based their status on white ancestry, social club membership, skin color, and the emulation of white cultural norms. More recent studies also find a link between skin tone and socio-economic status, and the health status and social functioning of African Americans.[13] In some cases, skin color enabled some African Americans to pass for white; in fact, Graham shares a list of the tips and rules once offered to the many who chose to do so.

The Politics of Gender

While race provided the overarching framework for black subjugation, the racial images used to exclude and control black people varied by gender, although sexual deviance, suitability for menial labor, and immorality were key aspects of these racialized and gendered stereotypes. One of the key criticisms of the newly freed African American population was that they were failing to embrace the respectable gender and family norms of the day, so their resistance to racial oppression included trying to do so. For example, many black men and women ideologically supported sexual chastity, marriage, and two-parent families, although those in the middle class were more apt to actually live these norms. African Americans often worked in gender-based organizations in their efforts to promote racial liberation, with black women seeing little contradiction between their social activism and their professed allegiance to marriage and even to patriarchy. Still, their historic lived experiences led them, as Paula Giddings notes, to "redefine the notion of womanhood to integrate concepts of work, achievement, and independence into their role of woman."[14] The remarkable record of community work and activism by African American women in dealing with the health, education, housing, and economic needs of their people has now been widely documented. Organizations such as Girl Friends, Inc., organized in 1927 and composed of the black society's most elite families, focused on raising money for charities and social and cultural activities. Similarly, Links, an elite, membership-by-invitation only club, donated millions of dollars to organizations like the National Association for the Advancement of Colored People (NAACP).[15] Freed from narrowly defined models of womanhood, black women have contributed notably to the survival of the race, their families, and their communities. Yet as these organizations imply, class differences also separated African American women from each other. In her study of the participation of black women in national organizations, Deborah Gray White concludes:

> Seldom did African-American women organize across class lines. Women from diverse class backgrounds formed national organizations, but mostly within their own groups. Although it cannot be said that black women always chose race over other aspects of their identity, it can be said that race, along with gender and class were variables always factored into whatever national organizations did.[16]

Thus, despite the saliency of race in the lives of African Americans, neither slavery nor racial subjugation managed to level intraracial class, gender, and status distinctions.

Coalescing for Racial Equality

African Americans reached the dawn of the civil rights era from decidedly different class, color, and gender positions, although these distinctions were often set aside or minimized in pursuit of racial freedom. That blacks as a group were relegated to a secondary status trumped concern over intraracial differences and, eventually, even discussing them became tantamount to "airing dirty laundry." The dual tasks of redefining blackness and abolishing racial segregation consumed the energies of civil rights activists, who challenged biological notions of race, created new images of African Americans, and blamed structural factors such as slavery, racial exclusion, and racism for the persistent gap between black and white people in economic and educational achievement. Race was acknowledged as a social construct, and the historically maligned meaning of blackness was confronted by embracing, redefining, and infusing it with pride and cultural uniqueness. New racial identities and a stronger sense of self-esteem emerged among African Americans, along with a fortified sense of racial solidarity. This solidarity helped ensure success in resisting injustice and inequality by enhancing the clout of black people as a political entity and elevating the importance of racial equality on the nation's agenda.

The plethora of civil rights laws passed during the 1950s and 1960s extended basic citizenship rights to black people such as access to voting, public accommodations, education, housing, and employment. Moreover, programs aimed at ending poverty, improving inner-city neighborhoods and schools, and promoting career and occupational diversity spawned optimism that racial equality was a viable goal. The concept of institutional racism, or that racism was embedded in hegemonic customs, norms, policies, patterns of thinking, and ways of behaving, moved the discourse beyond the issue of bigoted individuals and strengthened the mandate for equal opportunity and affirmative action policies. The policies seemed to offer an adequate path to racial equality, although support for enforcing them had waned considerably after less than two decades. Still, African Americans enrolled in college at unprecedented levels during the civil rights era, and the search for "qualified blacks" opened previously closed doors to professional and managerial jobs. Significant advances were made in economic mobility, educational attainment, participation in politics, and inclusion in dominant cultural and media spheres, yet that progress has been uneven, and racial equality remains an elusive goal. Eduardo Bonilla-Silva writes that arguing an absence of racial progress is a nonsensical position "which trivializes four hundred years of black resistance to racial oppression." While blacks remain at the bottom of the racial hierarchy, he maintains, "the bottom that they experience and struggle about today is better than that peculiar to the slavery and Jim Crow periods."[17]

Still, based on every objective measure—wages, wealth, occupations, education, health, criminal incarceration—the persistent racial gap between blacks and whites remains evident. The complex picture of racial gains and disparities makes it possible for scholars, lodged in divergent ideological camps and armed with specific political agendas, to argue opposing yet tenable views on the role of racism in perpetuating racial inequalities. Blatant forms of racism such as sitting in the back of the bus, entering through back doors, and facing "whites only" signs have ended, and policies and practices excluding African Americans from many occupations and institutions of higher learning have been legally abolished. Emphasizing these racial gains, an emerging group of scholars, described as "racial realists,"[18] argue that black/white differences are being exaggerated by those who remain wedded to a focus on racism, that race-specific policies engender hostilities, and that African Americans must accept more responsibility for lingering racial disparities.[19] Others, however, contend that racism is intrinsic in American attitudes and institutions, although it may have morphed into new forms. In the following sections, I discuss the racial disparities and gains by blacks since the civil rights era, and then turn to the more contentious debate over the changing nature of racism, the link between racism and racial disparities, and the consequences of the dominant racial discourse.

Progress, Stagnation, and Decline

Black Americans achieved notable socioeconomic mobility during the twentieth century due to northward migration, military service, a vibrant postwar industrial economy, and, later, the passage of equal opportunity/affirmative action legislation. Their initial mobility was mostly due to structural shifts in the economy from agriculture to industry; indeed, black people leaving the southern sharecropping system could scarcely avoid upward mobility, despite the segregated labor market they faced in the North. My father spent his early adult years in a sharecropping system that was practically a moneyless economy for blacks, most of whom could hope at best for enough sustenance (often rendered in food, used clothing, etc.) to see them through another year. Moving to Missouri, he and my mother took whatever maintenance/domestic work they were offered, but by World War II my father was virtually drafted into labor in an ammunitions factory. Even low-paying, dirty-work jobs enabled him to support his family and paved the way for him to buy his own home and eventually become self-employed.

The civil rights movement boosted African American progress, yet racial disparities in the economic arena have persisted, most obviously in differences between blacks and whites in rates of poverty and levels of income and wealth. Data from the U.S. Census Bureau[20] show that in 2002, nearly 23 percent of blacks lived below the poverty line, compared to less than 8 percent of whites. Based on money income figures, African American family households (28 percent) are much more likely to earn under $20,000 a year than are white family households (10 percent). In *White-Washing Race: The Myth of a Color-Blind Society*, Michael K. Brown and his colleagues note that the real median income of black families in 2001 was only 62 percent of that of whites, compared to 52 percent in 1947—reflecting a gain of only 10 points. Transitions in the industrial economy during the 1970s and 1980s displaced many African Americans, initially those at the low end of the occupational ladder but later many in middle-income jobs. Thus, while the wage gap between black and white men between the ages of twenty-five and thirty-four had been declining for several decades, it actually widened during the 1980s.[21]

The impact on African American women has received less attention, but a study by John Bound and Laura Dresser report relative declines in income and employment among young black women between 1973 and 1991, especially those who are college graduates. Many held jobs in declining industries and were forced to accept lower-paying, nonunionized jobs. The economic decline experienced by African Americans coincided with a rise in single-mother families, whose low earnings have contributed significantly to the racial gap in family income between African American and white families.

The racial income gap pales in significance when compared to wealth disparities. For example, Marcus Pohlman reports that African Americans are 13 percent of the population but have less than 0.5 percent of the nation's wealth. The National Urban League's *State of Black America 2002* report indicates that the average net worth of white households is $84,000, compared to only $7,500 for African Americans.[22] Wealth for the average American is primarily a reflection of home ownership, and here the racial gap remains especially sharp. Comparing homeownership among heads of households, Melvin L. Oliver points out that 47.3 percent of black and 75.2 percent of whites are homeowners and that homes owned by whites have more equity and market value.[23] The racial gap in homeownership and wealth is due largely to lending practices and persistent residential segregation. The federal government underwrote $120 billion in new housing between 1934 and 1962, according to Oliver, but less than 2 percent went to nonwhites. Federal policy once held that racial and class homogeneity was vital for neighborhood stability, thus validating racial segregation in housing. Even today, African Americans and Latinos— regardless of financial status, neighborhood factors, or employment—are about 60 percent more likely than whites to be turned down for home loans.[24]

Education has long been seen as the royal road to class mobility, and data on attainment reveal significant gaps and a troubling portrait of declining enrollment among African Americans in higher education and re-segregation in elementary and secondary schools. In 2002, slightly more than 21 percent of blacks over age twenty-five had not completed high school, compared to about 11 percent of whites. At the other end of the continuum, 17 percent of African Americans had a bachelor's degree or more, compared to 29.4 percent of whites.[25] While these figures reveal gains for African Americans since the civil rights era, residential segregation and waning support for busing have now virtually resegregated schools, with the majority of African American children attending predominantly black schools that are often severely deficient in quality. The Harvard Civil Rights Project reports that school desegregation peaked in the 1980s but that schools have now become almost as segregated as when Martin Luther King was assassinated.[26] The U.S. Supreme Court in 2003 offered some support for affirmative action in higher education by declaring admission policies at Michigan's law school as constitutional, but it struck down the policy of giving extra points to undergraduate minority students. This mixed support for affirmative action has left colleges and universities rethinking their commitment to racial diversity, with many eliminating race-based scholarships in favor of policies that focus on economic diversity.[27]

During the 1980s, African Americans experienced a class polarization paralleling that of the dominant society, with many moving into professional/managerial jobs and others losing positions as the number of industrial jobs shrank. In 2002, 26.2 percent of African American women (compared to 37 percent of white women) held professional/managerial jobs, as did 18 percent of black men and 33.4 percent of white men. Although African Americans have entered professional positions in many organizations, they are often relegated to marginal and often tenuous positions that deal specifically with "race issues," such as affirmative action officer. Even blacks in top-ranking positions, as Sharon Collins found in her 1997 study of Fortune 500 companies, have jobs that are often not linked to the organizations' occupational categories but are a byproduct of race-conscious policies and programs designed after the civil rights era "abate black upheaval and restore social order." Thus, much upward mobility occurs in situations where blacks are not fully integrated into the organization, and the strains of this mobility are further complicated by the race and sexism they experience on jobs.

Black women in middle-class positions face a unique "gendered racism," according to Yanick St. Jean and Joe R. Feagin, from supervisors and coworkers who assume they are incompetent and openly express surprise upon finding that they have suitable skills and language abilities.[28]

Upwardly mobile African Americans, especially those from modest class backgrounds, must negotiate a complex clash of class/cultural values and demands that prove physically and psychologically draining. Being labeled as beneficiaries of affirmative action, marginally qualified for the job, and representatives of their race intensifies their need to prove themselves (and the abilities of their race) by fitting in and succeeding. Many are uncomfortable performing middle-class identities, and are ever on the alert for cultural cues on appropriate behavior from dominant groups. Straddling mainstream and black cultural norms may foster an outsider within perspective, but it can also make African Americans vulnerable to an imposter syndrome where they question their own racial authenticity. Moreover, the gulf between their personal and professional lives is often significant, leaving them feeling marginalized on the job and among family and friends. Successful African Americans are also expected to "never forget where they came from" and willingly give back to the community. Black women who have experienced social mobility are much more likely than their white counterparts to feel a sense of obligation to family and friends, which in some cases detracts from the energy they can spend pursuing their careers.[29]

While class polarization has led to upward mobility for some African Americans (and the strains that accompany it), it has meant an almost durable place in the lower class for others who are likely to encounter blatant racial stereotypes in their efforts to find work. Black men, whose rate of unemployment in 2002 was twice that of white men (12 percent vs. 5.7 percent), are penalized by a focus among employers on "soft skills," defined by P. Moss and C. Tilly as "skills, abilities and traits that pertain to personality, attitude and behavior rather than formal or technical knowledge."[30] Employers not only see African American men as lacking these skills, according to Moss and Tilly, but also describe them as unmotivated, defensive, and hostile.

Similar racial stereotypes impede the ability of African American women to obtain jobs. Irene Browne and Ivy Kennelly found that employers hold stereotypes of black women as single mothers and thus apt to be unreliable employees—although the evidence shows they often have no more child care duties than men.[31] In 2002, black women were twice as likely as white women to be unemployed (9.9 percent vs. 4.4 percent). Among those who are employed, as Evelyn Nakano Glenn points out, the "new realm of public reproductive labor" remains stratified by gender and race:

Women of color are disproportionately assigned to do the dirty work, as nurses' aides in hospitals, kitchen workers in restaurants and cafeterias, maids in hotels, and cleaners in office buildings. In these same institutional settings, White women are disproportionately employed as supervisors, professionals, and administrative support staff. This division parallels the earlier division between the domestic servant and the housewife.[32]

The globalization of the labor market along race/gender lines, according to Rose Brewer, has left capitalist firms less reliant on the low-wage labor of black men or women.[33] Moreover, although many poor women faced welfare reform with a great deal of optimism, pressing them into low-wage jobs has benefited capitalism while undermining the stability of families and discounting the work women perform in their homes:

Black women perform a significant portion of the social reproductive labor. The socialization of children and the cleaning, cooking and nurturing functions are all disproportionately Black women's work. Indeed, poor Black women are often expected to do everything. Their work within the home is devalued, even though housework is accomplished under trying circumstances: substandard housing, no household washers and dryers, or few appliances. Yet these women are increasingly expected to work in low-paid jobs to qualify for Aid to Families with Dependent Children.[34]

Finally, racial disparities are seen in the disproportionate number of African Americans incarcerated in recent decades and the persistent racial gap between blacks and whites in health status. The largest single category of criminal arrests in the United States are from drug-related offenses, and much has been written about how inequities in sentencing and arrest have disproportionately affected African Americans.[35] B. Western and K. Beckett argue that the penal system during the 1980s and 1990s was a major way the government regulated the labor market and, at least in the short term, lowered rates of unemployment. In the early 1990s, $91 billion was spent on courts, police, and prisons, compared to $41 billion on unemployment benefits, and by 1996, 1.63 million people were in prison. The penalty associated with being black also takes a toll on the health and well-being of African Americans through social stigma, higher rates of poverty, inadequate access to health care, a greater prevalence of nearly every chronic disease, and shorter life spans. Regardless of age, class, or marital status, black Americans, compared to whites, are "less satisfied, less happy, more distrustful, more anomic, had less happy marriages, and rated their physical health worse than whites."[36]

As troubling as persistent racial inequalities have been efforts by public authorities to obfuscate the significance of racial inequality in official reports. In 2000, the Justice Department dropped support for employment discrimination suits previously settled during the Clinton era, and the overall number of new suits filed over the ensuing months declined dramatically.[37] The Union of Concerned Scientists, formed of Nobel laureates and others, recently criticized the Bush administration for essentially changing research findings on a range of issues that contradict its ideology.[38] For example, a White House report declared blacks were not longer getting inferior health care just as a major study found a persistent racial gap and less aggressive treatment for minorities. Health and Human Services Secretary Tommy Thompson said the report was changed to "accentuate the positive," yet others saw it as another example of facts contrary to the current administration's worldview being made to disappear.[39] In another case, a study of the Justice Department, charged with enforcing civil rights, found that racial minorities and women perceived their own workplace as biased and unfair. Yet the department's official posting of the report on its Web page excluded those sections highlighting significant diversity issues and the need for "extraordinarily strong leadership" to rectify them.[40]

Theorizing Racism and Racial Disparities

> White hearts know the status quo is racist; white hands are just having a hard time giving up all the goodies. Anyone would.
>
> —Debra J. Dickerson, African American lawyer[41]

While few people contend that racism is dead or inconsequential, much debate centers on its significance in perpetuating racial disparities. Racism maintains that certain racial groups are genetically/biologically superior to others (especially intellectually), and it is, logically, seen as leading to discrimination by individuals and institutions against those deemed inferior. Major surveys now show that 90 percent of Americans support policies such as equal access to jobs and integrated schools by all racial groups but they also provide plenty of evidence that significant numbers of whites think poorly of blacks. Lawrence Bobo and his colleagues report that a slight majority of whites (58 percent) rate blacks as less intelligent than whites, and 78 percent indicate that blacks are more likely than whites to prefer to live on welfare.[42] Other research finds that whites are more likely to express a desire for social distance from blacks than any other racial group and, contrary to the premises of integration theory, that the exposure of whites to sizeable black populations lessens their support for black opportunity and increases white hostility, racism, and prejudice.[43] Thus, racial hostility against African Americans exists along with widespread support for equal opportunity. How does one explain this?

The dominant racial discourse contends that the traditional meaning of racism, which linked biological racial traits to innate superiority or inferiority, has given way to a new strand of "liberal racism," defined as an "antiracist attitude that coexists with support for racist outcomes." As A. Gordon and C. Newfield have explained:

> Liberal racism rejects discrimination on the basis of race or color and abhors the subjection of groups or individuals on racial grounds. But it upholds and defends systems that produce racializing effects, often in the name of some matter more "urgent" than redressing racial subordination, such as reward "merit" or enhancing economic competitiveness.[44]

Liberal racism coincides with Bobo's notion of laissez-faire racism.[45] Bobo argues that the Jim Crow racism that served the political economy of earlier generations by insisting on black inferiority and segregation has been replaced with one that offers attitudinal support for equality but rejects virtually any mechanism that would bring it about. For example, while a majority of Americans express ideological support for racial equality, only about one-third are supportive of federal policies that would achieve these goals. I would argue, however, that using support for race-based policies such as affirmative action or school busing as litmus tests for who is racist risks casting the racism net far too widely and silencing those who feel most vulnerable to being disadvantaged by such policies.

Many racial stereotypes revolve around the concept of the black underclass that emerged during the economic decline of the 1970s. W. J. Wilson defines the underclass in both economic and behavioral terms by drawing a link between "individuals who are engaged in street crime and other forms of aberrant behavior, and families that experience long-term spells of poverty and/or welfare dependency."[46] As a result, while those in the public arena rarely speak disparagingly of racial minorities in an open fashion, Sanford Schram contends that the new racism, which is more discursive than ideological, "reinscribes race privileges implicitly through a euphemistic, encoded discourse" that associates blacks with economic danger and risk rather than inferiority.[47] The racial discourse described by Schram is strongly related to the increase in crime, violence, nonmarital pregnancy and childbirth, and welfare dependency that came to define the black underclass.

Wilson's work led him to proffer a class analysis of black progress, contending that while "talented and educated" blacks were rapidly moving into the middle class due to equal opportunity and affirmation action policies, deindustrialization had left many others trapped in poverty, unstable families, and deteriorating neighborhoods. His work has sparked controversy by proposing that class is now a stronger predictor of life chances than race. Marxist sociologists such as Oliver Cox, a prominent African American theorist of the 1940s, also emphasized the primacy of class, and saw capitalists as deliberately using racial prejudice as a tool to deflect attention from worker exploitation. For Cox, racism was mostly a divide and conquer strategy and "a social attitude propagated upon the public by an exploiting class for the purpose of stigmatizing some group as inferior so that the exploitation of either the group itself or its resources or both may be justified."[48]

Most theorists, however, focus on race and racism as transcending class divisions in its impact on African Americans, especially since middle-class status does not shield one from the impact of negative racial images. Critical race theorists, for example, argue that racial inequality is more an immutable, permanent feature of American society, as opposed to a mere aberration from its creed of liberty and justice for all. Rather than simply a form of institutionalized inequality, for example, Lee Collins sees race is a fabrication legitimized by the political structure, and thus a "fluctuating, decentered complex of social meanings, formed and transformed under the constant pressures of political struggle." As a major organizing tool of society, it shapes and constrains thinking, and allows at best only black progress that promotes white self-interest.[49] Eduardo Bonilla-Silva, however, criticizes critical race theory for failing to acknowledge that racism has been challenged effectively on some occasions, thus denying the efficacy of political reform and efforts to achieve racial equity. He offers the notion of racialized social systems as an alternative perspective, a term that "refers to societies in which economic, political, social, and ideological levels are partially structured by the placement of actors in racial categories or races," noting that "after a society becomes racialized, racialization develops a life of its own."[50] His theory ignores gender and class, but he argues that "[a]lthough racism interacts with class and gender structurations in society, it becomes an organizing principle of social relations in itself."[51]

Most race theorists argue that while racism has taken new forms, it continues to be the key factor in curtailing black progress. Although overt policies supporting racial segregation and exclusion have been declared illegal and open expressions of racist sentiment have become unacceptable, racism and negative stereotypes describing African Americans have by no means vanished. Studies show that race talk, defined by Toni Morrison as "the explicit insertion into everyday life of racial signs and symbols that have no meaning other than pressing African Americans to the lowest level of the racial hierarchy,"[52] is common in everyday conversations. Moreover, biological claims of black inferiority have not been put to rest even among those in the academic community, as evidenced by the controversial bell curve concept posed by R. J. Herrnstein and C. Murray in 1994 that linked intelligence and a host of other social ills to race. Thus, the dominant racial discourse asserts the continuing significance of racism and offers as evidence racial disparities, the prevalence of negative racial stereotypes, and the lack of support by most whites for policies such as affirmative action and school busing.

Others, however, have grown suspect of the claim that racism is mostly responsible for the continuing racial disparities between blacks and whites, insisting that welfare programs, nonmarital childbearing, inadequate effort at school, a poor work ethic, and generally pathological cultural values play a crucial role in racial inequality. Comedian Bill Cosby recently created a stir by openly criticizing the behaviors of many young African Americans and accusing them of failing to take advantage of the opportunities that were won during the civil rights movement. While Cosby's own success has been anything but normative, the ability of many blacks of his generation to succeed in an era of rigid racial exclusion has made them weary of the racism claim. Emphasizing the advances of many African Americans is another strategy for discounting racism by theorists such as Orlando Patterson, who complains that while the entire social science industry has learned to control for numerous factors to show that institutional racism exists, it remains "at a complete loss to explain the two-thirds of Afro-American people leading normal, uncursed lives, very much a part of the American mainstream."[53]

John McWhorter, a black professor at the University of California–Berkeley, has become an especially vocal opponent of attributing the problems and disparities of African Americans today to racism. While noting that racism has not ended, he sees it as dangerously overstated by those who perpetuate a "cult of victimology" by nurturing racial insults and inequities and promoting separatism, anti-intellectualism, and mediocre standards for African Americans. In *Losing the Race*, McWhorter claims that, despite notable progress, African Americans continue to be influenced by black leaders who "will maintain to their dying day that most black Americans are poor, that there is a racist at the heart of all whites, and that because of these things, regardless of class or opportunity, no black American is to be held to mainstream standards of morality or academic achievement."[54]

Thus, the persistence of racial disparities four decades after the civil rights era banned legalized segregation and extended more opportunity to black Americans has led to new theories and debates about race. The racism discourse has generated new terms, concepts, and arguments, and, despite an overall consensus that race matters, there is dissension over how much it matters and what should be done about it. Those focusing on the continuing significance of race in curtailing black progress imply that more aggressive efforts are needed to integrate African Americans into mainstream society, including extending and strongly enforcing affirmative action and equal opportunity policies. Those who believe the significance of race has waned are likely to place the onus of responsibility on African Americans by urging the need for them to work harder and take advantage the new opportunities they have gained. At a more practical level, Debra J. Dickerson, in the *End of Blackness*, urges black people to accept the reality that white America has done all its going to do address the consequences of historic and current racism, and to embrace the rights and opportunities they now have. Beyond that, she maintains, the assimilation of black people into the dominant society will occur only gradually through upward mobility and intermarriage.

Overall, it should not be particularly surprising that African Americans have not overcome centuries of racial disparities in the less than two generations after the civil rights era, especially given the saliency of race in American society, the changing economy and ambivalent support for enforcing equal opportunity legislation. In the end, neither race theories that posit the continuing saliency of racism nor those that herald its decline offer many viable solutions for gaining racial parity. Implying racism does not matter much anymore leaves us with practically nothing to talk about; more important, it plays into the hands of conservative politicians eager to ignore race, water down equal opportunity policies, and blame disadvantaged blacks for their plight. On the other hand, new theories that see racism as pervasive and as creating an almost impenetrable barrier to success flies in the face of practically everybody's observation that African Americans are now wealthier, more visible, more educated, and more likely than ever to hold high-level professional positions.

Given the agreement that race matters, enforcing equal opportunity laws is vital. But it would be fruitful to expand the dialogue beyond debates over its primacy in impeding black progress to a broader critique of new definitions of racism, analyses of how internalized racism and classism among blacks affect their perceptions of racism, and ideas about how to create spaces for open interracial dialogue. For example, the "everyone is a racist" thesis may draw little distinction among white supremacists, opponents of race-based policies, and those who simply buy into common racial stereotypes. Such theories have a chilling effect on the discourse on race; they not only hastily dismiss the significance of progress by blacks and the important changes in the racial attitudes of whites but offer far too many paths for whites to be labeled as racist—indeed, failing to acknowledge the pervasiveness of racism is, by some counts, a form of racism. That large numbers of Americans believe black people are less intelligent and more likely to want to live on welfare *is* racist, but black people *are* disproportionately found in low-level jobs and on welfare, and it has long been understood that racial inequality itself generates racist attitudes. Expecting the *average* American to astutely attribute that to racism may be unrealistic, and labeling them as racist nonproductive; even disadvantaged blacks rarely explain their situation in the context of racism.[55]

In fact, African Americans do not interpret every slight or episode of unfair treatment they experience as racism, yet efforts at interracial racial dialogue often encourage such thinking by obliging black people to identify instances in which they have felt marginalized, stigmatized, or excluded from mainstream society. The micropolitics of race sees all white people as innately racist and African Americans as innocent targets of racist abuse, but such thinking perpetually reenacts the white oppressor/black victim scenario and ultimately reinforces the power of whites by placing responsibility for change in their hands. In some cases, entire white organizations are indicted for racism based on the thoughtless comments or behaviors of a few, although racial minorities usually abhor such generalizations.

Focusing on white racism also deflects attention from a broader analysis of how social class affects interracial interactions. Whites and blacks are often from divergent class backgrounds, and the discomfort that African Americans who participate in predominantly white organizations experience may come from being pulled out of their comfort zones and/or expected to perform middle-class identities. Mainstream organizations *are* structured in ways that marginalize the class and race identities of many blacks, but that does not make them inherently racist. Unless altered by participation from multiple race-ethnic groups, they will continue to reflect their own specific class/cultural milieu—just as the Association of Black Sociologists does when it welcomes its members to their "annual family reunion" and opens its banquet with prayer.

An exclusive focus on white racism leaves little room for African Americans to examine their own internalized racism, yet it manifests itself in numerous ways, such as unconsciously privileging the presence and participation of white people in various activities. One example: A few years ago I entered a reception hosted by a women's organization with two white female colleagues. A well-known black scholar approached us with a welcomingly outstretched hand and introduced herself to both of my colleagues—but had to be reminded of my presence. The analysis of racial disparities also must acknowledge class divisions among black people and how the behaviors of many who are disadvantaged contribute to the perpetuation of racial inequality. Scholarly analyses of the racial hierarchy and its dynamics, however astute, offer few tools to those working to curb teenage pregnancy, substance abuse, and homicide in their communities. Teaching at a predominantly white university, I find that students understand how institutional racism results in things such as segregated housing, job discrimination, and inadequate educational institutions. Yet the premise that those inequities inherently lead to problems such as criminal involvement and poverty is more problematic, especially when the majority of African Americans seem to escape these negative outcomes. Still, questioning the link between racism and self-destructive behaviors means running the risk of being seen as racist, and most students either do their best to privilege the perspective of African Americans when it comes to defining racism or just remain silent. Reflecting on his teaching experiences, Bob Blauner, in *Still the Big News: Racial Oppression in America*, observes that black and white students tend to talk right past each other on the issue of racial inequality. White students, for example, agree that incidents like the Rodney King beating are racist, yet they do not see how the behaviors of a few police officers are indicative of institutionalized racism. Blauner argues that "the way we talk about racism more often reinforces the negative, divisive side rather than the positive possibilities for healing that an anti-racist movement must be centered around."[56] Those interested in fostering productive racial dialogues must move beyond polarizing language, broaden their analysis of the factors that continue to perpetuate racial disparities, and create spaces where people of all races can speak freely and honestly about their experiences.

Postmodern Diversity, Divisions, and Debates

Debate over the meaning of race and racism, growing class and political diversity, and black feminist thought have all shattered the monolithic blackness crafted during the civil rights era. The recent controversy over the movie *Barbershop*, where Cedric the Entertainer impugned such black icons as Rosa Parks and Martin Luther King and even suggested that Rodney King deserved a beating, provides one small example of the willingness of black people to challenge the legacy and perceived consensus of a bygone era. Age serves as another significant intraracial cleavage, with blacks of the civil rights generation often frustrated with the failure of the younger blacks to take advantage of the opportunities now available to them. Andrea Y. Simpson, in her recent study of identity and politics among the post–civil rights generation of African American college students, found that most felt connected with other blacks, but they rejected the idea that their own fates were intertwined with them. Some openly criticized what they saw as unwillingness by African Americans to help themselves and the insistence that the government must solve black problems. Most surprising for Hunter was discovering their lack of faith in black leaders, politicians, and organizations: The NAACP and Urban League were virtually never mentioned.

Intraracial diversity based on immigration and the growing number of people who claim multiracial status has made defining blackness more difficult. In 1996, participants in a sparsely attended Multiracial March on Washington demanded the inclusion of a multiracial category in census data, a move contested by most major civil rights organizations.[57] Professional golfer Tiger Woods's suggestion that his mixed racial heritage makes him "Cablinasian" is a prominent example of the refusal by many multiracial people to abide by the old "one drop" rule. Instead, as Kerry A. Rockquemore and David L. Brunsma report, biracial people identify themselves in diverse ways: Some choose a singular racial identity; some have fluid identities that shift based on their social location, while others claim to have no racial identity at all. The growing number of immigrants from Africa and the Caribbean also is altering the meaning of being black and diluting racial unity. While placed in the same racial category of African Americans, Revel Rogers's studies of Afro-Caribbeans in New York find that they usually have a transnational identity and are more interested in immigration policies than racial discrimination.[58] Most have gained a higher status and better opportunities simply by immigrating; moreover, they lack a collective memory of racial oppression in the United States and are fierce competitors with native blacks for low-income jobs. Those who have been in the country for a while are prominently represented in political life, and recent data show that African Americans trail Caribbean and sub-Saharan African immigrants in income and levels of education.[59]

The class polarization African Americans have experienced since the 1980s resembles that found in mainstream society: a demise in middle-income families and an increase in both those who are low-income and affluent. More than 15 percent of all black households (and 53 percent of black married couple households) earn more than $50,000 annually, yet the top 20 percent earn nearly half of all black income.[60] Class diversity has led to a splintering of political unity, with sharp differences in goals and strategies for achieving racial advancement. Many individuals and groups are questioning the long-standing allegiance by blacks to the Democratic Party, which began in the 1940 with New Deal policies and was later fortified, when Republicans failed to support civil rights initiatives. More blacks, however, now object to the implication by Democrats that welfare and minimum wage are "black issues" and contend that there is far too little talk about tax breaks, home ownership, and community development.[61] Others claim that black leaders have already forsaken the poor by focusing on policies such as affirmative action and professional advancement rather than eliminating poverty, improving inner-city communities, and creating quality schools. In either case, there is concern that the 22 million eligible black voters will be taken for granted by Democrats, ignored by Republicans, and thus essentially courted by no one.[62]

In reality, high-profile African Americans whose sentiments resonate with Republicans are quickly embraced by right-wing organizations/ sponsors such as the Heritage Foundation or the Hoover Institution.[63] Republican organizations are aggressively reaching out to black voters today, often through mass mailings to churches promoting faith-based funds and programs. Many note the discrepancy between the conservative social values of African Americans and their voting behavior; for example, most polls show that black people are conservative on issues such as gay rights, prayer in school, abortion, and drugs. Yet blacks often see Republicans as the "antiblack" party, an image President Bush tried to remedy when he spoke at an NAACP dinner and apologized for the Republicans' failure to be the "party of Lincoln." His speech drew the ire of black conservative Ward Connerly, a vocal opponent of affirmation action who criticized the administration for supporting racial preferences and quotas in government contracting programs and accused it of being "mesmerized with skin color diversity" and "tragically drifting toward the left."[64]

Finally, the divisions among African Americans include those based on gender. Black women have embraced feminism and expanded their focus to include analyses of race and gender, often implicating black men for their sexism and creating another barrier to black unity. Second-wave feminism emerged on the heels of the black protest movement, drawing parallels between race and gender by noting that both were social constructs that legitimized subordination and second-class citizenship. African American women had long devoted much of their energy toward helping poor women and their children, but, understanding the greater acceptance of male leadership in mainstream society, they had also had a tradition of trying to foreground black men. For example, Marian Wright Edelman, a founding member of the Children's Defense Fund, had urged Roy Wilkins to become the leader of the organization, noting, "Among other things, our children need the image of a strong black man running things, changing the course of events."[65] Yet African American women also understood the potentially adverse consequences of male domination for women and, despite facing issues of divided loyalty, were forced to acknowledge the blatant sexist ideologies of black nationalists and need to create a space for their own voices. While their analyses of gender has broadened and strengthened contemporary feminism, many in the black community remain concerned over its potential for undermining black unity.

Concepts such as black feminists, middle-class blacks, and black Republicans were once almost oxymorons, but they now contribute to the complexity and evolving meaning of being black. Such diversity has brought to the fore a search for black authenticity, or yearning to maintain what is seen as the real, natural, genuine traditional black identity. In *Authentic Blackness*, J. Martin Favor claims the legal status of blackness is "no more culturally important than people's everyday lived experience of their racial identity" and notes the definitions of blackness are "constantly being invented, policed, transgressed, and contested." Labeling black conservatives race traitors, sell-outs, and even house niggers, accusing middle-income blacks of having lost touch with their roots or of forgetting where they came from, and admonishing blacks to "keep it real" and "stay black" are policing strategies aimed at preserving and representing a common black experience. Favor notes that social class is often the key criterion, so blacks who are poor, southern, and rural are most likely to earn the status of authenticity. Beyond social position, P. H. Collins describes what she calls a search for the "essence of Blackness," or "a concern for harmony and connectedness between self, community, nature and spirit, a life where the material is not privileged over the spiritual."[66]

Thus, the twenty-first century finds African Americans united by a history of racial oppression, the legacy of a remarkable struggle for racial freedom and justice, a sense of intertwined fates, a yearning for greater racial equality, and, in many cases, an acute discomfort with their growing intraracial diversity.

Notes

1. Z. N. Hurston (1979).
2. W. E. B. Du Bois (1926:296).

3. Quoted in J. McWhorter (2003).
4. G. C. Loury (2002).
5. J. McWhorter (2003).
6. S. Lee (1993).
7. M. Nobles (2000).
8. K. M. Brown (1996:110).
9. J. E. Dabel (2002).
10. E. Franklin Frazier (1957:196).
11. K. Ringle (2002).
12. D. Franklin (1997:82).
13. M. E. Hill (2000).
14. P. Giddings (1984:356).
15. L. O. Graham (1999).
16. D. G. White (1999:17).
17. E. Bonilla-Silva (2001:13).
18. See M. Brown et al. (2003).
19. M. Brown et al. (2003).
20. U.S. Bureau of Census (April 2003) (www.census.gov/population/socdemo/race/black).
21. A. Cancio, T. Evans, and D. Maume (1996).
22. L. W. Diuguid (2004:B7).
23. M. L. Oliver (2004).
24. M. L. Oliver (2004).
25. U.S. Bureau of Census (April 2003) (www.census.gov/population/socdemo/race/black).
26. "Desegregation levels" (2004:A2).
27. A. Williams (2004:12).
28. Y. St. Jean and J. R. Feagin (1997:17).
29. See E. Higginbotham and L. Weber (1992).
30. P. Moss and C. Tilly (1996:253).
31. I. Browne and I. Kennelly (1999).
32. E. N. Glenn (1998:19–20).
33. R. Brewer (1993:19).
34. R. Brewer (1993:24–25).
35. See, for example, M. Mauer (1999).
36. M. Hughes and M. E. Thomas (1998).
37. M. Stearns (2002).
38. "Ideology trumps science" (2004:A8).
39. From *This Week* magazine, January 30, 2004, p. 14.
40. D. Johnston and E. Lightblau (2003).
41. D. J. Dickerson (2004:26).
42. L. Bobo, J. R. Kluegel, and R. A. Smith (1997).

43. M. Taylor (1998).
44. A. Gordon and C. Newfield (1994:737).
45. L. Bobo et al. (1997).
46. W. J. Wilson (1987:7–8).
47. S. F. Schram (2000).
48. Quoted in E. Bonilla-Silva (2001:23).
49. L. Collins (2002:154).
50. E. Bonilla-Silva (2001:37).
51. E. Bonnilla-Silva (2001:45).
52. Quoted in K. A. Myers and P. Williamson (2001:4).
53. O. Patterson (1997:85).
54. J. McWhorter (2000:214).
55. A. A. Young (2004).
56. B. Blauner (2001:217).
57. M. Nobles (2000).
58. R. Rogers (2000).
59. D. Fears (2003).
60. E. O. Hutchinson (2002a).
61. D. Goldstein (2002).
62. T. Cross and R. B. Slater (1998).
63. A. Pinkney (2000).
64. W. Connerly (2001).
65. Quoted in L. Olson (2001:378).
66. P. H. Collins (1998:162–63).

CHAPTER 3

Black Families

Beyond Revisionist Scholarship

In form, African American families have been some of the most flexible, adaptable, and inclusive kinship institutions in America. In function, they have been among the most accepting and nurturing of children, and the most supportive of adults.

—Niara Sudarkasa[1]

The latter half of the twentieth century witnessed a proliferation of revisionist scholarship on African American families, most of it aimed at challenging negative stereotypes and images and highlighting their strengths and diversity. Despite this work, the century began and ended with black people at the center of the country's most contentious family issue: the escalating number of single-mother families formed outside marriage, living in poverty, and dependent on welfare.

By the close of the century, the significant minority of black families historically headed by single mothers clearly had turned into a sizeable majority, a trend made even more alarming by the growing separation of marriage and parenthood, the economic decline of urban areas, the demise of extended family support, the growing number of black children placed in foster care, and an unprecedented expansion of the welfare rolls. By 2000, fewer than one-third of all African American women were married and living with a spouse, and a significant majority of black children—nearly 70 percent—were being born outside marriage.[2] Nonmarital childbearing was especially associated with welfare dependency for black women who, in the year prior to the elimination of the Aid to Families with Dependent Children (AFDC) program, comprised 40 percent of all welfare beneficiaries.[3] Never-married single mothers exemplified the concerns of political conservatives decrying a loss of "family values," and so wedded were race, poverty, and welfare in the minds of many Americans that the black family was often seen as consisting of a poor, single mother with several children, fathered by several different men. Claims by policymakers that a decline in family values and overly generous welfare benefits were fostering higher rates of single motherhood fueled support for ending the more than sixty-year-old AFDC program, which was originally designed to enable mothers to care for their own children, and for implementing new "workfare" (employment) and "wedfare" (marriage) policies.

The current focus on welfare and single-mother families represents the latest chapter in a long debate aimed at understanding why African Americans—or at least significant numbers of them—seem unable or unwilling to bring their sexual, marital, and family norms into compliance with mainstream cultural ideologies. While white slave owners had garnered immense economic profits for more than two centuries by insisting that enslaved black people disregard dominant family structures and ideologies, emancipation created the need to reorganize and stabilize the agricultural labor force, and it thus ushered in the first campaign to get African Americans married. The extent of their compliance to the marriage mandate became the focal point of scholarly work on black families, especially as the sociological study of families blossomed in the early 1900s. By then, most scholars had uncritically accepted the new ideology of marriage based on free choice and romantic love, and the family ideally as nuclear in structure with a breadwinner–homemaker division of labor. White, middle-class families were praised for their modernity and suitability for the new industrial economy, and the handful of researchers who turned their lens beyond that model of family saw only disorder, dysfunction, and pathology.

The early social scientists who unwittingly proffered a social deficit perspective on African American families were usually liberal scholars who failed to question the validity of dominant family structures. For them, the mission was to show that slavery and racism had crippled black families, leaving them with too few resources to form strong families and fostering the creation of matriarchal families. Indeed, marriage was unlikely to offer black women the option of full-time domesticity or economic security, as the southern sharecropping system demanded the labor of all family members.[4] Sharecropping and poverty diminished the resiliency of black families, but few championed decent jobs for black men as the solution to the dilemma, nor were there calls to exclude black women from their economic roles. Northward migration enhanced the number and visibility of single-mother families, and critics of "sexually promiscuous" black women who had children out of wedlock and ran their own families became more vocal. Not until the civil rights era was the "matriarchy" theme put to rest by revisionist scholars; however, much of their work has failed to stand the test of time.

In this chapter, I present a postmodern gender perspective on the cultural and structural forces that historically affected the marriage and family decision making of black women. I contend that, at least for a significant minority of black women, the cultural and economic resources they had garnered during slavery, their sense of autonomy and independence, and the viable female-centered families they had formed led them to resist efforts to force them to marry. During the post–civil rights era, the loss of these resources and traditions, due to factors such as public policies, racial integration, class polarization, and patriarchal leanings, fostered a proliferation of impoverished single-mother families that became the target of welfare reform initiatives.

Objectives of the Chapter

This chapter has three major objectives. The first is to bring a gender analysis to the study of African American families by focusing on the active, decision-making roles of black women in family formation. I maintain that while the concept of gender is prominent and well developed in most feminist work on families, it has remained in its nascent stages in research on African American families. In exploring the subordination of women, for example, feminist scholars have noted the significance of the breadwinner–homemaker family structure that emerged during industrialization. Casting women as homemakers marked an important change in their status, as in colonial American society they had combined productive and family work. Despite patriarchal ideologies, eighteenth-century marriages were often seen as economic partnerships between men and women, as white women's labor was required in the family-based agricultural economy.[5] While displacing white women from their productive labor roles and elevating their dependence on men and marriage undoubtedly helped spark the first wave of feminism, most evidence suggests that women accepted the new domestic code, as it enabled them to gain the status of being mistresses of their own homes and offered economic security for their children.[6] This gendering of the family, however, achieved its greatest success among those who were white and affluent, and even then it was being contested by a resurgence of feminism during the mid–twentieth century.

By then, the notion that being a full-time wife and mother was inherently gratifying was being increasingly challenged as more women were drawn into the labor force yet found that they were relegated to low-wage, dead-end jobs that assumed the primacy of their roles in the family. The dominant gender ideology suggested that white women were primarily wives and mothers (or would soon be), and those seeking employment faced discrimination, harassment, blatant sexism, occupational segregation, and an absence of family-friendly policies in the workplace. At home, their secondary, dependent status in their families often fostered abuse, neglect, and dissatisfaction, leading feminists ultimately to criticize families as oppressive to women. They contended that while the nuclear family had become enshrined as "traditional" and as the fount of love, support, and well-being, such families were often arenas of power and privilege for men, but of subordination and even violence for many women.[7] Rather than privileging marriage and heterosexuality, many argued that emotional bonds and commitments could be expressed in a variety of relationships, that men and women experienced marriage differently, and that families could take a variety of forms.[8] Their work led to the use of gender as an analytical framework for studying issues ranging from child socialization to family violence, yet the primacy of race in studying African Americans has resulted in a fairly truncated perspective on how gender affects their families.

While the substantial focus on single-mother families introduced the issue of gender to black family studies and produced a rich literature on the experiences of African American women, one rarely finds even a single chapter in black family books devoted to a discussion of gender; in fact, the word *gender* does not even appear in most indices. For the most part, research on black families has either praised the strength or criticized the behavior of poor single mothers or highlighted the ability of more affluent black women to combine their work and family roles with social activism. In some cases, black feminists have met the contention of families as a source of oppression for women with the reprisal that they can also be sources of support and encouragement—although the families they speak of are rarely the nuclear, gender-ordered ones criticized by feminists. African American scholars have also noted that being a full-time homemaker can be a cherished role for black women, as economic necessity has often forced them to work outside the home.[9] Considerable energy has been spent debating whether black women are matriarchal, simply strong, or victims of multiple oppression—yet the focus on these issues have done little to promote an understanding of how gender, and the resources and power associated with it, has affected their family and marriage decision making.

The second objective of this chapter is to provide an analytical overview of the history of black families and bring a gender lens to the two dominant perspectives—the legacy of slavery thesis and the revisionist approach. In addition, I articulate a third "postmodern perspective" that draws on themes from more recent research on the history of black families. While both the legacy of slavery and revisionist perspectives imply at least a modicum of support for diverse family structures, their central thrust has been to accept the legitimacy of hegemonic family and gender structures and explain why blacks have failed to embrace them. For example, early legacy of slavery theorists such as E. Franklin Frazier saw single-mother families as a source of poverty and disorganization among African Americans but also as testimony to the devastating impact of slavery, sexual exploitation, and economic exclusion. Although later criticized as offering a pathological perspective on black families, Frazier still deserves much credit for challenging the prevailing sentiment that the family traits of black people were a reflection of their innate inferiority.

Revisionist scholars challenged the legacy of slavery thesis by criticizing the cultural insensitivity and white, middle-class bias of most family research, which ignored the strengths of poor single-mother families, blamed the poor for their poverty, and disregarded the adverse impact of racist policies and practices on African American families. As black families were being recast as valiant survivors of racism and economic exclusion, historians pouring over plantation records and other archives were uncovering evidence that strong black families existed during slavery. Relying primarily on data from large plantations, they argued that black families had conformed to the dominant family model as best they could, given the vagaries of slavery and the century of legalized racial segregation that followed. Eugene Genovese claimed that to trace black family weakness to slavery was to incorrectly read history backward, and Herbert Gutman dealt what appeared to be a fatal blow to the legacy of slavery perspective with compelling evidence that black families were more likely to be composed of two parents during slavery than in the 1960s. These scholars rejected the black matriarch thesis, credited black couples with having egalitarian marital norms, and shifted the political discourse from how slavery had weakened black families to a focus on current patterns of racism and economic exclusion.

The postmodern perspective I articulate differs from both of these theories by contending that, at least for a significant minority of black women, centuries of slavery produced resistance to marriage by stripping it of its socially created sanctity, equipping them with resources that could be jeopardized by marriage, and fostering functional alternative family forms. While most theories highlight the significance of race and class oppression in shaping black families, I suggest that slavery did more than merely create structural obstacles to conformity. It also initiated a work–family–gender system that prioritized the work roles of black people and demanded that they transgress dominant conventions of family and morality, essentially denying that there was a crucial link among marriage, sexuality, and childbearing. Slavery and racism demystified hegemonic marriage ideals, exposing their patriarchal and economic underpinnings and serving to disabuse African Americans of the belief that intimacy and family had to unfold within the confines of a legal marriage contract. Slavery also endowed many black women with a strong work ethic, a sense of status from their more intimate interactions with and exposure to white families, and competence in the arena of family life. It paved the way for an incredible amount of autonomy for black women in deciding whether to marry and how to form families, and many resisted the strident marriage campaign that proceeded emancipation.

I describe this analysis as postmodern as it rejects the idea of uniformity in the family ideologies and experiences of black people, unmasks the gender experiences of women, and focuses on that segment of the black population that actively resisted compliance with family and gender systems that were foreign to their traditions and inconsistent with their status and resources. It draws on recent strands of research that show what slaves had in common was forced labor and a legal status of property; beyond that, they varied greatly in the marriage patterns, work demands, and gender relationships. While studies of black families have alternately castigated their deficiencies and trumpeted their resiliency, the objective here is to understand black women as active agents in their own lives who made decisions to protect themselves, their children, and their cultural and material resources by resisting conformity to dominant family norms. Thus, despite formidable forces urging them to do so, black women were often unwilling to forsake the kinship systems that evolved over centuries of slavery in favor of male-dominated marriage, not simply because of economic and racial barriers, but also because doing so was inconsistent with their cultural values and resources. The survival of black families has hinged on their ability to create a variety of family structures, and, drawing on their cultural and economic resources, they did so.

Single-mother and extended families have a long tradition among African Americans; however, the post–civil rights era saw a remarkable decline in the strength and well-being of those families. The epidemics of joblessness, gang violence, drug abuse, nonmarital childbearing, and welfare dependency in black urban areas mocked the implication of revisionist thought that removing racial barriers and creating greater opportunity would strengthen black families and bring them into conformity with the dominant societal norm.

Thus, the third and final objective of this chapter is to explore the decline in black families, especially those headed by single mothers, in an era where racial integration and equal employment policies have diluted racism and racial barriers to success. Structural theorists explained the problem in terms of a loss in the availability of industrial jobs for young African American men, while many embracing a cultural approach emphasized the changing and even pathological values of disadvantaged urban black people. I contend that a more complex array of factors have challenged the strength of single-mother families, including growing class diversity of black people and the decline in the traditional authority of black women.

The Legacy of Slavery Thesis

Whatever social organization may have prevailed in their native Africa, whatever family arrangements, forms, and usages found in the mores of the preexistent cultures, these were stripped from, or eventually lost, to the Negroes brought to America.

—S. A. Queen and R. W. Habenstein[10]

Family sociology emerged during the early 1900s, as concern over the disruptive impact of industrialization on family life gave way to ideologies of the modern, nuclear family as ideally suited to meet the needs of the new economy. Prior to the 1950s, however, many Americans lacked the economic resources to create such families, and racial and economic forces made such families even more elusive for black people. Nevertheless, racist ideologies attributing African Americans' inability to abide by these family traditions to their biological and moral inferiority were prevalent. In a series of studies initiated in the 1930s, E. Franklin Frazier worked tirelessly to redirect the focus of theories from racial inferiority to an analysis of the impact of slavery on black families. While Africans did not arrive on the shores of the Americas bereft of family traditions, slavery had taken a devastating toll on those traditions. Slavery had precluded the right of black people to marry legally, resulted in the sale of spouses and family members, undermined men as authority figures and providers in their families, and forced women to take on demeaning sexual and economic roles.

From the beginning of slave trade, ethnocentrism and the prospect of economic gain undoubtedly led the first white Europeans who encountered Africans to see them as savages and to misunderstand their family system, and these observations grew in significance as the slave trade flourished. Slavery destroyed the African heritage of blacks, claims Kenneth Stamps, and left them living in "cultural chaos" since the family patterns of whites were "meaningless and unintelligible" to them.[11] Moreover, the definition of slaves as property was one of many efforts to negate their humanity and deny the significance of their personal and family lives. Slaves' property status precluded them from entering a legal marriage contract, as the law recognized no form of marriage among slaves, "whether they 'take up' with each other by expression of their owners, or from mere impulse of nature, or in obedience to the command to 'multiply and replenish the earth.'"[12] With no standing before the law, slave marriages could be and were ended at any time at the discretion of slave owners.

Matriarchal Women and the Insignificant Black Male

Frazier acknowledges that slavery had given rise to both two-parent and single-mother families. While two-parent (male-headed) families appeared to function well, with some even achieving middle-class status, Frazier devotes most of his attention to single-mother or matriarchal families. Poor, female-headed families, Frazier argues, had their origins in the sale and separation of slaves, the definition of the black family as a mother and her children, and sexual relationships between female slaves and their owners. He understands that these maternal families had often functioned quite well in the rural South yet were being increasingly undermined by destabilizing forces such as northward migration. Implied in Frazier's analysis of the "black matriarchate," as well as the work of other legacy of slavery theorists, is the idea that slavery either abolished or severely curtailed dominant patriarchal traditions. One result, according to Frazier, was an unusual boldness and strength among black women, who often defied white authority in ways that black men would never have gotten away with. "Neither economic necessity nor tradition had instilled in her the spirit of subordination to masculine authority," writes Frazier, who describes these black women as playing a dominant role in families and seeking sexual satisfaction outside marriage.[13]

A similar theme is present in the work of Jessie Bernard, who argues that slavery had given black women an "unnatural superiority" over black men. Slavery was a more flagrant violation of masculinity than femininity, according to Bernard, as "enforced subordination and subservience was not so far out of line with the Western world's definition of a 'woman's place.'"[14] Highlighting the general sassiness of black women, for example, she notes that in matters of marriage, it "didn't pay, really, [for slave owners] to tangle with those spirited women. If they wanted a man, they seem usually to have got him; if they did not want him, it was . . . hard to force him on them."[15]

The flip side of the strong black women premise was the notion that slavery had deprived black men of their masculinity and rendered them irrelevant to family life. Slavery controlled the economic and reproductive labor of men and women; it denied men the right to provide for, protect, or be recognized as the heads of their families; and forced women to prioritize productive labor over their domestic roles. In doing so, it embodied numerous assaults of patriarchal families, including prohibiting slaves from entering legal marriage contracts, the sexual exploitation of black women by slave owners, the provision of separate housing for black spouses, the definition of black families as comprised of mothers and their children, and the sale of family members—all arrangements that allowed slave owners to maximize the exploitation of their slaves. Because black men could not protect their families from the abuses of slave masters, wrote one historian, some vowed either never to marry or to marry women from other plantations, as they did not want to "be forced to watch as she was beaten, insulted, raped, overworked, or starved without being able to protect her."[16]

Patriarchal traditions were also undermined by the frequent meddling of slave owners into the affairs of black families. To varying degrees, slave owners governed the marriage decisions and relationships, child-bearing and child-rearing practices, and the economic well-being of black families. They sometimes intervened heavily into the affairs of black families, whipping slaves for domestic discord and, ironically, for violating monogamous standards of sexuality.[17]

In Search of Freedom: Emancipation and Northward Migration

Innumerable tasks undoubtedly faced newly emancipated African Americans, not the least of which was survival in a society where racism was thoroughly entrenched and few were willing to hire, feed, or clothe black people. Emancipation diminished whatever stability slave families had achieved, as armies invaded and disrupted plantation life, setting thousands of black people adrift and leading many to abandon their spouses and children.[18] Although many African Americans had fought in the Civil War and had high aspirations for freedom, black men lost many of the skilled occupations they had held during slavery and, frequently charged with vagrancy, rape, and crime, faced an increased risk of being lynched, incarcerated, or forced into labor contracts with whites.[19] Most black people wound up on farms and plantations working under the sharecropping system, as the potential loss of their free labor was a major threat to the southern economy. For black men and women alike, the decision not to work after slavery was nearly impossible, as economic necessity and the power of whites forbade it.[20] To ensure an adequate supply of workers, some states created and enforced labor contracts between black workers and white landowners, justifying them on the premise that employment was essential to the transition from slavery to citizenship.[21]

The need for cheap labor also made it difficult for black parents to gain or retain custody of their children. Some states passed laws allowing former slave owners to "indenture" (or essentially reenslave) children under the age of twelve if their parents were either unmarried or unemployed.[22] Indeed, policymakers during the late nineteenth century often argued that children were generally better off living in orphan institutions than with poor, "immoral" parents, and, since black parents were often unemployed and unmarried, their parental rights were most likely to be under assault. Although these economic and family policies allowed some whites to profit from the absence of legal marriages among blacks, the abolition of slavery for the most part sparked a major campaign to get blacks married, as the long-standing patterns of nonmarital sexuality and childbearing that had served slave owners well were now seen as threatening.

The hope of escaping the racial caste system of the South and securing job opportunities fueled a massive northward migration of African Americans during the late 1800s and first half of the twentieth century. While the fortunes of a significant segment of the black population had risen after the abolition of slavery, these gains proved short-lived when Reconstruction ended, racial segregation became the law of the land, and southern blacks were disenfranchised and displaced from many jobs. By 1890, 90 percent of African Americans still lived in the rural South, and most of them worked in agriculture; less than a century later, 90 percent had migrated to urban areas, often in the North and West.[23]

As Carole Marks has explained, the active recruitment activities of northern industrialists played a major role in orchestrating this mass migration. Faced with a disruption in the flow of immigrants from Europe during World War I and growing labor unrest in factories, industrialists used black workers to perform low-wage, dirty work and to serve as strikebreakers. Black women were also actively recruited, sometimes signing domestic labor contracts in exchange for their transportation expenses and taking on jobs as cooks, laundresses, and maids that were crucial in supporting their families.

Black women often had an added incentive to migrate northward, as they were fleeing from the adversities of marriage and family life and sexual exploitation by black and white men.[24] While their maternal families and extended kin networks often functioned well in the South, the women who headed them were locked into low-wage agricultural and domestic jobs that were increasingly waning, and they were excluded from the benefits of social welfare programs. The northward migration of poor single mothers created a "moral panic" among black leaders in urban areas and state authorities, who often saw poor single black women as sexually and socially dangerous,[25] yet most survived by acquiring low-wage domestic or factory jobs and relying on the support of family networks. Migration brought higher wages, but northern families often insisted on live-in domestics,[26] making the work of black women more labor-intensive and keeping them away from their own families. As Jacqueline Jones has noted, in some cases their work in the homes of white families led to a re-creation of the mistress–slave roles that had existed under slavery. More often, black female domestic workers were exposed to the risk of being raped by employers, and they constantly instructed each other on "how to run, or always not be in the house with the white man or big sons."[27] "No white man had to fear prosecution for sexually attacking a black women," write Hines and Thompson, but "all black women, of whatever class or reputation, had to fear sexual assault, exploitation, and rape."[28]

Black women found their hopes for racial justice, economic advancement, and a more stable family life in the "promised land" of the North diminished by the racial oppression. Even the prospects for marriage were few due to black men's confinement in poor-paying jobs and their increasing criminalization for an array of petty offenses that dramatically increased their rates of incarceration during the early 1900s.[29] Abysmal housing, poor sanitation, malnutrition, and demanding, high-risk jobs increased rates of mortality and morbidity among African Americans, especially rates of infant and childhood mortality.[30] Thus, as Frazier points out, northward migration further undermined the two-parent family. As blacks moved north, negative portrayals of single black women as sexually degenerate, the rise in single-mother families in urban areas, and greater access by black mothers to government welfare policies all conspired in creating the image of the pathological, matriarchal black family.

Migration and concentration in urban areas significantly increased the visibility of black people, while the dashed hopes for racial and economic equality gradually ignited their political consciousness. The racial unrest that began to foment in the early 1900s gradually turned into an organized protest movement, as blacks became more openly critical of racial inequality. Yet in 1965, an official government policy report on black families issued by Senator Moynihan revived Frazier's matriarchy thesis by implying that female-headed families were thwarting black progress. Moynihan focused on the growing number of single-mother families in urban areas and saw them as the result of a slavery system that was "profoundly different from," and "indescribably worse than, any recorded servitude, ancient or modern."[31] Though issued at the height of the civil rights movement, the now-infamous study suggested that policy should focus on strengthening black families rather than eliminating racism, segregation, and poverty.

Although he focused on single-mother families, Moynihan also repeatedly recognized growing class diversity among black families, emphatically dismissed genetic explanations of black poverty, and championed greater economic opportunity for black men. He argued that while there was nothing inherently wrong with matriarchal families, they caused problems because they were out of step with mainstream society. Whether for practical or ideological reasons, he equated strong families with male-headship and argued that black children were often being neglected by employed mothers.

The Revisionist Perspective

Black women shared the doubtful advantage of greater equality with black men—usually the equal privilege of working with hoes and axes in the tobacco, corn, and grain fields.

—L. Walsh[32]

If slavery bred strong women, it hardly emasculated black men.

—P. Morgan[33]

The legacy of slavery and the black matriarch thesis deflected attention from the growing demand for racial justice by castigating black families as pathological and failing to abide by the family values of other Americans, thus sparking a genre of myth-dispelling research by revisionist scholars determined to provide a more accurate view of the black family. In his 1968 book *Black Families in White America*, Andrew Billingsley drew on functionalist theory to explain the adaptive nature of African American family structures, arguing that they should be evaluated based on their viability and survival rather than their stability and/or conformity to white cultural norms. Robert Hill delineated gender role flexibility, religiosity, a strong achievement orientation, and resilient kinship bonds as the particular strengths of black families. Similarly, Carol Stack provided a vivid ethnographic portrait of black, single mothers that made a lasting contribution to our understanding of the complex networks of exchange and reciprocity they used to survive. Other scholars criticized the seeming inordinate focus on poor, single-mother families as perpetuating a distorted, stereotypical image of the "typical" black family. Noting that most black families were neither poor nor headed by single women, researchers such as Charles Willie, Bart Landry, John Scanzoni, Walter Allen, and Harriette McAdoo extended the research lens to middle- and working-class black families, usually pointing out that they were quite similar to their white counterparts. Speaking of the diversity of black families, McAdoo contended that, "contrary to what many people seem to think, there is no such thing as 'the' African-American family."[34]

While revisionist research constituted a thorough reassessment of black families, such as recasting single-mother families as strong and functional and highlighting the diversity of black families, its most enduring legacy has been to reject the notion that slavery had destroyed the black family. John Blassingame became the first of many scholars to document the strength and importance of slave families:

> The family, while it had no legal existence in slavery, was in actuality one of the most important survival mechanisms for the slave. In his family he found companionship, love, sexual gratification, sympathetic understanding of his sufferings; he learned how to avoid punishment, to cooperate with other blacks, and to maintain his self-esteem.[35]

Similarly, Eugene D. Genovese claimed that "slaves created impressive norms of family life, including as much of a nuclear family norm as the conditions allowed, and that they entered the postwar social system with a remarkably stable base" and a "healthy sexual equality" between men and women.[36] More recently, historian Philip Morgan explained that it was with family life that slaves "continually demonstrated that they had wills of their own [and] that they were sentient, articulate human beings."[37] Despite their efforts, slave owners could not negate the humanity of their African slaves, and, according to Morgan, nowhere was their humanity more evident than in the great importance they placed on their families; indeed, exploiting family ties was a powerful mechanism of social control over slaves.[38]

Thus, slaves were allowed to experience some of the gratifications of courtship, marriage, and family life, as such relationships fostered loyalties and boosted the morale and stability of the slave population. These factors became especially vital to the survival of slavery after 1807, when importing additional slaves into the United States was officially prohibited. While the family lives of slaves were scarcely allowed to interfere with their profitability, the few prerogatives they received were shaped by gender.

Rediscovering the Patriarchal Slave Family

An accurate portrait of the African women in bondage must debunk the myth of the matriarchate.

—Angela Davis[39]

Notable in the work of revisionist scholars was the rediscovery of patriarchy, with the linchpin being Herbert Gutman's argument that a majority of enslaved black families living on plantations were composed of two parents. Other research has contributed to constructing the patriarchal black family by emphasizing how male prerogatives shaped patterns of courtship, marriage, freedom of mobility, and occupational diversity. Historian P. Morgan, for example, finds evidence of patriarchy in the fact that, as customary in some African traditions, husbands were often seven to eleven years older than their wives, thus strengthening male-dominant marriages. Men usually initiated courtship and proposed marriage, and they were often described by slave owners as domineering husbands.[40] Families were organized along gender lines, with slave women doing most of the domestic chores and caring for children, and men often buttressing their status in the family by providing additional material resources. The greater geographic mobility of black men also hinted at male privilege: Compared to black women, men traveled more, either to run errands for their masters or to visit families on other plantations, and naming practices often favored men. Black masculinity was also expressed through social protest; for example, while there is ample evidence that women were also involved, men dominated when it came to organizing slave rebellions and conspiracies.[41]

Work assignments and other privileges granted slaves were also organized along the lines of gender, usually giving men greater privileges than women. Black men, for example, were given opportunities for more varied jobs, while women spent more time in monotonous drudgery. The greater occupational diversity and training available to black men is illustrated by data from South Carolina showing that by the late 1700s, nearly 25 percent of rural slave men worked outside the fields, compared to only 5 percent of rural slave women. Not only was the occupational structure for women narrow, but nearly all skilled and privileged positions were held by men.[42] Their occupational roles often enabled them to provide special gifts for their wives and children:

> Slave ironworkers in the Chesapeake purchased small luxuries and domestic items for their wives. During the 1730s, one skilled hand . . . used his overwork pay to purchase a bed, two blankets, and a rug for his wife and children. In 1797, a slave named Phil, who worked at John Blair's foundry in Virginia, bought shoe leather and seven and half yards of ribbon for his wife. Even ordinary field hands could provide for their womenfolk.[43]

Thus, enslaved black men made symbolic and important economic contributions to their families, as patriarchal traditions enabled them to claim the most prestigious occupations available to blacks and to be recognized as authorities in their families.

Free black families also took advantage of a gendered labor system that favored men, according to Thomas Bogger, who studied the family and occupational structures of free blacks in Norfolk, Virginia, during the mid-1800s. During this era, black men were listed as employed in nearly fifty different occupations, compared to only nine for black women. A slight majority of black families were male headed, despite a significant shortage of men, and only 25 percent of free black women worked outside the home—all of whom were married to men with low-paying jobs.

Drawing on the West African legacy of black families further strengthened the revisionist account of patriarchy, often by showing that male dominance could exist even when women had strong productive and family roles. Most prominent among those scholars linking black families to their African ancestry are Afrocentric theorists such as Wade Nobles, who has argued that the structure and function of the black family is "ultimately traceable to its African value system and/or some modification thereof."[44] That value system described patriarchy, polygyny, extended families, respect for the elderly, the primacy of mother–child relationships, and women as economic providers as characteristic African family life, and it noted that all were practiced and even reinforced to some extent during slavery. Despite their economic roles, African women were subordinated to men in virtually every aspect of life, from denial of the best food to enforced sexual chastity to female circumcision.[45] Polygyny itself is usually indicative of male domination, although the short supply of black women, especially during the early decades of slavery, curtailed the practice and heightened the status and importance of black women. Some have argued black women were less likely to be slated for slavery because of the value of their work roles in West African society.[46] Overall, however, the dual family and economic roles of African American women were not seen as diminishing the significance of men in families.

Feminist Analysis of the Family

Despite its revival of black masculinity and implicit support for two-parent families, the work of revisionist scholars often dovetailed nicely with the feminist critique of families. Gender as socially constructed based on economic factors and patriarchy was the cornerstone of modern feminist thought, and the experiences of African American families offered ample evidence of this contention. Barrie Thorne summarized feminist family policies as endorsing a broader array of sexual and household arrangements as families, supporting women's right to abortion, and ending male authority, female dependency, and the relegation of nurturing to women in families.[47]

Claims by revisionist scholars that black families took a diversity of forms, that female-headed families could be strong and viable, that black women had effectively combined labor market and family work, and that black marriages were based on relative equality between men and women embodied much of the feminist vision for families. Black feminists expanded the revisionist focus on racial oppression as shaping African American families by placing it within the larger framework of intersectionality theory. Rose Brewer, for example, asserted that poor, single-mother families could not be understood unless historically grounded in the "social construction of a racist/sexist social order," noting that:

> gender, race, ideology, culture, state, and economy operate simultaneously and interactively in the family formation and change process. Capitalist

racial patriarchy profoundly shapes male and female relations generally but is also conflated with cultural and ideological realities. I mean by capitalist racial patriarchy a structure of White male-dominated social arrangements. These institutional arrangements severely disadvantage Black women, men, and children.[48]

Rethinking the Revisionist Paradigm

Born of the civil rights era struggle to control images of the black family and contest racist explanations for the proliferation of single-mother families among African Americans, revisionists highlighted the strengths and survival of black families, rejected the notion that most were headed by single mothers, and eventually challenged the dominant paradigm contending that slavery had destroyed black families. They essentially argued that African Americans had conformed to the dominant family model as best they could and sought to refute the theme of matriarchal families with evidence that slavery did not thwart the patriarchal inclinations of black men. Yet this claim itself, advanced to redeem black families from the accusation of deliberately ignoring dominant family conventions, offers significant implicit support for the superiority of two-parent families and introduces a "masculinist bias" into the study of black families. Moreover, attributing their family structures solely to racism denies any active decision making on the part of African Americans in assessing the value of white cultural family forms.

In many cases the revisionist perspective also inadvertently produced a more "humane" version of slavery, countering evidence of the harsh realities of slave life with the notion that it honored or at least sought to sustain the family ties of slaves. Genovese wrote that slaveholders "rarely if ever denied the moral content of the [marriage] relationship" between their slaves, and credited them with often showing "tender concern for black women who suffered abuse from their husbands."[49] He additionally claimed that slaves were fed well and that married life served effectively to keep the white sexual aggression to a minimum, contributing to a revisionist view of slavery recently described by Wilma A. Dunaway as more of a "Disney script than scholarly research."[50]

Perhaps more important, the notion that black people managed to maintain a reasonable semblance of the two-parent family during slavery produced a monolithic picture of the black family during slavery. Postrevisionist historians, criticizing earlier work as drawing too heavily on documents from large plantations, have produced a much more complex picture of the family lives of black people during slavery. Moving beyond debates over matriarchy and patriarchy, they have sought to show how an array of factors, such as region and size of plantation, affected black families. Dunaway, for example, criticizes the dominant revisionist paradigm as having neglected the study of family life on small plantations, although 88 percent of slaves resided in locations where there were fewer than fifty slaves.[51] In doing so, she argues that revisionists have overstated the prevalence of two-parent families and exaggerated the agency of slaves in resisting family breakup. On small plantations, enslaved black people experienced more family separations, greater brutality, and more sexual exploitation. The following postmodern perspective builds on emerging research by highlighting how structural forces gave rise to cultural traditions and resources that often empowered African American women and led to a great deal of activism and autonomy in their family decisions.

A Postmodern Gender Perspective

In *Cane River*, Lalita Tademy weaves a wealth of archival data into an eloquent, poignant story of her African American foremothers that dates back to the 1800s. These four valiant black women—Elizabeth, Suzette, Philomene, and Emily—endured the numerous indignities of slavery on plantations in central Louisiana where they often worked side-by-side with their white slave owners. Seldom able to marry or sustain marriages with freely chosen partners or to control their own sexuality, all had children fathered by white men they are unable to marry, yet they mustered the courage to manipulate their dire life situations and their relationships with white male partners to their own advantage. Tademy writes that her research led her to challenge everything she thought she knew about slavery, race, class, and Louisiana, where blacks in some areas were as likely as whites to own slaves. Slavery undoubtedly played itself out in a multitude of unique dramas, and Tademy's focus on the family decision making of her female ancestors stands in sharp contrast to male-centered revisionist accounts of black enslaved families doing their best to mirror their white counterparts. It highlights the saliency of female bonds and the agency of black women in forming families, and it resonates with postrevisionist research showing that slavery produced a diversity of black families, not simply because of the inclinations and whims of individual slave owners but also because it evolved differently based on region and economic factors.

The impact of slavery on the black family structure, argues Donna Franklin in *Ensuring Inequality*, depended on the plantation's size, work organization, and economic solvency. African customs, restrictive sexual norms, and stable slave marriages were more characteristic of large plantations, where there were more potential marital partners, less likelihood of slaves being sold, and greater segregation between whites and blacks. Slaves living on smaller plantations had fewer marital partners, more interracial interaction with their white owners, and were more likely to be sold to resolve economic crises. On these plantations, early sexuality, teenage childbearing, master–slave sexual relationships, and single-mother families were common. Moreover, while revisionist writers have often drawn on the systematic records of large plantation owners,[52] the dominant image of slaves living on large, wealthy plantations is countered by the fact that by 1860, the 10 percent of whites still owning slaves had an average of seven to nine slaves each.[53] Tademy's story stands as a case in point to the diversity of family experiences among slaves. Her female ancestors lived on a small plantation where they worked alongside their owners and faced the constant threat of family members being sold and of coercive sexual encounters with white men.

In this postmodern gender perspective on African American families, I try to illustrate some of the diversity in black women's responses to freedom and the opportunity (and often demand) that they marry, based on their own appraisal of their resources and their active decision making. Theorists agree that blacks were neither allowed to enter legal marriages during slavery nor guaranteed that the unions they formed would not be separated by sale, yet revisionists insist that emancipation produced heroic efforts by black people to legalize marriages, and they have marshaled evidence in support of that claim. Missing from their work, however, has been a critical analysis of the relevance of the marriage contract to the newly freed blacks, the coercive state policies and class politics that urged marriage, the fragility of black marital unions, the frequent failure by early census takers to determine if couples living together were married, and the resources of African American women that militated against their entry into patriarchal marriages. Marriage and patriarchy are essentially universal institutions and are "naturalized" as the bases for family life; so, it is certainly not surprising that scholars have found substantial ideological support for both among black people. Still, neither the African heritage of black people nor centuries of American slavery had prepared them for the marriage-centered family arrangements of mainstream society.

By forbidding legal and/or permanent marital ties among black people, slavery curtailed access to the rights and benefits of marriage but also sanctioned the separation of sex, marriage, and childbearing. It diminished patriarchal power among enslaved African men, yet revisionists have found that male prerogatives existed in that they initiated courtship and marriage, married younger women, enjoyed more freedom of movement, engaged in a broader array of occupations, contributed economically to their families, led rebellions, and expected their wives to perform the bulk of the domestic work. Less, however, has been said about how the resources garnered by black women during slavery may have thwarted their interest in marriage. Slavery not only reinforced West African traditions that valued women's economic and reproductive work, privileged the mother–child relationship, and focused on female-centered kinship ties and blood ties more than marriage; it also equipped black women with a sense of autonomy and authority that did not bode well for marriage. Thus, while the freedom to formalize marriages after slavery ended undoubtedly held appeal for many African Americans, I argue that black women had often garnered important gender, cultural, and economic resources that precluded a simple rush to get married.

Despite its romanticization and cultural sanctification, marriage is a quintessentially gendered institution, embodying expectations of male dominance and female subservience inherently at odds with the race and class position accorded many African Americans and their long-standing cultural traditions. These factors led to an abiding nonmarriage ethos among a significant number of black women and a tendency among women who did marry to define their marital roles differently. Resistance to families that relegated women to a dependent status and the nonmarriage cultural ethos that emerged among blacks reflect the tension between dominant families ideologies and the cultural norms and economic resources of African Americans. This resistance was strengthened by the fact that enslaved black women had often garnered significant tangible and intangible resources that afforded them some autonomy in their family decision making. Most important of these were their important economic roles, as many had performed labor as arduous and valuable as that of men. Despite a gender division of labor, slavery had equally appropriated the productive work of black men and women, treating them as "almost equal, independent units of labor."[54] The importance of their labor is reflected in the fact that by the mid-1600s Virginia had declared the labor of black women as "tithable" (or taxable), making an important distinction between the labor of white female indentured servants and African women by defining the latter as having the productive capacity equivalent to that of men, and imposing a special tax on free black men who married them.[55]

In addition to their work roles, black women's sexuality, reproductive work, communal-oriented family systems, and closer association in the intimate, daily activities of white family life were important sources of power. Jacqueline Jones's seminal work on the historic labor roles of black women found that most black women worked in the fields, but those performing domestic work often had a higher status and gained more cultural capital through their contact with the plantation mistress, whose "privileged status . . . rested squarely on the backs of their female slaves."[56] Domestic service gave black women greater access to food and other resources than was available to those who worked in fields, which they used to help their own families and communities. House servants were often privy to vital information about most issues or events on the plantation and were intimately involved in caring for and nurturing white children. Most legendary was the image of the "mammy"—the black woman who held a vital position in the white family by performing domestic work, child care, and generally ruling the household with a "rod of iron." Deborah Gray White has described the stereotypical mammy "as a woman who could do anything, and do it better than anyone else. Because of her expertise in all domestic matters, she was the premier house servant and all others were her subordinates."[57] Few male roles provided black men similar entry into white society or comparable respect and authority.

The communal organization of family work among slaves also empowered black women by giving them the opportunity to socialize and build relationships with each other. Sex-segregated living situations in Africa were replicated in the United States, in that women worked together and often shared child rearing and domestic work. In many cases, spousal visits were confined to the weekends, so black men were only marginally involved in the daily work of family life. Older black women were especially relied on for child care and support, as well as for their practical and philosophical wisdom. Their special knowledge of the use of roots and herbs in healing earned them power and respect as conjurers, and they were often seen as usurping the position of white physicians by delivering babies.[58] For many African American women, family was more about sharing the work of feeding and rearing children with other women than marriage. Stevenson writes that matrifocality was widespread among Virginia slave families in the 1800s, with a malleable extended kin unit as the only discernable ideal. Single-mother families were also common among free blacks: Steven Ruggles had found that in 1850, nearly half of all free black children lived with one or neither of their parents, and by the 1880s, parental absence was five times more likely among blacks than whites.

The power African American women gained through their work roles, reproductive activities, family work, and intimate relationships with white families often made them "ferocious and formidable" in dealing with slave owners, despite their marginal roles in organized social protest.[59] Many also had children fathered by white men, which gave them a source of power and privilege not available to black men. Children fathered by white men and free or slave black women were often referred to as "natural children" and left in the will of their fathers.[60] Black children stood to lose the advantages of their mixed racial heritage if their mothers married black men; moreover, since mothers passed their free status on to her children, children could sometimes fight for freedom based on their maternal descent.[61] Thus, black women had reason to distance themselves from black men, especially those who were enslaved. As Kathleen Brown has written:

> As free parents, black women often formed the first line of defense against encroachments upon the freedom of children, making possible free black family and community life. Many free women may have participated in relationships unrecognized by white courts and churches, either because marriage ceremonies were not conducted according to white law or because white or enslaved men could not legally become their husbands.[62]

Affluent black women whose wealth and status were tied to their relationships with white men whom they were unable to marry usually had nothing to gain by marrying a black man. Darlene Clark Hine and Kathleen Thompson have pointed out that French men in New Orleans, for example, customarily had black mistresses who inherited land and wealth, although laws forbade any formal recognition of these interracial unions. These relationships "gave a large group of free black women in New Orleans—and their children—a considerable degree of independence, wealth and power. . . . Property records of the second half of the eighteenth century list dozens of free black women who owned prime real estate in New Orleans in their own names, had houses built on the properties, and passed them on to their children."[63]

Among the less privileged, emancipation had a destabilizing effect on the black family and/or marriage relationships that had existed during slavery, as it led to starvation, separation, and the desertion of spouses and children. Yet the reorganization of slave labor into the sharecropping system yielded few protections from the abuse of black women. The dominant cultural mandate became the crusade to get African Americans married; however, the impact of the marriage campaign was mediated by the long-standing cultural and gender traditions of black women, the resources they had garnered during slavery, and their active agency in defining and protecting the well-being of their families.

The Marriage Campaign

> Us had de preacher but us didn't have to buy no license and I can't see no sense in buyin' a license nohow, 'cause when dey gits ready to quit, dey just quits.
>
> —Ex–slave woman[64]

After slavery ended, the state, the Freedmen's Bureau, and practically every element of respectable black society (e.g., the church, the press, social organizations), scrambled to convince the newly freed blacks of the virtue of formalizing their marriages, sometimes forcing them to legalize fairly casual sexual relationships and, as Noralee Frankel has shown, at other times simply declaring those living together as husband and wife to be married. An 1870 Mississippi law (later repealed as being overly strict), for example, declared that all African American couples "who have not married, but are now living together, cohabiting as man and wife, shall be taken and held, for all purposes in the law, as married."[65] Fueling the marriage campaign were efforts to reorganize the labor of black people and curtail state responsibility for their care. Marriage was described as necessary to elevate "freedpeople to a new level of civilization"—that is, legitimate children, properly transfer property, and regulate black sexuality.[66] Slavery was seen as having had a civilizing influence on blacks, who were now described as quickly regressing to their primitive state in its absence—black men by becoming vagrants and rapists and black women by giving in to their natural tendency toward lasciviousness and immorality.[67] The legalization of marriages became especially important as a way of controlling female sexuality and reorganizing black families as efficient work units for sharecropping.

The marriage campaign was often undergirded by coercive state policies, as well as class and gender politics among blacks. The private family lives of black people came to the attention of public officials in several ways, such as their involvement in the military. Nearly one hundred thousand African American men fought in the Civil War, and their military careers made their private lives subject to scrutiny. The army demanded that the marriages of soldiers living on military bases be legalized, despite also forcing black women to leave the cities where their husbands were stationed due to accusations that they interfered with military procedure or posed a health risk.[68] The efforts of the state coincided with the patriarchal yearnings of black men, who sought to solidify their power and authority, at least in their own homes.

Acutely aware of a diminished claim to masculinity, African American men launched their campaign for the "ownership" of their wives, children, and property before slavery ended. As D. Franklin has pointed out, their move to reorder the gender relations in their homes after slavery ended was supported by state policies and apparently sparked an alarming increase in wife battering. The Freedmen's Bureau designated black men as the legal heads of their households with the right to sign labor contracts for the entire family and endorsed policies that allocated less land to single women and their families.

Emancipation thus created the legal basis for patriarchal families among black people, although continuing economic and racial exploitation undermined the viability of such families. By 1867, black men (in theory) could vote, hold office, serve on juries, and participate politically—all rights that black women did not have.[69]

Class politics also played a pivotal role in the marriage campaign. Through embracing the patriarchal traditions of the dominant society, more affluent and educated African Americans sought to gain greater acceptability and respect. Institutions such as Spelman College insisted on domestic training for every female student, so she could "preside intelligently over her own household."[70] More privileged blacks, fearful of their status being tarnished by the behaviors of poor blacks, actively professed and promoted the value of marriage to the black masses. The self-interested nature of their work was expressed by Mary Church Terrell, president of the National Association of Colored Women, who explained to her middle-class peers in the early 1900s:

> Colored women of education and culture know that they cannot escape altogether the consequences of the acts of their most depraved sisters. They see that even if they were wicked enough to turn a deaf ear to the call of duty, both policy and self-preservation demand that they go down among the lowly, the illiterate and even the vicious, to whom they are bound by the ties of race and sex, and put forth every effort to reclaim them.[71]

Like many middle-class black women who called on women to do their work in the "sacred domain" of the home, Terrell supported patriarchy in principle and the ideal of domesticity for women.[72] Such themes were also central in black newspapers, which urged black women to marry and thus achieve true womanhood, and sought to tame aggressive women by generating negative stereotypes of single women with "unruly tongues."[73]

The bastion of support for patriarchy was found in the black church, starting with the Free African Society established by Absalom Jones and Richard Allen in 1787. As Christopher Booker has noted, long before the abolition of slavery, the church had sought to rid black men of derogatory images such as that of the childlike/docile "Sambo" or the threatening/dangerous "Nat." Portraying African American men as responsible, moral heads of their families was critical to dispelling these stereotypes and the penalties associated with them, and Booker contends that the patriarchal ideal was "virtually unquestioned" among African Americans during Reconstruction, an era when black men gained dominance over black women in political and social life. In their effort to solidify this dominance, according to Evelyn Brooks Higginbotham, the Black Baptist Church especially "sought to provide men with full manhood rights, while offering women a separate and unequal status."[74] African American women, especially the "female talented tenth," worked to pass white, middle-class family values on to all blacks, especially those who were poor. Driven by the "politics of respectability," they tried to dispel images of black women as "immoral, childlike, and unworthy of respect or protection"—a stereotype that was being used to disenfranchise black people and one that clearly respected no class boundaries when it came to affecting the lives of black women.[75] The black church had traveling clergy who performed marriages among the newly freed slaves, linking marriage to morality and in some cases even to church membership.[76] Their growing authority was widely condoned in communities and churches, and it was often seen as needed protection against the historic abuse of the labor, bodies, and sexuality of black women.[77]

Given these efforts to promote marriage among African Americans, it is not surprising that Gutman found the majority of blacks of all social classes living in nuclear families between 1880 and 1925. Yet, by the early 1930s, African American scholar Charles S. Johnson provided an insightful glimpse into the reluctance of southern blacks to marry by writing:

> Married life imposes certain obligations which are, in the feeling of this element of the community, more binding than necessary or practical. It gives license to mistreatment; it imposes the risk of unprofitable husbands; and it places an impossible tax upon freedom in the form of a divorce.[78]

Cultural Resistance and the Nonmarriage Ethos

> How shall I so cramp, stunt, simplify, and nullify myself as to make me eligible to the honor of being swallowed up into some little man?
>
> —Anna Julia Hayward Cooper, 1892[79]

Efforts to transcend the painful legacy of slavery and racial denigration and gain social acceptance and respectability undoubtedly led many African Americans to marry and proffer support of dominant family norms. Marriage held the promise of creating stable, satisfying relationships, protecting women from sexual and economic exploitation, and providing proof that black people could abide by the conventions of morality and were worthy of participation in civil society. Yet despite the intense pressure to marry created by efforts of the marriage campaign, the cultural, economic, and institutional support for marriage remained weak among a significant portion of black people. Many continued to live in the nonmarital, cohabitating "took-up" relationships that existed during slavery and were widely accepted in black communities.[80] For others, slavery had fostered a freedom from the strictures of gender and family conventions; moreover, it had disabused them of idealized notions about the sanctity of marriage and womanhood and taught them that love, sexuality, childbearing, and family need not be tied to legally sanctioned contracts. Black men had often been exempt from providing for their families and excluded from the day-to-day operations of families, and ideas of female modesty and passivity had been thoroughly impugned by the hard labor and sexual assaults endured by black women.

The gender expectations of the marriage contract made it inherently less viable for black people, as did its traditional focus on legitimately born children and the ownership and transfer property. For black women, marriage entailed a massive and unacceptable reordering of gender privilege, power, and property, all based on the slender hope that the benefits of patriarchal families would exceed their costs. Poor African American women who entered the sharecropping system quickly learned that marriage would not shield them from economic exploitation; indeed, entire families were expected to perform field labor, and black women who tried to confine their labor to the home were "severely criticized by whites . . . because they were seen to be aspiring to a model of womanhood that was considered inappropriate for them."[81] Their efforts to embrace the breadwinner–homemaker family model were thwarted by labor demands and often resulted in more condemnation than praise. But black women had other reasons not to take the risk of marrying, such as the stability of their maternal families, the potential deterioration of their social status caused by marriage to a black man, the paucity of economic resources available to black men, and the protection of their children and property.

Enthusiasm for marriage was diluted by the reluctance of black women to forsake the kinship systems that evolved over centuries in favor of male-dominated marriages, not only because of economic and racial barriers but also because it was inconsistent with their cultural values. Maternal families had been the norm for many blacks, even those who were free. For example, a majority of freed blacks in eighteenth-century Virginia did not live in male-headed households, not solely because they lacked the opportunity to form such bonds but because they chose not to. In her study of more than seven thousand African American households in New York City between 1850 and 1870, J. E. Dabel found that two-thirds of free black women did not marry.[82] Not only had most New York slaveholders owned only a few slaves (by 1790, half of these slave owners had only one slave), but the state's abolition of slavery in 1799 left most black women working as live-in domestics for white families and often relying on the extended female unit for the care of children. Freed from the West African system of marriage, which was based more on lineages, community ties, and patriarchy, and equipped with the ability to survive on their own, many chose to establish matrifocal residences. In her study of the transition from slavery to freedom among black women in South Carolina, for example, Leslie Schwalm has argued that "marriage was not the only, or even most important, familial relationship" to the newly freed slaves. She suggests that the bonds of sisterhood were not easily relinquished in favor of marriage:

> Freedwomen insisted on working "in their own time, as they see fit"; on reconstructing their families in ways that made sense according to their own standards and expectations; on meeting their obligations and responsibilities not only as wives and mothers, but also as sisters, aunts, grandmothers, and as women who knew too well the costs of slavery.[83]

Despite the respectability promised by conforming to marriage and patriarchy, a culture of resistance emerged among many African American women who were skeptical of the benefits of marriage. Marriage rendered fewer economic and gender privileges to African American women, as black men were ill prepared to support them financially or protect them from the onslaught of racist and sexist stereotypes. Moreover, while the rate of family violence is difficult to assess, black wives often complained that "freedmen felt that freedom brought to them the right to beat their wives,"[84] and, despite their reputation for going "blow for blow" in domestic disputes, 5 percent of the complaints brought to the Freedmen's Bureau in Mississippi were by female victims of partner abuse.[85] After centuries of slavery and sexual assault at the hands of black and white men, it is not surprising that many opted to control their own lives and sexuality, often by evading patriarchal marriage. Women often rebelled against any form of patriarchy by choosing to live alone, work their own farms, and enjoy male companions on their own terms or, as Barbara Omolade has argued, to live with other women as "emotional and sexual companions" and thus avoid being controlled or defined by black men.

While black middle-class women did marry in large numbers and voice support for patriarchal families, their employment roles and the call for social activism and community service to advance the cause of racial justice militated against their confinement to wife–mother roles in patriarchal marriages. Thousands of black women joined the women's club movement, which was often the sole provider of social services for community members who were poor, elderly, and sick, and their participation helped pave the way for political activism.[86] In his 2000 book on black marriages, Bart Landry argues that African American women starting in the late 1800s pioneered an egalitarian ideology that anticipated modern feminism by combining domestic and employment roles. Here, I contend that the roles of poor and working-class black women, though often less heralded, were similarly notable in maintaining both families and freedom from male domination. However, the once-legendary authority of black women waned gradually over the course of the twentieth century.

The Declining Well-Being of Single-Mother Families

The precipitous rise in the number of single mothers has dominated scholarship on the families of African Americans. In 1940, slightly more than 20 percent of black families were headed by single women; however, with northward migration, the rates of singleness, separation, and divorce grew. All of these factors helped destabilize black families and led to more despair among those living in them. The birthrate of single black women tripled between 1940 and 1957,[87] and, by the end of the twentieth century, a significant majority of black children—nearly 70 percent—were being born to single mothers who headed their own families. Moreover, the surge in births among poor, single teenagers during this period was blamed for the growing number of health impairments, cognitive deficits, and behavioral problems of black children,[88] and studies were increasingly documenting the demise of black family ties and high rates of depression, isolation, and despair among single African American women.[89]

By the 1980s, concern over the declining status of poor black families had dwarfed the focus of revisionist research on their strength, diversity, and functionality; indeed, such visions of black families rang hollow as marriage rates fell to an unprecedented low, and rates of single mother-hood, poverty, and welfare dependency escalated. The once-well-functioning kinship units of black mothers were challenged by dwindling economic resources, declining employment opportunities, neighborhood deterioration, the drug epidemic, and the spread of AIDS. One indicator of the decline was the record number of black children being placed in foster care. Although African American children were nearly three times more likely to live with grandparents than were white children, the tradi-tional voluntary nature of extended family ties had weakened, and many grandmothers were taking on these responsibilities under the duress of child abandonment and drug use by their own children.[90] Clearly, the ex-tension of civil rights and equal opportunity policies had failed to uni-formly improve the lives of African Americans. Moreover, given the legal and economic gains that had been made by many other African Ameri-cans, the potency of arguments linking black poverty and family instabil-ity to institutionalized racism was diminished.

Explaining the Decline in Poor Black Families

Theoretical explanations of the decline in black families fell into the two familiar camps of structure and culture. Structural theorists emphasized the massive loss of decent paying industrial jobs during the 1970s, which disproportionately affected young black men, as the source of the prob-lem.[91] In fact, as early as the mid-1950s, for the first time ever, rates of un-employment among African Americans were twice as high as those for whites, and this continued to be the case throughout the twentieth cen-tury.[92] Facing the specter of unemployment, menial work, and poor wages, black men were described as having turned to crime, drugs, and gang violence—all activities that rendered them less eligible for or inter-ested in marriage. Black urban neighborhoods were increasingly seen as war zones, plagued by crime, drive-by shootings, the selling of illicit drugs, and gang violence. Amid the epidemic of violence, their high rates of homicide and incarceration led to young black men being referred to as a "vanishing species." Mandatory sentencing and antidrug statutes that specifically targeted African Americans resulted in an unprecedented ex-pansion of the prison population, with nearly one-third of black men in their twenties under the supervision of the courts and others significantly overrepresented among the nearly 1.5 million incarcerated Americans.[93]

Structural theorists thus maintained that the economic marginality and actual numerical shortage of men had sparked the retreat from marriage, leaving black women single and impoverished.

A broader portrait of economic changes shows the demise in the viability of poor families linked to a pattern of class polarization among African Americans that evolved over the course of the twentieth century. Although the number of black middle-class families grew after both world wars, and even more substantially as a result of the civil rights movement, by the 1980s, the overall economic portrait of black Americans paralleled the trend found in the dominant society: a small gain in the number of wealthy families, a shrinking of the middle class, and a significant increase in the number of working and nonworking poor families.[94] Many middle-class black families, whose grasp on economic solvency was often tenuous at best, lost ground during this era, but the impact on poor families was much greater. While economic transitions diminished the rate of employment and marriage, racial integration drained poor urban areas of middle-income residents and the resources they once brought to communities. One manifestation of these changes was an increase in poor, single-mother families: Between 1950 and 1990, the number of black families headed by single mothers rose from 17 percent to 56 percent, resulting in only 38 percent of black children (vs. 73 percent of white children) living with two parents.[95]

While the dominant structural argument has focused on the work experiences of black men, feminist explanations have highlighted the lack of structural and policy support for poor, single-mother families. In her critique of mainstream society's insistence on defining black single-mother families as "unlawful" and maligning the women who head them, Willa Mae Hemmons redirects responsibility for their plight to the economic and racial forces that have impoverished and marginalized them:

> Ironically, the blame for [black families'] substantially diminished viability is primarily placed not upon the shoulders of the discriminatory society, but upon those of the Black woman. The Black woman is called emasculating, promiscuous, domineering, excessively fertile and lazy; it is she who fails to rear her children to avoid the lure of drugs, crime, violence, and more children in lieu of jobs, education, self-discipline, obedience, and abstinence.[96]

Various strands of the cultural perspective have also been used to explain poor black families. In some cases, theorists ignore the decline of single-mother families and continue to trumpet them as a viable cultural alternative or link them to black people's African heritage,[97] but others see structural inequalities as resulting in cultural behaviors inimical to marriage. Douglas S. Massey and Nancy A. Denton, for example, argue that racial segregation and inequality produce an "oppositional culture that devalues work, schooling, and marriage,"[98] and W. J. Wilson, although a key proponent of the structural approach, concedes that there has been a change in cultural values of poor African Americans. Such evidence is consistent with the claims of researchers who have found that, historically, those blacks with the fewest resources were the most tolerant of marriage. Despite their meager access to good jobs, prior to 1950, black men married at a younger age than white men, leading H. Koball to speculate that they found marriage and family life appealing precisely because they lived in the South and had little education, few expectations of economic advancement, and few appealing life options.[99] S. Ruggles's research also supports this cultural view: His data show that in the 1880s, blacks with the highest rates of illiteracy and living in the poorest areas were most likely to be residing in two-parent families.[100]

The cultural perspective in the dominant political discourse, however, frames the issue in terms of cultural degeneracy, insisting that black women have simply refused to control their own sexuality and childbearing and embrace the family values of other Americans. Black women are denigrated for their efforts to raise children without the help of the men who fathered them; moreover, the efforts to do so are seen as fostered by generous welfare policies. The controversy surrounding single mothers reveals our gendered assumptions about sexual morality, marriage, and family roles and, when directed at black women, amplifies long-standing racial/sexual myths and stereotypes. Even when single fathers are scolded for being derelict in their economic support of children, the bulk of the blame for the plight of black families is reserved for women, who are expected to be the guardians of morality and cultural values. Thus, single mothers are vilified as economically irresponsible and sexually promiscuous, and as dismissing the importance of fathers, jeopardizing the welfare of their own children, and swelling the welfare rolls. Despite their struggles with multiple inequalities, they are held responsible for the fragility of their families.

Single motherhood challenges cherished conservative ideologies about sexual morality, family, child welfare, and patriarchy, but perhaps most objectionable has been its link to poverty and welfare dependency. The AFDC program was created in 1935 and by 1940 had fewer than 400,000 beneficiaries; however, the number of beneficiaries had grown to 12.5 million by 1995.[101] Moreover, with northward migration and political activism supporting the right of poor black women to claim benefits, the proportion of AFDC clients who were black grew from 21 percent in 1942 to 40 percent by 1960.[102] Welfare, race, and single motherhood became wedded in the minds of most Americans, and, while scholars could accurately claim that a majority of recipients were not blacks, African American women were significantly overrepresented in their participation in and reliance on welfare programs. For example, between 1994 and 1996, more than 30 percent of black households received some type of public assistance from a means-tested welfare program, and African Americans were much more likely than other groups to receive 50 percent or more of their income from such a program.[103]

While the growing welfare budget was a point of contention, studies were also documenting the adverse impact of welfare, poverty, and single motherhood on poor women and their children. Women who rely on welfare, as well as those who grew up relying on it, experience more chronic burdens, psychological distress, and lower self-esteem,[104] and children in fatherless families have higher levels of poor academic performance, early sex, and pregnancy.[105]

The Postmodern Gender Perspective Revisited

Neither the structural nor cultural perspective has paid much attention to the complex, interrelated social forces that have proven so devastating to the status and autonomy of black women and the resiliency of their families. The postmodern gender perspective posited here offers a more integrated framework for understanding how intertwined structural and cultural forces merged in leading black women to resist patriarchal marriages, and that perspective is also useful in explaining the declining viability of poor black families during the mid- to late decades of the twentieth century. More specifically, if slavery allowed black women to develop a tradition of self-reliance and even equipped them with cultural and material resources to run their own families, more recent social forces, policies, and ideologies have certainly undermined those traditions. The declining labor market position of black men and their high rates of incarceration have lessened the prospect of black women receiving much help supporting families from their male partners, regardless of marital status. In addition, the attention focused on the economic losses of black men has ignored the fact that black women, many of whom were the sole support of their families, have experienced significant downward career mobility. The earning potential of African American women, especially those who were young, decreased between 1973 and 1991, regardless of their education. Declines were even greater for college-educated black women because of their disproportionate representation in declining industries.[106]

Also of significance has been the demise of female-centered support systems for poor black women and a general loss of the cultural power and authority black women once held. As historian D. G. White has noted, "If [black women] seemed exceptionally strong, it was partly because they often functioned in groups and derived strength from numbers."[107] Many factors—public policies leaving blacks with less to share, the class polarization heightened by integration, a surge in black nationalist and patriarchal thinking—have curtailed the status of black women in their communities. The civil rights movement and revisionist scholarship, for example, served to emphasize masculinist doctrines, giving new life and validity to notions of gender subordination that are now promulgated by everyone from religious leaders and state officials to rap artists and black nationalists. The fierce rejection of the black matriarch thesis created a new determination to emphasize the leadership roles of black men; indeed, some theorists claimed that the strong black woman had outlived her usefulness.[108] Political activist Angela Davis was criticized by black men for assuming a key role in organizing a protest rally; they called her behavior a "matriarchal coup d'état" and suggested that women should focus on inspiring men and educating their children.[109] African American women have contributed to patriarchal thinking by "pushing their men forward" and trying to maintain racial solidarity rather than, as P. H. Collins noted, appropriately engaging in personal advocacy.[110] Several writers have noted the loss of cultural power by black women, as did the Million Woman March held in Philadelphia in 1997. These participants called for greater solidarity among women as the solution to improving the life situations of women.

Welfare policies also grew more punitive throughout the twentieth century, shaping the choices black women made about work and family and reducing the resources they were able to share with each other. African American women were historically denied welfare benefits or at best considerably underserved by them, especially in southern areas. As Kenneth J. Neubeck and Noel A. Cazenave have documented, welfare racism ranging from policies that blatantly denied benefits to black women when laborers were needed to pick cotton to the implementation of "suitable home" and "man in the house" policies gave welfare workers broad discretion in scrutinizing the personal lives of black mothers. Still, the steady migration of blacks from the South and the National Welfare Rights Movement gradually increased the participation of African American mothers in the program.

Moreover, eligibility guidelines came to shape many of their family decisions. For example, I spoke with mothers of chronically ill children who wanted to work outside the home but could not afford to lose their Medicaid benefits if they did so—a powerful incentive for choosing non-work for those with sick children. Another earlier policy insisted that mothers establish their own household to become eligible for benefits, which worked against extended families. Restrictions on the eligibility for public housing also undermined poor black families, even more so with the implementation of punitive drug policies. A law passed in 1988 called for the eviction of tenants when their guests and relatives were involved in drug-related activity on the premises—even if they did so without their knowledge. In one case, a grandmother who had lived in public housing in Oakland, California, for thirty years was evicted because her grandson had smoked marijuana in the complex parking lot.[111] Thus, women, as the primary recipients of government welfare benefits, have become less able to use their benefits in support of their families.

The expanding welfare budget and research documenting the deficiencies in poor, single-mother families strengthened support for the controversial Personal Responsibility and Work Opportunity Act of 1996, which sought to discipline single mothers by abolishing the AFDC programs in favor of temporary assistance policies and stronger incentives to work and marry. While liberal scholars (like myself) railed against removing the safety net for poor families, studies show that many welfare mothers felt trapped by the old system and viewed change optimistically as an opportunity to move toward economic independence. As a black mother who moved from welfare to work told Sharon Hays, many people were abusing the system:

When I was younger, years ago, anybody could get on welfare. And I think that's what's good about welfare reform. People have to show some sort of initiative. Before, the welfare office didn't pressure you to find a job, but now they do. And I think that's a good system. They've really helped me out a lot.[112]

In reality, a stronger economy, initiatives by states to curtail welfare participation, and the debate over ending AFDC had already begun to curb the number of welfare beneficiaries: Nearly 7 million women left welfare between 1996 and 1999, half to two-thirds of them for jobs. In most cases, workfare policies have not been as onerous as imagined by some political activists; for example, most states opted out of the federal work policy that urged putting poor mothers to work in the community to earn their welfare checks, and some successful programs have eased the transition to work by providing families with support such as child care assistance, food stamps, and public health insurance. Welfare reform has been credited with a 56 percent reduction in the welfare rolls and with bringing child poverty to its lowest rate in twenty-five years;[113] however, its ultimate success depends not merely on whether poor women get jobs but on their ability to keep those jobs and improve the quality of life for themselves and their children. Hays's work has led her to view welfare reform as a mixed bag. She sees it as based on a set of honorable principles such as "independence, productivity, conscientious citizenship, family togetherness, social connection, community, and the well-being of children," but it may also be potentially punitive in the context of "massive changes in family and work life, deepening levels of social distrust, rising social inequalities, and an increasingly competitive and global capitalist marketplace."[114]

Welfare policies focusing on employment may harm poor women with little education and few marketable skills, especially in the absence of training programs, as well as those who are in poor health or face labor market discrimination. Many women who left welfare for work found themselves in low-wage work and deprived of benefits such as health insurance, and, with the changing economy, at least some states have experienced an increase in the welfare rolls in 2001, as women lost their jobs, lacked day care, or simply could not maintain financial sufficiency.[115] In many cases, those deficits correlate with race. Kathryn Edin and Kathleen Harris report, for example, that while work is the most common way off welfare for all women, black women have fewer skills and less education, as well as more restricted access to employment due to racial discrimination and residential segregation, and they are more likely to cycle frequently between welfare and work.[116] Moreover, the most successful route off welfare, according to Sandra Hofferth, usually entails finding both a job and a partner—another factor that may disadvantage black women. Wedfare policies promote marriage as a solution to poverty and seek to give grants to nonprofit and religious groups to teach its virtues. These policies, however, do little to provide jobs for men—the foundation of the marriage contract—nor do they offer much critique of the patriarchal families that are increasingly unacceptable to women.

Single-Mother Families: The Big Picture

While speaking of crises and declines is essentially the norm when studying African American families, economic, social, and cultural forces are challenging the ideology of male-headed families nationally and even worldwide. Economic transitions, technologies, worker migration, and the global labor market are deskilling and displacing multitudes of workers, diminishing the economic prospects of men and increasingly pulling women into the labor force. The trend toward delayed marriage, smaller families, employed women, high rates of divorce, impoverished women, and single-mother families has been evident in the United States for several decades, as well as in other countries. Women are less tolerant of gender inequality in families and much more confident in their ability to head families. More than one-third of all American children are now born to single mothers (about 70 percent of African American children), and at least half of all children born in the 1990s will spend some time in a single-parent family.[117] While single-parent families headed by women and men have higher levels of poverty (34 percent and 16 percent, respectively), the more than 10 million single-mother families in the United States are extremely diverse, and making generalizations about the quality of life of their members is difficult.

Despite these national and global changes, and the long history of African Americans living in single-mother families, the issue remains contentious in the broader culture and among black people. As discussed in the following chapter, the root of the problem may lie in the contradiction between the lived experiences of African Americans and gender ideologies of the dominant culture. Indeed, such contradictions have produced consider-able gender trouble in the intimate relationships of black men and women.

Notes

1. N. Sudarkasa (1996:1).
2. W. M. Hemmons (1996).
3. See, for example, R. A. Moffitt and P. T. Gottschalk (2001).
4. J. Jones (1985); B. T. Dill (1988).
5. K. Brown (1996); L. Tilly and J. W. Scott (1978).
6. L. Walsh (1985).
7. See, for example, M. Andersen (2000).
8. R. Rapp, E. Ross, and R. Bridenthal (1979:22).
9. D. King (1988).
10. S. A. Queen and R. W. Habenstein (1967:315).
11. Quoted in H. Gutman (1976:304–5).
12. S. A. Queen and R. W. Habenstein (1967).
13. E. F. Frazier (1966 [1939]).
14. J. Bernard (1966:68).
15. J. Bernard (1966:68).
16. J. Blassingame (1972).
17. K. Brown (1996:360).
18. E. F. Frazier (1966 [1939]:313).
19. C. B. Booker (2000).
20. J. Jones (1985).
21. D. Franklin (2000).
22. R. J. Scott (1985).
23. A. Billingsley (1992).
24. D. Hine (1995).
25. H. V. Carby (1995).
26. C. Marks (1989).
27. D. C. Hine and K. Thompson (1989:215).
28. D. C. Hine and K. Thompson (1989:215).
29. C. Marks (1989).
30. C. Marks (1989).
31. L. Rainwater and W. L. Yancey (1967:15).
32. L. Walsh (1985:13).
33. P. Morgan (1998:315).
34. H. McAdoo (1990:74).
35. J. Blassingame (1976:261).
36. E. Genovese (1974:451–52).

37. P. Morgan (1998).
38. E. Genovese (1974).
39. A. Davis (1995:201).
40. T. Bogger (1997).
41. J. Sidbury (1997); C. B. Booker (2000).
42. L. Walsh (1985); T. L. Bogger (1997).
43. P. Morgan (1998).
44. W. Nobles (1974).
45. D. C. Hine and K. Thompson (1998).
46. R. Terborg-Penn (1986).
47. B. Thorne (1982:7).
48. R. Brewer (1995:166).
49. E. Genovese (1974:453, 484).
50. W. A. Dunaway (2003:270).
51. W. A. Dunaway (2003:3).
52. H. Gutman (1976), for example, draws heavily from the records kept for nearly one hundred years by the Good Hope plantation in South Carolina, which still had 175 slaves when slavery ended.
53. C. Hurst (2004).
54. B. T. Dill (1988a).
55. K. Brown (1996:118).
56. J. Jones (1985).
57. D. G. White (1985:47).
58. J. Jones (1985).
59. J. Sidbury (1997).
60. C. Clinton (1985).
61. J. Sidbury (1997).
62. K. Brown (1996:229).
63. D. C. Hine and K. Thompson (1998:59).
64. Quoted in F. Butterfield (1995:44).
65. N. Frankel (1999).
66. L. Schwalm (1997:239); also see E. B. Higginbotham (1993) and P. Giddings (1995).
67. P. Giddings (1995).
68. D. C. Hine and K. Thompson (1998).
69. D. Franklin (1997).
70. E. Higginbotham (1993).
71. Quoted in S. L. Smith (1995:18).
72. C. B. Booker (2000).
73. J. E. Dabel (2002).
74. E. Higginbotham (1993:3).
75. Also see N. Frankel (1999).

76. N. Frankel (1999).
77. B. Omolade (1995).
78. Quoted in D. Franklin (1997:36).
79. Quoted in G. E. Gilmore (1996:189).
80. N. Frankel (1999).
81. B. T. Dill (1988a).
82. J. E. Dabel (2002).
83. L. Schwalm (1997:268).
84. L. Schwalm (1997:262).
85. N. Frankel (1999).
86. D. C. Hine and K. Thompson (1998:166).
87. D. Franklin (1997).
88. A. Pinkney (2000).
89. M. E. Ensminger (1995).
90. S. A. Hill (1999).
91. W. J. Wilson (1987).
92. A. Billingsley (1992).
93. M. Mauer (1999).
94. A. Billingsley (1992:46).
95. A. Pinkney (2000).
96. W. M. Hemmons (1996:188).
97. B. Dickerson (1995).
98. D. Massey and N. Denton (1993:8).
99. H. Koball (1998).
100. S. Ruggles (1994).
101. R. A. Moffitt and P. T. Gottschalk (2001).
102. K. J. Neubeck and N. A. Cazenave (2001).
103. R. A. Moffitt and P. T. Gottschalk (2001).
104. M. E. Ensminger (1995).
105. S. McLanahan and D. Schwartz (2002).
106. J. Bound and L. Dresser (1999).
107. D. G. White (1999:119).
108. J. Ladner (1972).
109. P. Giddings (1984:316).
110. P. H. Collins (1998).
111. W. Rickey (2002).
112. S. Hays (2003:217).
113. F. Kiefer (2002).
114. S. Hays (2003:21).
115. P. Loprest (2002).
116. K. Edin and K. Harris (1999).
117. P. R. Amato (2000).

CHAPTER 4

Love, Sex, and Relationships

The Pursuit of Intimacy

> As long as African Americans remained outsiders, we were forced to concentrate on the central issue of getting in and, in the process, to downplay the many problems that beset us internally. I think the time has now come to confront these problems squarely. When we do so, we find that at the top of this internal racial agenda is the crisis-ridden problem of gender relations between African-American men and women.
>
> —Orlando Patterson[1]

While one might squabble with Orlando Patterson's assertion that African Americans are no longer "outsiders" who must focus on "getting in," the fact that their gender relations seem to be "crisis-ridden" is now recognized in practically every genre of popular and scholarly literature. Historically, scholars gave only sporadic attention to what P. H. Collins calls the "love and trouble" tradition among black men and women, as necessity demanded a sustained focus on the broader forces of inequality, such as institutionalized racism, segregation, and economic exclusion. In light of such issues, explorations of relationship troubles between black women and men were seen as nothing more than inappropriately airing dirty linen or, even worse, contributing to literature that impugned and stereotyped African Americans.

In recent years, however, relationship analyses have moved from the margins to the center in African American scholarship, novels, and films. John Singleton's movie *Baby Boy* provides one example. The central theme of the movie is that centuries of racism have retarded the psychological and emotional development of black men, many of whom see themselves as overgrown children and behave accordingly. *Baby Boy* centers on the life of Jody (Tyrese Gibson), a young African American man who still lives with his thirty-six-year-old mother and her cohabiting boyfriend, with whom he has a hostile relationship. Jody is immature, unfaithful, abusive, and unemployed, but he is absolutely in demand by several young, employed, attractive women, two of whom already have had "his baby." These young women have tapered their expectations to match the reality of what Jody can offer; rather than economic support, shared child care, or even marriage, they expect good sex, fidelity, and cohabitation.

Movies like *The Brothers, Waiting to Exhale,* and *Two Can Play That Game* suggest that relationship trouble is not confined to poor, inner-city black people with dismal employment and marriage prospects; instead, neither class mobility nor greater material resources do much to ease the distrust and conflict so prevalent among black men and women. Movies, of course, are profit-seeking ventures apt to promote images that distort and exploit real-life experiences, and it is clear that there is little money to be made by noting that African Americans overwhelmingly choose and marry each other and in many cases form stable, satisfying relationships. Yet the fact that these popular movies are so widely discussed and debated, along with the high rate of singleness and marital failure among African Americans, makes it difficult to dismiss their relevance. They expose crucial issues that challenge black love, such as the economic impotence of many black men, the stereotyping of black women, the relationship between love and self-esteem, the viability of marriage in postmodern society, and the issue of gender in relationships. Yet for the most part, this surge of interest in analyzing the intimate relationships of African American women and men, sparked more by popular artists and authors than scholars, had been stunted by a lack of contextual and structural analysis of the issue. In this chapter, I explore the search for intimacy among African Americans in the broader context of race and class. I contend that the very heart of the troubles that proliferate in black intimate relationships is the inability to resolve the tension between their own cultural traditions and resources and Eurocentric notions of love, gender, courtship, and marriage.

African Americans often embrace dominant societal definitions of masculinity and femininity, ideals about female attractiveness, and gendered prescriptions of male–female relationships, despite the fact that their race and class position preclude conformity to such norms. Dominant societal rules about courtship, for example, sanction men as the aggressors, protectors, proposers, and providers and cast women as passive recipients of male attention that is gained largely through their physical attractiveness, sexuality, and coyness. The courtship process is seen as logically culminating in romantic love and marriage, despite the fact that marriage is essentially a legal contract based on property rights, legitimate heirs, and gender-defined roles for men and women. The historically marginalized class and racial status of African Americans has compromised their ability to meet the economic and gender expectations of marriage, thus reducing the relevance and stability of marriage. Heroic efforts aside, black men have often found themselves unable to shield women from the hostilities of the public arena, foot the entire bill for dating, or provide economic support for their families. Black women have had to fend for themselves, work outside the home, and rely on female kinship networks for support, and they have thus developed a strong sense of independence. This disjuncture between the historic experiences of African Americans and the gender norms of courtship and legal requisites of marriage have pitted black women and men against each other in patterns of resentment, mutual blame, and denigration, each blaming the other for failing to create successful relationships.

African American women criticize black men for being unfaithful and exploitative in relationships and often deride them for being "less than a man" when it comes to earning money and supporting their families. Black women are also criticized and penalized by their men for violating white female codes of behavior, especially for spoiling intimacy by failing to be submissive and depriving men of the dominance they deserve. In their reflective moments, African Americans understand that race and racism shaped their dilemma, but such insights do not produce healing or peace, nor do they exempt African Americans from the stigma of having disordered gender relations. Although explicitly invoking the black matriarch concept has become almost verboten in scholarly literature on African Americans, its enduring legacy is evident in the frequent charge that black women are "simply too strong, too independent, and too self-sufficient for their own good or for the good of their relationships."[2] Contention over the strong women/weak men premise remains a central theme among blacks in their everyday talk, with many embracing and idealizing the very models of family and gender that they have never been able to implement and that are now being rapidly abandoned by other races. Black couples who have experienced enough class mobility and assimilation to carve out a comfortable niche for themselves between dominant societal and black cultural norms are seen as exceptions to the rule, but even they find themselves playing out their relationships against the backdrop of palpable tension between race/gender myths and realities.

In this chapter, I deepen our understanding of African American intimate relationships by showing how gender expectations operate in class and race context and how black people have tried to challenge and reconstruct those expectations. Marriage relationships among blacks remain especially understudied, and I draw on my own and other research to explore factors that affect marital stability. Intimacy and companionship are increasingly found outside the boundaries of marriage, and I look at the lives of those who are single, gay/lesbian, and in cohabiting relationships. I conclude with a discussion of the marriage bust among African Americans and the viability of new "marriage campaign" instituted by welfare reform policies.

Pursuing Gendered Intimacy

> Every black woman I knew growing up dreamed of having a black male partner who would give her financial support and allow her to be a housewife.
>
> —bell hooks[3]

Delia Williams is a fifty-six-year-old African American divorced mother of three children who has recently earned a doctorate degree and teaches at a predominantly black community college. Concerned about the prevalence of early sex, childbearing, and welfare dependency among her young, mostly female students, as well as the way the men in their lives seem to exploit and abandon them, she offers her students a few rules on how to remedy the problem. According to the advice she shares with her students, male–female relationships should go this way: The man asks for a date, picks you up at home, meets your family, pays for the date, does the pursuing, proposes marriage, and provides economically for the family. Her advice is only partially tongue-in-cheek and strictly at odds with her own marital and class background: She has always been in the labor force, is divorced from a husband who did not support her values and career ambition, and has worked hard to raise her children as a single mother while advancing her education. Yet her advice reflects attitudinal support among blacks for dominant norms in love, courtship, and marriage—despite her own inability and even unwillingness to live such norms. Even blacks who proffer strong support for gender equality at work and in marriage often embrace traditional norms of dating and courtship.

Evidence that seemingly outmoded notions of courtship continue to hold sway as the solution to the rift between black men and women is apparent in the growing number of publications proffering relationship advice. Most are directed at African American women and take as a given that they are misbehaving by being too assertive and independent. The title of Zondra Hughes's recent article in the annual women's edition of *Ebony* magazine poses the question "Who says sisters can't be nice in relationships?" Hughes applauds black women for being "strong, resourceful, and tenacious African Queens" yet also criticizes them for being "overbearing, attitudinal and, most notoriously, the Queens of Mean." Being an "aggressive lioness" in the public arena is fine, advises Hughes, but a black man wants his woman to be a "soft and cuddly kitten" at home. Another relationship expert cited in the article suggests that black women learn to fight for their rights in a passive-aggressive way like white women do and cautioned that those who fail to do so will find themselves "alone, bitter, and unfulfilled." "Proper" gender behavior is especially crucial for black women who want to marry affluent men: In *Trophy Man: The Surprising Secrets of Black Women Who Marry Well*, Joy Elroy interviewed one hundred women who married well and offers that doing so requires women to work hard at looking and acting feminine and making sure they are not more successful or financially secure than their men.

Such advice apparently resonates with many African American women, who often feel rejected and denigrated by black men and see adherence to dominant gender expectations as a way to restore their relationships. Yet in buying into a gendered scenario of love and marriage, they place unrealistic expectations not only on themselves but also on men, as traditional values tend to measure their masculinity by their economic achievements. Black women's weariness of male partners who do not measure up in the economic arena has made money a central issue in relationships. A recent study of college students found that, compared to their white counterparts, black female students were ten times more likely to say that a man should pay for the date (regardless of who initiated it), twice as likely to say that it was insulting for a man to even expect a women to share the cost of a date, and twice as likely to say that it was improper for women to initiate intimacy. Black men and women both indicated that upward mobility was an important trait in their partners, but women placed much more value on the social status of their partners than did men.[4]

Support for traditional gender expectations also runs high among African American men who, deprived of other legitimate sources of power, often cling tenaciously to the ideology of male dominance and see controlling black women as crucial to their claim to masculinity. Stung by the "black matriarchy" thesis, many black men appear to have become even more blatantly sexist in their demand for female subordination. Even Black Power militants missed the irony of advocating violence to overthrow racial injustice, while insisting on the subordination of women. "What makes a woman appealing is femininity," says black nationalist Maulana Ron Karenga, "and she can't be feminine without being submissive."[5] All too often, the physical and personality characteristics associated with black women were denigrated as deviant and destructive, and they found themselves pushed aside by black male leaders who were frequently accused of "talking black but sleeping white." As one black female law student pointed out, "We black women are always being reminded of how marginal and unworthy we are. We're never smart enough or beautiful enough or supportive, sexy, understanding, and resourceful enough to deserve a good black man."[6]

Endorsing dominant societal norms fosters the dismaying idea that relational harmony hinges on the economic success of men and the ability of women to assume submissive, secondary, and dependent roles. While black women are applauded for the active, strong, vital roles they have played in their families and communities, they are contradictorily told that such roles are improper in their intimate relationships with men. Moreover, dominant societal norms of femininity uphold exclusionary, Eurocentric images of female attractiveness that are defined in terms black women rarely can meet. A recent study found that African American males (33 percent) were nearly twice as likely as black females (17 percent) to say they preferred to date a person with light skin and even more likely to want to marry such a person.[7] These attitudes help account for the sixfold increase in interracial marriage between blacks and whites between 1960 and 2000, with black men twice as likely as black women to marry outside their race.[8] While less than 1 percent of marriages are between blacks and whites, this low rate of marriage may mask the growing rate of interracial dating and relationships: A 2001 survey found that two-thirds of black men and half of black women have dated someone of another race.[9]

Revisioning Love and Gender

The dilemma facing African Americans is scarcely addressed in theories of heterosexual love and partner selection. Most emphasize the values of reciprocity, equity, and homogamy in forming successful relationships, although social exchange theorists (and some feminists) have seen marriage as essentially an exchange of a woman's sexuality and physical attractiveness for the economic resources of a man. Theorists such as Afrocentrist Molefi Asante have addressed the strain between black women and men by providing an African-based vision of the ideal relationship. Asante argues that four major value components—sacrifice, inspiration, vision, and victory—shape successful black unions, yet his model is clearly more prescriptive than analytical. Most black cultural theorists have fallen short of reconciling dominant societal traditions of love with the material realities and racial status of African Americans, often even insisting on the propriety of patriarchal relationships.

The civil rights era ushered in a burgeoning of black pride and support for black cultural traditions, such as an emphasis on the strength and self-reliance of women, alternative standards of beauty, attire, and attractiveness, and oppositional expressions of masculinity and womanhood. At least publicly, strength was an appreciated and embraced characteristic of black women, and many devised styles of beauty and sexuality that challenged the emphasis on long, straight hair, small bodies, and sexual passivity. Black magazines are filled with images of women donning strikingly black cultural hairstyles and clothing, and popular singers often depict the sexual freedom of black women by depicting them as "independent, strong, and self-reliant agents of their own desires, masters of their own destiny."[10] The black cultural tradition of valuing women with big bodies has also been noted in publications like *Ebony* magazine, whose cover recently featured three plus-size African American female celebrities above an article title that read, "The full-figured revolution: If you got it, flaunt it." Yet, most efforts by black women to embrace the traditions that arise from their cultural, material, and gender experiences are rebuffed by white society as reflecting class deficits, sexual promiscuity, a lack of self-discipline, or behaviors that are detrimental to health and well-being. Thus, images of a distinctively black womanhood have often failed to gain currency in the dominant society and have been discredited and devalued by many black people who embrace white standards of style and the dominant society's almost fanatical dieting culture.

Forging alternative expressions of black masculinity has been equally difficult, especially for the vast majority of men who are not celebrity-status athletes, successful rap artists, or members of the inner-city underclass. Unique styles of dress and behavior are often cultivated as reflecting authentic black masculinity, and they often revolve around displays of power and sexuality. As Cornel West explains:

> For most young black men, power is acquired by stylizing their bodies over space and time in such a way that their bodies reflect their uniqueness and provoke fear in others. . . . In this way, the black male search for power often reinforces the myth of black male sexual prowess.[11]

Hip-hop artists are often the trendsetters for performances of black masculinity, but most of the penalties that accrue from such behaviors fall to the poor, young black men who imitate them. Such displays of manhood are less available for black middle-class men, who do not fit or embrace these versions of masculinity. Their class achievement brings prestige but also deprives them of being seen as either authentically black or particularly masculine. Performances of black masculinity by low-income men are associated with pathology and failure in the dominant society and are seen as socially threatening. Moreover, they enact the very stereotypes social activists have condemned as erroneous portrayals of black men as violent, criminal, and hypersexual. bell hooks argues that although "popular culture has made the black male body and presence stand for the apex of "cool," it is a death-dealing coolness, not one that is life-enhancing."[12] These dangerous behaviors further isolate young men from mainstream society, and the emphasis on hypersexuality, cool pose, game playing, and violence renders them ill equipped for stable relationships with women.

Courtship and Marriage Class Context

Analyses of the intimacy dilemma faced by African Americans has often focused on the plight of young, economically marginal women and men, whose fragile ties to marriage are most evident. Young black females living in poor, urban areas, for example, are especially vulnerable when it comes to hanging all of their hopes for a better life on finding the right man. The paucity of fatherly love and male attention in their lives, coupled with their own dismal prospects for escaping poverty through educational or career success, heightens their search for a male partner to validate their self-worth and provide them with a home, a family, and adult status. Nothing in their background prepares them to demand respect from their potential suitors, and most of the males they encounter lack the emotional maturity, material resources, or inclination to marry or form stable relationships. These young women use their sexuality to negotiate the lives they yearn for—freedom from parental control, womanhood, and a secure relationship with their male partners—yet they rarely fully realize their dreams. An exclusive relationship with a woman who they are accountable to but unable to support holds little appeal for disadvantaged young men, who are more likely to gain respect among their peers by being seen as "players." Elijah Anderson's insightful work explains the pattern of relationships between young men and women in inner-city areas this way:

> The girls have a dream, the boys a desire. The girls dream of being carried off by a Prince Charming who will love them, provide for them, and give them a family. The boys often desire sex without commitment or babies without responsibility for them. . . . Yet the boy knows what the girl wants and plays that role to get sex. In accepting his advances, she may think she is maneuvering him toward a commitment or that her getting pregnant is the nudge he needs to marry her and give her the life she wants. What she does not see is that the boy, despite his claims, is often incapable of giving her that life. For in reality he has little money, few prospects for earning much, and no wish to be tied to a woman who will have a say in what he does.[13]

Black teenage girls in poor families *do* face relentless pressure from their male partners for sex, but Anderson's analysis falls short by portraying them as helpless victims who are easily duped by their male counterparts, as this view ignores their sexual desires and efforts to garner power through their sexuality. Nearly all research reports a racial gap in the sexual patterns of blacks and whites, although class may hold as much explanatory power as race in understanding it. For example, although the percentage of sexually active high school students has declined in recent years, it still remains much higher among blacks (73 percent) than among whites (44 percent).[14] Studies show that the onset of sexuality is earlier for blacks than for whites and that being African American is associated with having more sex partners and higher rates of marital infidelity.[15] Nonetheless, exploring the racial gap in sexual behavior is generally thwarted by concern over reinforcing negative view of black sexuality, and most researchers steer clear by focusing on the outcomes of sexuality, such as pregnancy, teenage motherhood, and sexually transmitted diseases.

The pursuit of intimacy among older, more affluent African Americans is also shaped by economic factors, class-based relationship expectations, and gender factors. The traditional norm of women "marrying up"—or marrying men who have more status, education, and income than they do—is complicated among blacks and increases the fragility of their relationships. Black men as a group have higher earnings than black women, mostly because they are concentrated in male-typed jobs but also because they are more likely to hold high-paying professional positions. Nonetheless, during the 1950s and 1960s, the actual educational, economic, and employment gains of black women began to exceed those of black men, as did their entry into white-collar jobs (albeit mostly female-typed jobs, such as teaching and social work).[16] The status of African American women is also based on the fact that they have held jobs that have more fully integrated them into mainstream society. This situation was exacerbated during the economic decline of the 1980s, intensifying what D. King describes as a "low-level gender war" between black men and women.[17] Black women today hold more bachelor's degrees and especially more graduate degrees than black men and more jobs described as managerial/professional.[18] Black men often argue that black women are less threatening to the dominant culture and have an easier time getting good jobs—fueling dissension with the suggestion that their "double minority status" (rather than their merit) allows them to get ahead. Some African American women feel ambivalent about their own success, but others contend that black men are simply insufficiently motivated. As one women I interviewed asserted, black women "are just more go-getters than black men are. . . . [A black woman] has more of a driving force to succeed in what she wants to do, because black women overall are like that compared to black men."

The economic advantage of black men often does not compensate for the status and educational advantage of black women, who often find themselves "marrying down." In 1996, only 46 percent of college-educated black women were married to college-educated men, compared to 70 percent of white women, and college-educated black women were twice as likely as other black women to be interracially married.[19] The higher education of women, especially in relation to their spouses, increases marital instability, as it plays itself out as key differences in values about family life. The class background of women is likely to predict certain attitudes about child socialization, how money is spent, and how gender is organized; moreover, educated women are more likely to demand companionship, equity, and emotional intimacy in their marriages. As Robert Staples admits, meeting such needs "is not the forte of American males," and this may be even more likely to be true for less educated and economically disadvantaged men. Men and women thus often find themselves in separate and hostile camps; indeed, as a black woman with a doctorate degree and married to a white man said: "I never ran across a lot of black men who liked women, who really liked women and appreciated women. Perhaps because of upbringing, because of society, black men haven't been allowed to, or just don't know how to like women and how to value them."[20]

Although they are still considerably less likely to marry interracially, the actual increase in black–white interracial marriages involving black women has grown faster than that of black men. Still, "A good man is hard to find" is virtually a mantra among black women, as high rates of underemployment, low-wage work, incarceration, and mortality have diminished the supply of African American men. Moreover, the number of available women has decreased black men's incentive for fidelity and marriage and increased the vulnerability of women in relationships. As Robert Staples admits in his 1994 book, the gender ratio favors men and reduces the bargaining power of women: "In a sense," he writes, "black women often find themselves in the position of sexually auditioning for a meaningful relationship. After a number of tryouts, they may find a black male who is willing to make a commitment to them."[21] To rectify the shortage of black men, the notion of polygyny has been offered as a way to organize and institutionalize extramarital and other relationships.

The Love Connection

Cultural ideology assumes that dating and courtship processes eventually lead to falling in love and getting married; indeed, no matter how compatible couples may be, most claim that romantic love is a vital requisite for marriage. Modernization idealized women as experts in romantic love, which was once seen more as a sentimental feeling than a pragmatic decision, but the idea that love naturally propels couples toward marriage has long been refuted. Patriarchy itself can undermine love as the basis for marriage, leading men to prioritize fading virtues such as physical beauty and sexuality and women to gauge their love based on the status and power of the man. Rather than falling blindly in love, women have understood that they were choosing a lifestyle as well as a life partner, and they engage in considerable "emotion work" to fall in love with the right person. Black women have often had to be even more cautious in weighing the merits of marriage; as Joyce Ladner told us nearly three decades ago, love and emotional needs are often subordinated to practical considerations among young black women, as they make "a more realistic cold assessment of the chances of succeeding [and] use more sophisticated and rational reasons for entering the marriage contract."[22] The high rate of marital failure that began in the 1970s led theorists, theologians, and scholars to ponder the meaning of love and wonder whether basing marriage on something as fleeting as romantic love was a good idea.

While the need to be loved is probably universal, most social scientists contend that the ability to love is learned, primarily through processes whereby children bond with their parents or primary caregivers. Such processes are flawed in families where children are not nurtured, held, loved, or cared for properly, and these developmental deficits mean that many reach adulthood essentially unable to connect with others in deep and meaningful ways. Children's self-esteem may also be diminished by inadequate family processes and further undermined by racism and exclusion from mainstream society. bell hooks (and others) argues that in a "white supremacist society it makes sense that internalized racism and self-hate stand in the way of love."[23] That black children suffered deficits in their self-esteem was once accepted as an article of faith—how could it be otherwise in a society that systematically denigrated every aspect of blackness? Studies now challenge the idea of race-based differences in self-esteem, yet growing up poor, experiencing a deprivation of parental support and love, receiving an inferior education, and being bombarded by images equating whiteness with success and attractiveness undoubtedly have a corrosive effect on one's self-esteem. The claim of pride in blackness as a racial identity and high levels of self-esteem in children is simply not consistent with their high levels of sexual promiscuity, teenage pregnancy, substance abuse, and the glorification of street toughness and violence. Thus, economic, gender, and psychological factors often hinder the creation of genuinely loving relationships.

Marriage: The Culture, Contract, and Reality

Modern marriage has been seen as the natural outcome of heterosexual love, as proof of commitment and value conformity, and as the only legitimate arena for sexuality, reproduction, and rearing children. Despite undergoing significant revolutions in the past few decades, Karla Hackstaff argues that the "marriage culture" remains particularly strong in the United States. At least 90 percent of Americans plan to marry, and most still believe that married people are happier than single people. The dominant culture romanticizes marriage as an expression of committed love, free choice, intimacy, sexuality, and security. As the highly idealized nucleus of the family, it is entered into with elaborate ceremonies, celebrations, and solemn vows. The vision of a lifelong relationship with a soul mate, with someone to love and share life with, is probably universally appealing—even among those who are divorced, more than 80 percent of whom say marriages ought to be permanent. The marriage culture is inspired by Western Judeo-Christian religion, notes Hackstaff, which regulates marriage and divorce, gives meaning to family practices, reinforces the notion of male dominance, and accepts divorce only as a last resort.[24] The cultural romanticizing of the value of marriage is also heralded by scholars who document its numerous benefits, including better health, greater sexual satisfaction, more financial affluence, and better social, academic, and psychological outcomes for children.[25]

The idealized view of marriage as the locus of love and sexuality sharply contrasts with the reality of marriage as a legal contract that upholds male domination and female dependency, assures property rights, and sanctions the legitimacy of children. Traditional marriage has been described as the linchpin of gender inequality in families, rigidly defining the roles of husbands as legal heads of their households and economic providers and obliging women to provide unpaid domestic work and child care. Women were seen as owing their husbands complete obedience, as common law held that "the husband and father had nearly absolute authority over his wife and children, including the right to administer physical correction."[26] The concept of marital rape did not exist, as women were expected to accept the sexual overtures of their husbands under all circumstances, and husbands could sue a third party who interfered with his exclusive right to the sexuality and domestic work of his wife. Marriage was also a property arrangement based on legitimizing childbirth and inheritances, offering significant economic benefits to women and children. As such, it has been less relevant to African Americans.

Although the majority of blacks historically have gotten married, economic strains and female independence made it difficult for them to reap the usual benefits of marriage—that is, household authority and exemption from domestic work for men and economic solvency and the ability to engage in full-time domesticity for women. Black Americans have not, of course, been completely exempt from such marital arrangements. The working-class family in which I was born and reared, for example, consisted of a blue-collar, wage-earning father and a full-time homemaker mother who had full responsibility for the housework and caring for six children. My father embodied the strong male head of household: He earned the money, laid down the law, demanded obedience, and meted out punishment, all of which was uncritically accepted by us as normal. My mother deferred to his authority, and the marriage lasted until her death (nearly forty years), although I never thought much about whether she was happily married or satisfied with the relationship. Two-parent working-class families like my own remain fairly invisible in most scholarship, which tends to dichotomize African American families as either poor and headed by single mothers or as dual-income, middle-class families. In neither case is gender viewed as much of an issue, as men were absent in the former and the latter were held out as models of gender egalitarianism. The notion that married black couples had achieved gender equality in the domestic arena has now been challenged by systematic research, but few studies have offered much insight about other factors that might affect marital satisfaction among African Americans.

Feminist research implies gender equality is the key to marital stability and happiness, as seen in Pepper Schwartz's emphasis on "peer marriage," defined as one in which "each [partner] has equal status and is equally responsible for emotional, economic, and household duties." For the most part scholars have settled on studying the division of housework and child care as the most important determinant of gender equality, documenting repeatedly that women of all races do much more of it than men. Age and level of education appear best at predicting male partners' contributions to family work, with young, educated men being more involved than other men. In 1997, D. John and B. A. Shelton found that black men spent only about half as much time doing housework as their partners; moreover, although black and white women spent a comparable number of hours each week on housework, black women worked longer hours on their jobs and had more children. The myth of gender equality between black spouses may stem from the fact that African American men have been shown to be more accepting of their wives' employment than are white men; yet, they are also more conservative in other gender beliefs[27] and experience more conflict over work–family responsibilities, especially when the wife has a career.[28] At best, the handful of studies conducted during the 1990s suggest that blacks are moving toward a more egalitarian pattern, since in some cases black women do less of the housework than white women.[29]

African Americans often hold seemingly incongruent gender ideologies; my research, for example, finds strong support for the idea that men and women should share housework and child care equally *and* that mothers should be in the home and fathers in the labor market.[30] For the most part, gender ideologies are probably less potent predictors of behavior than economic factors. There is no conflict between believing in gender equality and being a stay-at-home wife and mother, but women whose husbands earned enough money to exempt them from the labor force did most of the domestic work and were often quite satisfied with the relationship. The impact of age and education on sharing domestic work was evident among dual-income couples with young children, even when couples professed belief in male headship and authority in the home. One employed mother I interviewed made it clear that gender had little bearing on the distribution of work in her household, saying:

> Norman [her husband] does about everything. He has always cooked—
> he's a better cook than I am. . . . I think men and women should share
> equally in the responsibility of the home, but it depends on what the

strengths and weaknesses of the two people are. Like if a person cannot cook, I don't want them cooking for me. But I think there should be an equal sharing—child care, definitely.[31]

Middle-class married African American men are often quite *happily* involved in the care of children—in many cases eager to become the fathers they never had—although there tends to be a gender division in the work they perform. The owner of a day care center, who was married to a physician, described her husband this way: "My husband is incredible . . . he's just a great help. He loves to help the kids with their homework, and as they get older he takes more responsibility. And he loves to plan our vacations and go on field trips with the kids at school."

Beyond the sharing of family work, other factors undoubtedly shape marital satisfaction among African Americans, although little research has explored the issue. One interesting (and contested) article by R. E. Ball and L. Robbins reported that being single produced more happiness among blacks than being married.[32] Black men who were single, divorced, or separated were happier in life than those who were married, and among black women, widows had the highest level of life satisfaction. A more recent study found that, compared to white women, black women felt they were receiving fewer benefits from being married; they also expressed less trust in their spouses and had lower levels of marital well-being.[33] In their study of divorced black men, Erma Jean Lawson and Aaron Thompson found financial strain and male unemployment to be the most frequently mentioned causes of divorce, and that these factors were also associated with wife abuse. But while an overall higher standard of living predicts marital satisfaction among blacks,[34] higher earnings by wives than husbands place some black marriages at risk.[35]

Frequent participation in religion is apt to strengthen black marriages, despite the fact that churches support patriarchy in principle and often disperse antifeminist rhetoric. The pastor of a large church I visited recently, for example, mocked women in sports and described strong black womanhood as simply being out of the will of God and as opening up black sons to the "spirit of homosexuality"—another topic of widespread derision. Yet such polemical teachings by Christian fundamentalists are frequently accompanied by marriage enrichment classes that teach men to sacrifice practically every male privilege in supporting their wives, and they define male headship in seemingly benign ways. For example, an African American man endorsed male headship of families but explains:

My views in terms of gender—I think that spiritually I'm head of the home. All that means is that the ultimate responsibility of how well things go and the quality and the peace, and so forth, is ultimately my responsibility . . . but that in no way means that women are lesser of an entity, lesser in terms of responsibility, lesser in terms of importance.[36]

Thus, understanding how religion affects marriage and gender will require looking beyond the polemical literature supporting patriarchal norms.

Race translates into cultural patterns that also affect the quality of black women and men's relationships, often in class-specific ways. African American women have historically been known to place more value on blood than marriage relationships, and the bonds of mutual aid and support formed by low-income black women often militate against marriage and long-term relationships. Research has found that wives in kin-centered units are less likely to discuss their problems with their husbands and more likely to experience marital dissatisfaction.[37] The strong emphasis on extended family relationships may explain why black wives' closeness with their in-laws correlates with marital happiness for both spouses but has no impact on white marriages.[38] Family bonds also seem to matter in that husbands' close contact with their fathers is associated with their having greater love for their wives and with greater marital satisfaction among wives.[39]

The challenges facing African Americans historically did not keep most of them from marrying and trying to create viable relationships, yet the fragility of those marriages is seen in the fact that even in the 1950s and 1960s, their rate of divorce was four times higher than that of whites.[40] Since then, it has been about two times higher, but the reduction in the racial disparity is largely the result of high rates of nonmarriage among both blacks and whites. In 1998, 80 percent of white adults had been married at least once, compared to only 61 percent of blacks.[41] Combining those who have never married and those who are separated, divorced, or widowed reveals about 65 percent of black women are single. Black men have a higher rate of marriage than black women but a lower rate than white men.[42] These trends in black marriage rates parallel and amplify patterns of singleness, delayed marriage, cohabitation, and divorce evident in the broader society. Yet while whites are often seen as delaying marriage until they acquire adequate resources to sustain families, blacks are seen as irresponsibly making lifestyle choices that undermine family stability and increase rates of crime, poverty, and welfare dependency. In reality, the same forces that have weakened black marriages are increasingly affecting white marriages.

The Declining Legitimacy of Gendered Marriage

The emergence of the postindustrial economy challenged the viability of gender-based marriages, especially the breadwinner–homemaker family that prevailed among whites during the 1950s. Feminists criticized such marriages as based more on patriarchal traditions and economics than the power of love, while the declining wage-earning abilities of men and the massive entry of white women into the labor force shifted the balance of gender power in families. As had always been the case for black women, white women found that their entry into the labor market increased their independence, power, and workload, and diminished their tolerance for gender inequities of marriage. Male prerogatives such as exemption from housework and child care in exchange for economic support came under fire as many white women faced the "second shift" dilemma for the first time. Despite their labor market work, it has been difficult for women, especially in their lower-paying jobs, to negotiate equitable sharing in the domestic arena effectively. But even having a low-wage job has allowed women to bail out of relationships lacking equity, as well as emotionally unfulfilling and abusive relationships. By the mid-1970s, the rate of divorce in the United States reached a record high, and, while declining somewhat during the 1980s, it continues to exceed that of most other countries. Thus, the economic factors and gender inequities that had historically made marriages less viable for black people had begun to take a toll on those of white Americans.

The economic decline of the postindustrial era has had an even stronger impact on African Americans, reinforcing their ambivalence toward marriage. As I have argued, societal norms sanctioning heterosexual marriage as the quintessential intimate relationship and the cornerstone of stable families have always been somewhat at odds with black peoples' resources and traditions, as seen in the resistance of many to the marriage campaign that followed emancipation (see chapter 3). By the end of the civil rights era, marriage rates were notably plummeting; for example, in the 1970s, about half of all blacks had married by age twenty, but by 1990, only 10 percent had done so.[43] Federal census data show that the overall rate of nonmarriage among black women more than doubled between 1970 and the mid-1990s, from 17 percent to 40 percent. Rates of marriage also fell among white women, but in 1990, they were still nearly 80 percent higher than for black women. For more privileged blacks, those with steady working-class or middle-class jobs, marriage may make sense economically, yet poor women are not apt to want to sacrifice what little autonomy they have in exchange for a man who is unable to significantly improve their standard of living.

Economic decline offers the easiest explanation for the current demise in marriage, yet high rates of marriage among other economically marginal groups (such as Latinas) suggest that there is a cultural angle to the story. While blacks are at least slightly less likely than whites to say marriage and a committed relationship are desirable,[44] some research shows that many black people have simply lost their confidence in marriage, often due to the high rates of marital failure they witness.[45] In some cases, young black females see marriage as having fewer advantages now than in the past,[46] while those who are older and more affluent believe that marriage should take a backseat to their career goals. Interviews with professional black women revealed that they were more likely to see marriage than motherhood as an obstacle to their career.[47]

Living Single

Delia Williams, the African American sociology professor introduced earlier, divorced her husband after nineteen years of marriage as conflict elevated over her career success and growing differences in their values. Moreover, he was unwilling to make any compromises to save the marriage, assuring Delia that she should do whatever she wanted to do, because that was what he planned to do. Only after divorcing her husband and becoming involved in a new relationship, says Delia, did she really find out that it was possible to have intimacy with a man:

> I was married for nineteen years, and I really, really loved my husband—
> we had good times, we both liked to party, and we had great sex. But it
> was only after we divorced and I started dating that I learned what intimacy was. In a two-year relationship with [James], I felt he knew me at

every level—sexual, spiritual, intellectual. I just don't think my husband was really capable of that kind of relationship.

The ideological connection among intimacy, love, and marriage has been weakened by growing rates of singleness, delayed marriage, and nonmarital cohabitation. Black adults are more likely to be single than whites, but just as marriage does not assure intimacy, being single does not exclude it. Asked where she finds intimacy now that her relationship with her male partner has ended, Delia said:

> I have intimacy with my children, especially my youngest [twenty-two-year-old] son. We can really share things emotionally—even when he was a child we had that special connection. I always thought he was destined to be something special in life. I'm extroverted and find a lot of intimacy in teaching. I also have lunch with one of my girlfriends almost every Friday—you know how they say a spouse has to be your helper, your companion, your counselor? I find that in my girlfriends, although each relationship fulfills some different aspect of it.

African American women have a long tradition of relying on each other for assistance in raising families, and the deepening of those relationships today both includes and transcends the swapping of child care and economic resources. Black women pull together in religious and myriad other ways to bond and support each other—whether through prayer groups, community uplift, and recreation activities. *Ebony* magazine wrote on the growing importance of the "sister circles" that black women are engaged in, and they are proliferating informally and through organized single groups, offering women much of the companionship and intimacy of marriage. Most of the single women I know are quick to say they still may marry—if they find the right man—but they find themselves willing to make fewer and fewer concessions to do so. Delia, for example, toys with the idea of having a man in her life, although she says she's left it entirely "up to the Lord." After all, she has raised three children—mostly by herself—and she loves her teaching job and leisure time, saying that she truly has peace of mind for the first time in her life. She also enjoys her freedom and doesn't want anyone coming home asking, "What's for dinner?" As Delia notes:

> I guess I'd be willing to make some changes to have a man in my life, but not very many. I think men my age are really into that "better half" stuff—they want you to be there, doing things with or for them all the

time. I almost believe that familiarity like that breeds contempt—after a while, you've heard each other's stories. I am a whole person, and I need to have a whole person. I have a life and I need someone who also has a life and interests of his own. We'd be like two parallel lines but come together and share sometimes.

Sexual intimacy can be a problem among single women regardless of how many friends they feel close to, but, as Delia points out, "all the sexual promiscuity and sexually transmitted diseases makes it hardly worth the risk." Terry McMillan's popular 1992 novel *Waiting to Exhale* vividly portrays the search for sexual satisfaction and intimacy among a group of accomplished black women, who engage in one-night stands, have affairs with married men, and even tolerate drug-abusing partners—only to find themselves relying on each other in the end. Many criticized the movie for its negative depiction of black men, but few questioned the portrayal of successful, intelligent black women who were unable to figure out why they could not find true love despite giving generously of their sexuality to men who were adulterers, abusive, and sometimes virtual strangers. Today, more black women (and some black men) are considering the benefits of celibacy as a way to achieve greater respect for themselves and control over their bodies. Efforts to convince young African American girls of the virtues of sexual abstinence have been widespread in churches and communities for decades, and a spate of new books—mostly by Christian authors—now argue that many older single women should be more circumspect in their sexual choices, since relationships have often left them feeling used and abandoned. As M. M. Hammond writes:

> People are tired of giving themselves, not getting anything in return, and feeling used at the end of the experience. For a woman, it's crucial that she keeps herself until she is in a committed relationship because her body is her power base. When she gives her body, her mind, heart and strength go with it.[48]

Many African American women, of course, form sexual relationships with other women, although doing so openly often leads to criticism and stigma. B. Omolade argues that the historic homosocial ties between black women have often had a sexual dimension, as they sought to free themselves from sexual exploitation by white men and the patriarchal leanings of black men.[49] In other cases, black women take heterosexual orientation for granted rather than exploring their sexuality. In *Women's Untold Stories*,

Tangri and Browne introduce Laura, an African American woman in her fifties, who had never even entertained the thought of being lesbian, despite growing up with distinctive "tomboyish" interests. Laura endured a heterosexual marriage with an abusive husband for twenty-five years before finally collapsing into mental illness and homelessness. She found the safest place on earth for her was an all-male gay support group, saying, "I needed hugs, but I didn't want someone to think the hugs were going to lead somewhere."[50] She found a sense of community among gays and lesbians that led her to accept her own sexual orientation.

Black Americans today are depicted as especially homophobic,[51] and, while such attitudes seem consistent with their educational and religious background (see chapter 6), it appears that they may have grown more openly intolerant of gays and lesbians since the civil rights era. The black nationalist movement, for example, was especially hostile to gay men, even arguing that homosexuality was unknown in Africa and was a European strategy for destroying black people. Beverly Greene argues that internalized racism also heightens homophobia among blacks, who see it as another basis for their denigration. Black religious leaders today align themselves more closely with the new Christian Right and their fundamentalist views of the Bible. Together, black nationalism and conservative religious thought may have fostered more antigay and antilesbian attitudes. J. Battle and M. Bennett find that blacks are less likely to disclose their homosexuality and that those who do have more negative mental health outcomes than whites. Still, black leaders like Al Sharpton, Coretta Scott King, and Carol Moseley Braun are among those who support the rights of gays and lesbians as a civil rights issue, and polls show that issues of social justice and jobs are more likely to sway black voters than politicians' stances on gay issues.[52]

Cohabitation, another alternative to marriage, rose dramatically among singles during the 1990s, increasing nearly 50 percent to more than 4 million couples. For poor people, cohabitation has been described in some studies as the "budget way" to start a family[53] and it can produce relatively stable relationships. As one black mother said, "I'm not married. I got three kids. But their father is there with the kids. He's been there since I was 16. . . . I been with the same guy since I was sixteen years old and I'm still with him now. I only had really one man in my life."[54]

Since the 1960s, cohabitation can no longer be the explicit basis for denying welfare eligibility, and states have become fairly lenient about relationships between welfare recipients and their partners.[55] Those in long-term cohabiting relationships often feel they have less to gain from marriage, especially if they are unable to meet the financial obligations of marriage. Moreover, cohabitation among single mothers improves their economic standing and decreases the rate of childhood poverty by about 30 percent.[56] K. Edin finds that low-income women place much emphasis on the financial stability and respectability of potential mates in considering marriage, and they may even have a "pay and stay" rule for coresiding male partners to ensure that they contribute to household expenses. Their mistrust of men, fear of domestic violence, and concern over losing control of their own households also affect their marital decisions.[57]

Despite the risk poor women face in their intimate relationships, the past few years have seen the emergence of a new campaign to solve poverty and single motherhood by getting them to marry. Welfare reform policies designated $300 million to promote marriage among the poor, in many cases through premarital counseling and making marriage education a part of the high school curriculum.[58] Whether welfare reform or marriage will reduce poverty and births to young, single mothers remains to be seen. A recent study by D. T. Lichter and his colleagues found that poverty rates would still be more than twice as high among black women if they had the same family background and rates of marriage and unwed childbirth as whites. Moreover, they noted that among economically disadvantaged black women, marriage is associated with downward educational mobility, and those who marry and then divorce have even higher rates of poverty than never-marrieds.[59] L. Hao and A. Cherlin found that welfare reform has failed to decrease teenage births for girls in welfare families; in fact, rates of unwed pregnancy and high school dropout had increased slightly in those families.[60] More important, marriage promotion policies seem to miss the significance of economic solvency and gender equity in creating viable unions.

Summary

This chapter has explored the clash between the black cultural traditions of love and marriage and those of the dominant society. For African Americans, racism and poverty have stripped marriage of much of its facade, exposing its economic and patriarchal underpinnings. Still, many have accepted the gendered scenario of love and marriage, although doing so has been especially perilous, as few black men have achieved the economic prowess sufficient to warrant female subordination, and black women have a long tradition of employment and independence. The gender dilemma, coupled with racial and economic oppression, has made marriages fragile and left African Americans leading the way in creating alternative family systems that are now becoming common in the broader society. While social conservatives champion marriage as compatible with family values and as a strategy for strengthening the economic base of poor families, research so far has not supported the efficacy of this strategy. Families need a solid economic base if they are to succeed and outmoded traditions of notions of male dominance must be put to rest.

Notes

1. O. Patterson (1993:4).
2. D. Franklin (2000).
3. b. hooks (2001:158).
4. L. E. Ross (1996).
5. Quoted in M. Marable (2000 [1983]:97).
6. Quoted in D. Bell (2001).
7. L. E. Ross (1997).
8. D. Franklin (2000).
9. R. C. Romano (2003).
10. R. A. Emerson (2002:116).
11. Quoted in M. B. Zinn and D. S. Eitzen (2002:253).
12. b. hooks (2004:155).
13. E. Anderson (1990:113–14).
14. B. Risman and P. Schwartz (2002).
15. C. F. Scott and S. Sprecher (2000); D. Franklin (2000).
16. D. Franklin (2000).
17. D. King (1999:434).
18. "Marriage Dilemma" (1997).
19. "Marriage Dilemma" (1997).
20. E. Cose (1995:51–52).
21. Quoted in M. B. Zinn and D. S. Eitzen (2002).
22. J. Ladner (1972:247).
23. b. hooks (2004:18).
24. K. Hackstaff (1999).

25. L. Waite (2000).
26. L. Walsh (1985:4).
27. K. M. Blee and A. R. Tickamyer (1995).
28. J. S. Bridges and A. M. Orza (1996).
29. J. Veroff, A. Young, and H. Coon (2000).
30. S. A. Hill (1999).
31. S. A. Hill (1999:121).
32. R. E. Ball and L. Robbins (1986).
33. P. Y. Goodwin (2003).
34. T. L. Orbuch and L. Custer (1995).
35. R. Staples and L. B. Johnson (1993).
36. Quoted in M. T. Carolan and K. R. Allen (1999).
37. R. M. Milardo and A. Graham (2000).
38. J. Veroff et al. (2000).
39. E. Burger and R. M. Milardo, cited in R. M. Milardo and A. Graham (2000).
40. D. Franklin (2000).
41. R. S. Oropesa and B. K. Gorman (2000).
42. W. M. Hemmons (1996).
43. C. A. Fitch and S. Ruggles (2000).
44. R. S. Oropesa and B. K. Gorman (2000).
45. A. G. Hunter (2002).
46. A. O. King (1999).
47. C. B. Leggon (1983).
48. Quoted N. A. Foston (2004).
49. B. Omolade (1995).
50. S. S. Tangri and J. M. Browne (1999:134).
51. J. Battle and M. Bennett (2000).
52. K. Boykin (2004).
53. F. F. Furstenberg (1996).
54. R. Jarrett (1994:39).
55. R. A. Moffitt, R. Reville, and A. E. Winkler (1998).
56. J. A. Seltzer (2000).
57. K. Edin (2000).
58. K. Campbell (2002).
59. D. T. Lichter, D. Roempke Graefe, and J. B. Brown (2003).
60. L. Hao and A. Cherlin (2004).

CHAPTER 5

In Search of the Village

Black Motherhood in Transition

> Motherhood meant everything to Mildred. When she was first carrying
> Freda, she didn't believe her stomach would actually grow, but when it
> did she felt it stretch like the skin of a drum and she'd never been so
> happy. She felt there was more than just a cord connecting her to this boy
> or girl that was moving inside her belly. There was some special juice and
> only she could supply it. And sometimes when she turned over at night
> she could feel the baby turn inside her too, and she knew this was magic.
> . . . She was so proud of Freda that she let her body blow up and flatten
> for the next fifty-five months. It made her feel like she had actually done
> something meaningful with her life, having babies did.
>
> —Terry Mcmillan[1]

Mildred, the central character in Terry McMillan's 1997 novel *Mama*, has
her first child at age seventeen and is awed by the sheer power and mys-
tery of pregnancy and childbirth. Although a work of fiction, McMillan's
vivid portrait of the significance that childbearing can have in the lives of
young and poor African American females resonates well with scholarly
research. While few girls actually plan to have babies during their teenage
years, doing so often elevates their feelings of pride and self-esteem.
Asked to recall a time or an event that made them feel really good about
themselves, nearly half of the black teenage mothers in one study replied,
"Having a baby." Attributing her elation to the birth process itself, one
young mother explained, "I don't think it really hit me at first, but at the
hospital when I had him, I told myself, WOW, I'm a mother! I was happy;
I was excited; I was really totally excited. . . . I just gave birth to a baby!"[2]
My research with low-income African American mothers also shows that
childbearing and motherhood hold a special meaning in their lives, even

when it entails the risk of passing an incurable and potentially fatal disease on to their children and coping with the demands of a chronically ill child.[3]

Poor women of color often have few sources of hope or fulfillment in their lives, but the oppression they experience usually does not deprive them of their procreative abilities, and pregnancy and giving birth are profoundly powerful acts. Moreover, motherhood is a significant marker of womanhood. It provides a respectable social identity, an important set of child-rearing tasks, access to kin resource networks, and a space where authority, a sense of control, and self-expression can be cultivated. Thus, childbearing and motherhood often loom large as sources of gratification among poor and less advantaged women, even when it is not always planned or intentional.

For African Americans, the fusion of motherhood, power, and activism is deeply rooted in a confluence of social forces stretching from precolonial African societies through slavery and its aftermath. Despite the diversity of African societies, the value of procreation was nearly universal because one's eternal spiritual existence was seen as nullified by the absence of descendants. As Barbara Christian explains, "The African mother is a spiritual anchor; thus she is greatly respected in African societies. By giving birth to children, African women ensure their people's continuity, both here and in the hereafter."[4] Thus, while patriarchy and the practice of polygamy suggest that female subordination was the norm among Africans, their consequences were buffered by the premium placed on women's fertility and the economic responsibility of mothers for their children.[5] The power of motherhood was further enhanced by African norms emphasizing the primacy of consanguineous (rather than marital) relations, the mother–child relationship, and female-centered kin networks. All of these traditions were both degraded and reinforced by slavery, but even in that setting—where motherhood was often involuntary and based on sexual coercion—childbearing had its advantages: It could be a route to freedom, a guarantee of not being sold, an important source of social standing, or a strategy for gaining access to valued resources.

Recognizing the significance of motherhood, revisionist writers provided the framework for a black cultural ethos of motherhood that challenged the concept of legitimacy and portrayed black mothers as authoritative and effective child-rearing agents.[6] African American feminists have also underscored the cultural value of mothering work in black communities, arguing that it differs from that described by white feminists as oppressive, privatized labor that keeps women tied to the private arena of life.[7] P. H. Collins, for example, acknowledges that motherhood is a contradictory institution that is experienced in diverse ways by black women but also contends, "Motherhood can serve as a site where Black women express and learn the power of self-direction, the importance of valuing and respecting ourselves, the necessity of self-reliance and independence, and a belief in Black women's empowerment."[8]

An accurate reading of black women's history shows that they have managed the work of raising children—their own and those in white families—with courage, confidence, wit, and skill. They have often mothered effectively under extraordinarily difficult circumstances and have made an invaluable contribution to sustaining families in a racially oppressive society. Yet, while I applaud the research that has made the experiences of black mothers visible, I contend that it has also given rise to what I call a black cultural ethos of motherhood that is narrow in scope, often contradictory, and inherently politically risky. It represents at best one model of black motherhood, and even then can inadvertently minimize the challenges black mothers face, their valiant fight for reproductive rights, and the perils of motherhood, especially for the poor. Drawing on the implications of literature on the mothering work of African American women, I construct and then critique what I call the "black cultural ethos of motherhood" by examining it within the framework of changing societal and family resources.

Overview of the Chapter

I begin this chapter by looking at the historic, cross-cultural reproductive mandate—the valuing of women based on their ability to have children—and discuss how this often meant that neither enslaved black women nor free white women in colonial America had control over their childbearing or their children. Slavery thoroughly degraded black women's sexuality and childbearing, yet the economic value of their progeny in some cases brought them benefits, such as more status, food, and relief from work.

Fertility, thus, was a tool through which at least some enslaved black women could challenge the authority of white slave owners; for example, some resisted the mandate to reproduce, and others used it to gain privileges, status, or even freedom or to win advantages for their children. With emancipation and modernization, the birthrates of middle-class women of all races fell, as they fought for the right to gain control over their own reproductive processes. Such control was especially difficult for African American women, who navigated the difficult terrain between eugenicists and policymakers who insisted that they curtail their births and even endorsed involuntary sterilizations and black males who equated any form of birth control with white-inspired genocide. The post–World War II procreative ethic increased rates of childbirth, leading to the birth of the baby boomers, but the notion that all women were slated for motherhood soon met with resistance from feminism.

I discuss contested visions among feminists over whether motherhood and the oppression of women were inherently linked and how that contention was further exacerbated when placed in class and race contexts. Low-income and poor women often naturalize childbearing and express a great deal of pride in their roles as mothers, yet they are less likely than more affluent women to see themselves as having made an explicit choice to become mothers and more likely to encounter hardships in their child-rearing work. Racism further intensifies the hardships of motherhood and challenges the reproductive rights of women, and African American women have often criticized the white feminist analysis of motherhood as failing to address the host of issues they have faced in gaining control over their own childbearing. Motherhood among poor black women has been seen as the result of sexual irresponsibility or flawed cultural values or as motivated by a generous welfare system. Early birth control clinics were disproportionately located in black neighborhoods, and coercive state policies have threatened their right to bear children through involuntary sterilization, court-ordered medical screenings, and the loss of welfare benefits. In the late 1970s, one federal district court found "incontrovertible evidence" that "an indefinite number of poor people have been improperly coerced into accepting a sterilization operation under the threat that various federally supported welfare benefits would be withdrawn unless they submitted to irreversible sterilization."[9]

In addition to the unique reproductive struggles of African American women, many also saw the account by some white feminists of motherhood as inherently oppressive as being inconsistent with their own experiences. Drawing on their historic experiences in West African societies and during slavery, they contended that motherhood had been organized differently among black women—more as work shared by a community of women rather than privatized labor that transpired in the household. Moreover, they maintained that in black cultural tradition, being a mother had often been a central identity and a source of status and power.

In this chapter, I analyze the black cultural ethos of motherhood, which I define as the assumption that African American women are somehow endowed with an innate capacity for mothering work, that they experience motherhood as natural and intrinsically gratifying, and that they have organized mothering work in less oppressive ways. The cultural ethos of motherhood, I contend, constructs black women as authoritative, confident figures who easily manage the responsibilities of child rearing; effectively integrate mothering, employment, and social activism; and willingly share with other women the work of caring for children. These ideas resonate with the lived experiences of many black Americans, and they legitimize and value the mothering work in which black women have invested heavily. However, while finding examples of valiant black motherhood poses few problems, I see generalizing this model to all African American women as problematic. I revisit the "takes a village" philosophy based on my own experiences and what I have learned from other black mothers, and I conclude the chapter with a look at how motherhood is a perilous journey, especially for poor black women who face elevated health and social risks in having and raising children.

From the Reproductive Mandate to Voluntary Motherhood

Children are a woman's constituency with the narrow political world of the family; the more she has, the stronger her clout. If she is infertile, her status plummets, and she often falls victim to polygamy, desertion, or divorce.

—Betsy Hartmann[10]

Having and caring for children has almost universally been the purview of women, whether based on choice, powerlessness, ineffective birth control, labor demands, or the need to perpetuate the species. The reproductive mandate sharpened with the advent of agriculture and private property, and complying with it has often been the only source of social acceptance, security and status for women. Cross-cultural research has found that while infertility and barrenness were historically sources of shame and stigma for women, the birth of a child (especially a son) officially consummated marriages, solidified a women's status as wife, and in some cases even meant that a woman could change her dress, demeanor, hairstyle, or name to signify her new status.[11] Thus, for much of human history, the dominant demand placed on women was to produce a sufficient supply of children, ideally in the context of a marital relationship that ensured paternity and an orderly transmission of property. Producing children enhanced women's worth, especially in traditionally sex-segregated societies, where patriarchal ideologies often precluded property ownership by women. Betsy Hartmann describes children as a hedge against an uncertain future for women in Kenya, for example, since women are not allowed to inherit land but are given the right to use it through male family members, including sons. In societies where women are seen as inferior and as unsuitable social companions for men, children become important economic, emotional, and political capital for mothers. Motherhood gave women a source of authority, allowed them to establish intimate relationships with children, and validated their position in the family and community. In some societies where women seem virtually powerless, they have been able to use their roles as child producers and mothers to enter the political arena.

Childbearing in colonial America was driven by a similar scenario: Children were economic assets in farming communities, and producing them the cultural expectation for black and white women alike. White women had an average of six to eight children, while enslaved black women were expected to have as many children as possible. Married white women and virtually all black women shared a legally sanctioned lack of control over their own bodies, sexuality, and children; white males felt entitled to have sex with and children by whomever they pleased, and they were legally the custodians or owners of all children. While black and white women were expected to produce children and most had to combine childbearing with productive labor, motherhood for the two groups of women differed sharply: As Bart Landry succinctly notes, white women gave birth to heirs, while black women gave birth to property.[12]

Enslaved black women faced tremendous pressures to have children, and, with rates of voluntary conception elevated by sexual coercion, rape, and deliberate breeding, it has been estimated that nearly one-fourth of those of reproductive age gave birth each year. Black mothers had little choice but to prioritize their work roles, which often meant carrying infants into the fields on their backs while working or leaving older children in the care of elderly slave women. Their maternal authority was further eroded by the fact that children were owned by slave masters and destined to become their coworkers, and they could be taken, sold, or abused. As one ex-slave recalled, "During slavery it seemed like your children belonged to everybody but you."[13]

Although slavery created immense anguish and hardships for black women, motherhood remained one of the few social roles they could attain and even be rewarded for despite pervasive race and gender oppression. While there is evidence of deplorable treatment of enslaved black women during pregnancy,[14] the value of human chattel also meant that having children could result in special privileges for black women. Pregnant women and the mothers of young children often received extra food supplements and reduced workloads, and children fathered by white slave owners were sometimes allowed to learn to read and write or given their freedom once they reached adulthood. Childbearing could also lead to greater family stability, since women who gave birth frequently were less likely to be sold. As Thomas Jefferson aptly stated, "I consider a woman who brings a child every two years more profitable than the best man of the farm," noting that her production added to capital rather than mere consumption.[15] On the other hand, freedom could be a reward to women in exchange for the production of numerous children.

Despite the benefits garnered by their child-rearing and domestic work, enslaved black women frequently resisted the reproductive expectations foisted on them by their owners. Many drew on African folk knowledge to avoid and abort pregnancies—so effectively, in fact, that entire families of black women sometimes failed to have children. In response to slave owners' complaints of barren slave women, one physician explained that "blacks are possessed of a secret by which they destroy the foetus at an early stage of gestation," leaving frustrated slave owners in the position of trying to control access to such knowledge or offering greater incentives and privileges for childbearing.[16] Thus, having children or refusing to do so could be a significant source of power for at least some enslaved black women.

Fertility rates plummeted among African American women once slavery ended, a fact that population scholars used as proof of blacks' general inferiority and poor health.[17] Instead, blacks also saw the link between birth control and racial progress: Fewer children meant greater mobility and freedom to pursue educational and occupational goals. Lower rates of childbearing were also touted as a weapon in gainsaying the pernicious idea that the abolition of slavery had left black people descending into their primitive ways. The use of abortion and abortifacients (e.g., alum water, turpentine, powders, suppositories, vaginal jellies, nails, pins and needles) was widespread,[18] especially among black women who migrated northward in search of a better life. Birth control clinics—often sponsored directly or partially by black community organizations—proliferated in African American neighborhoods between 1925 and 1945,[19] despite protest among a handful of black male militants who vociferously condemned these clinics as white efforts to promote black genocide. The black press supplied an abundance of birth control information, including reporting cases of abortion that had resulted in death and the arrests of physicians who had performed them.

Black health organizations, the women's club movement, and community organizations strongly supported family planning, their efforts coinciding with Margaret Sanger's early twentieth-century birth control movement. One of eleven children born to a mother who died before reaching age fifty, Sanger criticized the "marriage bed as the most degenerating influence in the social order" and heralded birth control as a means of social mobility for women and reducing reproduction among the "unfit." Middle-class blacks embraced the message, despite its classist and racist implications, including noted scholar W. E. B. Du Bois, who wrote in a 1932 edition of Sanger's *Birth Control Review*, "[T]he masses of ignorant Negroes still breed carelessly and disastrously, so that the increase among Negroes, even more than the increase among whites, is from that part of the population least intelligent and fit, and least able to rear their children properly."[20] An enthusiastic supporter of birth control, especially among poor African Americans, Du Bois later praised black women for moving toward "economically independent motherhood," noting that they were marrying later and having fewer children and that a significant percentage (a full 25 percent) were childless.[21]

Racialized Constructions of the "Good Mother"

The white women of this country are about the worst enemies with which the colored race has to contend . . . [but] if anything can make all women sisters underneath their skins, it is motherhood.

—Angelina Weld Grimké,
African American playwright and poet[22]

The abolition of slavery and growing interest in reproductive control among black people paralleled industrialization, modernization, the rise of science, and the eugenics movement—all of which created a broad context for new definitions and ideologies of motherhood. White children, increasingly freed from farm or factory labor, became the emotional commodities of their mothers, who were expected to invest heavily and often solely in their care, upbringing, and well-being. Women, especially those who were white, middle-class, and in conformity to the new definition of motherhood, were idealized as innately endowed with a yearning for children and described as self-sacrificing beings who willingly placed the needs of children ahead of their own. Aiding this ideology was the creation of the "doctrine of tender years," which shifted the legal custody of children from fathers to mothers, particularly in cases of divorce. The dominant cultural ideology held that good mothers were stay-at-home wives who had nearly full responsibility for child rearing and also mothers who availed themselves to the advice of the growing number of child-rearing experts. Motherhood itself became a scientific enterprise between 1890 and 1950, according to Rima Apple, who documents a steady rise in the emphasis on the need for mothers to be trained. Many affluent women accepted the ideology that motherhood made them inherently virtuous and morally superior to men, but they also used that ideology to justify their public roles and to advocate for policies that were advantageous to women, such as voluntary motherhood, birth control, better prenatal care, education, and the entry of women into the caring professions. They clearly equated having fewer children with greater freedom and opportunity, and birthrates dropped sharply as the new modern woman emerged, from a national average of six children per family in 1840 to three in 1900.[23]

Although African American women also experienced lower fertility rates and advocated for birth control, their class and race status precluded them from meeting the dominant requisites of being good mothers. A majority worked outside of the home, for example, and many were poor, uneducated, and single. Black motherhood was associated with a lack of sexual restraint and morality, and those who were poor were especially described as incompetent at raising children—at least their own. Moreover, they were apt targets for the eugenics movement that, fueled by the growing prestige of science, advocated selective breeding as a strategy for eliminating social problems.[24] The interests of eugenicists often ran counter to those of women of all races: They urged white, middle-class women to have children they did not want, condemned poor women of all races for having any children at all, and advanced heavy-handed interventions into the private affairs of women and their families. Eugenicists endorsed involuntary sterilization and/or confinement of "unfit breeders" (e.g., poor, race-ethnic minority, and immigrant women), proffered a "reproductive morality" that urged prospective parents to consider whether their offspring would improve the quality of future generations, and provided "preventive gynecology" by doctors who screened couples for diseases and defects and counseled them about childbearing.[25] The U.S. Supreme Court upheld the rights of states to engage in involuntary sterilization in 1927, declaring that it would be better "for all the world, if instead of waiting to execute degenerate offspring for crimes, or to let them starve for their imbecility, society can prevent those who are manifestly unfit from continuing their kind."[26] The eugenics movement contributed to the deviancy discourse on black motherhood by characterizing black women's childbearing as irresponsible and their mothering as incompetent. Indeed, as Jackie Litt has noted, the scientific era equated black motherhood with biological inferiority and maternal inadequacy, and medicine freely used black women as "objects of study and control rather than improvement and assimilation."[27]

Despite the blatant racism found among eugenicists and even some white feminists who advocated voluntary motherhood, middle-class black and white women found common ground in their support for reproductive freedom. In *Mothering the Race*, Allison Berg examines fictional portrayals and public debates surrounding black and white motherhood in the early twentieth century, when declining birthrates among more affluent women sparked heated controversy. Berg points out that for white women, the issue was producing a sufficient supply of children to offset the growing population of poor and race-ethnic minority children; that the children of white natives improved the genetic makeup of the population was taken as a given. Black leaders saw a relationship between the problems of children and racial progress, and felt it could be ameliorated through birth control and better mothering. Early activist Anna Murray pointed out, "The children of any race are the hope of that race, [and] it is doubly true of all backward races, and especially true of American children of African descent."[28]

Middle-class women of all races contended that women should control their fertility, and they used motherhood as a springboard for political activism. Nonetheless, the procreation ethic gained new vitality during the post–World War II era, when economic affluence enabled many Americans to actually live the breadwinner–homemaker family ideology. Between 1950 and 1957, fertility rates in America rose 50 percent, while the age at marriage declined.[29] As the wage-earning abilities of men increased, the ideology of motherhood again grew in prominence, as did social pressure on women to immerse themselves in producing and rearing children.

Contested Visions of Motherhood

To me the only answer a woman can make to the destructive forces of the world is creation. And the most ecstatic form of creation is the creation of new life.

—Jessie Bernard[30]

The heart of woman's oppression is her childbearing and childrearing roles.

—Shulamith Firestone[31]

Although Jessie Bernard, a founding mother of family sociology and early critic of gender inequality in marriage, seemed to embrace the glorification of motherhood that blossomed during the war era, the procreation ethic was short-lived, and the naturalization of motherhood was soon contested by feminists. Disenchantment among housewives and stay-at-home mothers, a changing economy, the entry of women into the labor force, and the second wave of feminism all gave rise to renewed critiques of motherhood as the central identity and source of satisfaction for women. Feminists contended that motherhood is more than simply a role or relationship but rather an institution embedded in patriarchal dominance, economic systems, power relations, and the distribution of resources, as well as the linchpin to gender inequality.[32] They debunked the notion of a "maternal instinct," noting that historically women did not opt to become mothers to fulfill biological yearnings but complied with the cultural mandates of reproduction because children were important for economic and inheritance purposes. The modern celebration of motherhood and child rearing, Sheila Kitzinger has argued, masks a very real antimother culture that evolved with industrialization.[33] Mothering became a second-rate activity after children lost their value as a form of wealth, Kitzinger notes, and was performed in the isolation of homes by women who were cut off from other important elements of social life. The modern ideology of motherhood calls for "intensive mothering," according to Sharon Hays, since mothers are expected to sacrifice their own needs for child-rearing work that is "exclusive, wholly child-centered, emotionally involving, and time-consuming."[34] Intensive mothering provides women little time or resources for engaging in other activities outside the home, and those who attempt to do so are often seen as "bad mothers." Numerous studies have found that motherhood entails substantial costs for women. For example, childless married couples have higher levels of satisfaction than those with children, and the onset of motherhood has been shown to result in a decline in women's psychological well-being and marital power.[35]

Despite a relatively coherent feminist critique, the discourse on motherhood is evolving and marked by divergent and competing voices. The assertion that motherhood is inherently oppressive and the radical call by a handful of scholars for its abolition have been countered by the work of a number of scholars and prominent women who are reasserting its significance and even suggesting a link between biology and the social aspects of mothering. Mary O'Brien, for example, argues that childbearing is a potential source of power for women. She faults feminists for devaluing the "intimate, humane, exasperating, agonizing, and proud relations of women and children"[36] and theorizes that an important "female reproductive consciousness" emerges from the bodily childbearing work of women. Sara Ruddick's contention that mothering work itself (whether performed by men or women) engenders an important strand of "maternal thinking," and, in a book that borders even more on essentialist views of motherhood, Robbie Kahn explains that a "maialogic connection" exists among mother, child, and nature.[37]

Affirmations of the power of biological events such as pregnancy, childbirth, and nurturing children in shaping women's thinking are also found in experiential accounts of motherhood, such as that recently written by author-feminist Naomi Wolf.[38] Wolf claims to have overcome infertility through a "heart-induced alchemy of her bodily chemistry" and describes pregnancy as altering her personality, leading her to rethink her support for abortion, and causing her to feel more "girly," dependent, and protective. Similarly, Chris Bobel finds that the quintessentially female tasks of bearing, nursing, and nurturing children firmly embraced by a group of white, mostly middle-class women engaged in "natural mothering." Her interviews with these women reveal that, although most support feminist principles, they relish their investment in mothering and see it as the best way to cultivate a "gentler, less material, more family-centered social environment."[39]

While a sense of power, creativity, and authority may be engendered by the biological processes of bearing and breastfeeding children, the social role of mothering is demeaned by gender inequality and the general devaluation of women and unpaid labor. Many cultures have linked the "potency of fertility and the awareness of loss" as the dual themes of motherhood, according to Wolf, because they have "recognized that pregnancy and birth had a foreground that was joyful and miraculous, and a background with strokes of what was dark and traumatic."[40] In the past, that "dark and traumatic" background often featured a lack of effective contraception, the cultural demands on women to produce children, relentless childbirth pain, and high rates of maternal and child mortality. Today, women lose control over the processes of birth because they are expected to conform to medical advice, diets, and technologies of questionable value. As Barbara Rothman points out, motherhood and childbirth are increasingly commodified, with pregnant women who engage in behaviors such as smoking and drinking being held responsible for their "flawed products."[41] The superficial honor and esteem accorded mothers fails to mask the powerlessness most women experience when they try to gain control or autonomy in managing pregnancy and childbirth or the absence of support for mothers in families or the public arena.

Feminists have criticized an array of social policies that either penalize mothers or ignore their needs. Yet advocating for gender equality, the protection of women's reproductive rights, and special provisions for motherhood can be difficult. As Patrice DiQuinzio explains in the *Impossibility of Motherhood*, favoring women's complete autonomy over reproductive matters seems to conflict with the call for full participation by men in the domestic life.[42] Similarly, the insistence that social institutions treat women and men alike rests uneasily with the demand that the needs of mothers be accommodated.

Overall, the demystification of motherhood as a sacred and vital aspect of womanhood and the critique of medical and social policies that adversely affect mothers seem to have done little to quell enthusiasm for motherhood. Although there is no evidence that motherhood is a role that women instinctively desire or have an inborn aptitude, most women plan to have children and are usually unable to explain exactly why.[43] Undaunted by evidence of the cost of motherhood, they forge ahead in their missions to become mothers, even when it entails costly and elaborate social and medical interventions.[44] Still, it is the dilemma of difference, notes DiQuinzio, that poses the "impossibility of motherhood": While feminism argues for gender equality by disavowing difference, it also finds that it must embrace difference to analyze specific experiences of mothers based on race and class status.

Motherhood in Class and Race Context

If you're poor, you got no safety. Anything can drop you back in the pit. You get pregnant, you're back in the pit. You get sick, you got no job. But the hardest part is being poor with too many children. It not only affects your physical health, but your mental health. You are despondent, living in the project. You are blaming your kids for just being there. You are looking at them and thinking of all the things you could have been if they weren't there.

—African American mother of four[45]

Contested visions of motherhood among middle-class white women are amplified when the motherhood critique is explored in class and race context. Class is consistently inversely related to rates of fertility, with poor and lower-income women having the highest rates of childbearing. Working-class women are more strongly tied to their identities as mothers; for example, one who became a mother at age sixteen said, "I'd be heartbroken, empty," without motherhood; "I don't think I'd feel whole. . . . I wouldn't feel like I could be a *woman*."[46] Yet, while class background and the restricted access to opportunity it implies heighten the appeal of motherhood, the notion that these women simply "choose" to have children warrants further examination. Choice assumes that women "reflected on the options or weighed the costs, benefits, and consequences of having or not having children;"[47] it implies that women have control over their bodies and fertility and that they reflect "rationally" (i.e., in a middle-class fashion) on the costs and benefits of having children. The contention that motherhood is or should be a choice runs counter to the class experiences of poor women, according to Rickie Solinger, as they have fewer resources and often less control over their own sexuality. Solinger argues that the concept of choice is highly individualistic and fraught with class privilege, as it neglects the impact that poverty, racism, sexism, and powerlessness has on the reproductive behavior of the poor.[48] While choice rhetoric is consistent with the position of privileged women, it can be inverted in the discourse of conservative politicians who blame poor mothers for having made the bad "choice" of having children they are unable to support and who justify forcing them into the labor market.

Racism intensifies class disadvantage, heightening the difficulties of motherhood and the deficits children born to poor mothers are likely to encounter. A few years ago I interviewed Shawn Branson, a twenty-one-year-old, never-married unemployed mother of four children, the oldest a six-year-old daughter named Leah.[49] Leah was in kindergarten but had already been identified as a slow learner. Her language skills have improved since receiving speech therapy in an early childhood education program, but, as Shawn explained, "she's not retaining like she should, she's not keeping information, not holding it real good." Managing four children, including one with special educational needs, is clearly a challenging task for Shawn, even with the help of her boyfriend (the father of the last two children), who occasionally coresides with Shawn. Watching her struggle to create some semblance of order during the interview, I asked why she chose to have her children at such an early age. The notion of "choice" elicited a laugh from Shawn, as though she had never even considered the issue. She replied:

> I don't know. I didn't want to have them young; it was just something that happened. I do wish I was doing something different, like being in college somewhere. Now everything is on hold. . . . I think if I wouldn't

have started having my kids so young, I would have had my goals together and I could have become whatever I wanted to if I had strived for it. But as far as right now, I am struggling, because my kids are so young.

Although she was pregnant at age fifteen, Shawn spoke with amazement of some teenage girls she had seen on a talk show who actually *wanted* to have children. She saw herself as different from those teenagers, because she had not particularly decided to get pregnant. I asked, then, why she had three more children: "Well, I *did* have three more. [It was] just something that happened, not using protection like I should have, like taking birth control. But really not caring, not being cautious. Something I brought on myself. . . . I made an awful lot of mistakes."

Shawn almost fits the stereotypical profile of the welfare mother: a black, single, unemployed teenager with multiple children who have different fathers. Nothing in her story, however, validates the myth of early pregnancies as inspired by flawed cultural values or welfare checks. Rather, Shawn simply grew up in poverty, became disengaged from the educational system, found herself without any particular goals, and started having babies before she had time to think about what she really wanted to do with her life. She blames only herself for her plight, admitting that she "made an awful lot of mistakes," but she is proud of her children and hopeful about their future. In fact, her lack of education, employment, and other life activities increase the saliency and focus on her role as a mother.

Although the majority of single black mothers are poor and many became mothers at an early age, I do not share Shawn's story as a typical example of how or why most of them became mothers or as reflective of their sense of efficacy and control over their own lives. Indeed, single black mothers are an incredibly diverse group in terms of their economic status, resources, support networks, and child-rearing abilities. I do, however, think that the dominant construction of black motherhood that draws heavily on the experiences poor, single mothers pays too little attention to mothers like Shawn. Class and race are also conflated in studies contributing to the notion of distinctive black motherhood. A 1996 study by M. R. Polatnik, for example, argues that motherhood was the most divisive issue among black and white feminists during the late 1960s; however, Polatnik notes that these divisions were between low-

and working-class blacks and middle-class whites. Since the 1960s, racial integration and class diversity have created a similar gap between poor and middle-class black mothers. The tradition of sharing the work of mothering that originated for blacks in West Africa and was strengthened by slavery and, to some extent, by class and racial oppression is now in a state of transition that challenges the black cultural ethos of motherhood. In what follows, I define that ethos and then examine some of its implicit assumptions.

The Black Cultural Ethos of Motherhood

The black cultural ethos of motherhood tends to valorize African American mothers as tough, competent, authoritative women who excel at the work of raising children. It can also be read as implying that they have an almost innate capacity for mothering work and find it natural, gratifying, and unproblematic. Situated in a matrifocal family system, which Bette Dickerson describes as an "extended line of female kin: mothers, daughters, and their children pooling resources and often sharing a household,"[50] African American mothers are said to have a community of supportive "other mothers," thus enabling them to combine child rearing, family, employment, and social activism.

While most would agree that structural forces created distinct mothering patterns among blacks, the motherhood ethos goes further by offering almost essentialist views of black women as naturally equipped with child-rearing skills. It resonates with images of them as mammies, versions of which still are reinforced in the media. In *Bringing the House Down*, Queen Latifah becomes another addition to the lengthy list of black women characterized as adept at mothering and mending the strains in white families. Although cast as a tough, streetwise, single, childless woman with questionable links to the criminal world, she handily advises a middle-class white father (Steve Martin) on how to relate to his daughter. Latifah's maternality goes beyond counsel to a confused single father; she also rescues the daughter from a boyfriend who tries to force her into an unwanted sexual encounter by physically assaulting him and forcing him to apologize for his bad behavior. Rarely are black mothers portrayed as being this nurturing and protective when rearing their own children.

I contend that while explicating these distinct mothering experiences have helped us understand the impact of race and the adaptive abilities of black women, the cultural ethos has many troubling aspects. Besides the promotion of a single, valorized image of black mothers, it tacitly promotes a comparative framework that suggests African American women are *more* interested than other women in having children, that they place *more* value on children, and that they are somehow innately endowed with mothering abilities. The cultural ethos of valiant black motherhood may unwittingly encourage procreative attitudes while also giving credence to stereotypes of black women as "reckless breeders." While the racial gap in fertility between black and white women has reached a historic low and even ceased to exist among women between the ages of twenty-five and forty-four, black teenagers are still twice as likely as whites to become mothers,[51] and research indicates that a significant number of them believe that early, nonmarital childbearing is acceptable.[52] Despite this naturalizing of motherhood, studies showing that black women are especially interested in mothering are scarce. One comparative study of college students notes that blacks are more likely than whites to agree that a woman's real fulfillment comes from motherhood, while another suggests a pattern among black women of prioritizing motherhood over marriage.[53]

The black cultural ethos of motherhood risks casting black women as perpetual mothers, often with little regard to the costs incurred by those who find themselves unable to move beyond the parenting stage of life. Mothering work too often becomes a lifelong obligation for black women, regardless of age, occupation, or progeny. It prescribes a shifting and sharing of mothering work among black women who are always available to serve as nurturers and providers for children. Far too many African American women have been pressed into perpetual motherhood, with their ability to advance normally through the stages of life or take on other meaningful pursuits compromised. Having lost her own mother at age ten, a good friend of mine practically raised her younger siblings and later her own three children. She now feels compelled to assume the care of her grandchildren who badly need a stable family environment. Caring for her grandchildren often means foregoing other activities she and her husband enjoy, yet she receives little appreciation for her efforts.

Today, many factors compete with the satisfaction grandmothers might once have experienced in caring for their grandchildren, such as having to rescue children from substance-abusing parents, being less respected in their families and communities, and passing up opportunities to further their own education and careers. Describing the new generation of young black grandmothers that emerged during the 1980s, J. A. Ladner and R. M. Gourdine write:

> grandmothers complain about unmet emotional and social needs. They appear to feel powerless in coping with the demands made by their children. They comment frequently that their children show them no respect, do not listen to their advice, and place little value on their roles as parents.[54]

Elaine Bell Kaplan found that African American mothers had become especially rejecting of their teenage daughters who became pregnant: They saw the unwed pregnancies of their daughters as diminishing their own community standing, and nearly all of these grandmothers had advised their daughters to get abortions.[55] Black grandmothers who are young and in the labor force see their struggle for upward mobility compromised by the ongoing responsibility for children, and many older, retired grandmothers have health issues that make caring for young children especially difficult.

This ethos of motherhood also releases African American men from the responsibility of caring for children based on the belief that black women can simply rely on each other. In many cases, fathering is seen as optional or of minimal importance, as there is always a supply of women who can do the work of parenting. The fathers of children born to single, poor teenagers provide very little support; only about 20 percent provide any type of monetary support, and fewer than half spend time with their children.[56] But it is important to point out that class matters: Many middle-class African American men prize and prioritize their roles as fathers and are heavily involved in the lives of their children. The roles of black men as "other fathers" also gets scant attention, although those who are brothers, uncles, grandfathers, and boyfriends often contribute to the care of children.[57]

While the ethos applauds black mothers for their long history of integrating labor market and mothering work, welfare reform policies that insist they do so are criticized as punitive and undervaluing motherhood. Overdrawn racialized images of motherhood may do much to obscure the growing stress and social isolation experienced by many poor mothers; studies increasingly challenge the idea that blacks receive more support from their families than other racial groups, and a few find that extended kin networks among blacks are detrimental to mental well-being.[58]

When the ideology of strong black motherhood is seen as essential to authentic womanhood, those who are childless, infertile, or who simply do not fit the model of confident, kin-supported motherhood may be silenced or distanced from the concerns that face all mothers. In addition, the emphasis on motherhood can mask the historic and contemporary efforts of black women to control their own fertility and make the decision not to become a mother more difficult. Yet African American women have always been active in the reproductive rights movement, often challenging the agendas of both white feminists and black male nationalists on issues of childbearing. As longtime reproductive rights activist Loretta Ross has noted, "It is both wrong, and racist, to assume that African-American women had no interest in controlling the spacing of their children and were the passive victims of medical, commercial and state policies of reproductive control."[59]

Revisiting the Village

Writing this chapter has led me to think deeply about my own mothering experiences, as well as those of other women in my family and community. I find a long tradition of extended families that typically included grandmothers who were respected and integrally involved in the rearing of their grandchildren. My mother never knew her father and was reared by her maternal grandmother, and one of my grandmothers lived with us until the time of her death. But even in the racially segregated neighborhood where I grew up, which had a strong sense of community, frequent interaction with neighbors, and close bonds with extended family members, I found no appreciable sharing of mothering work. Many mothers were single and employed; they often relied on their older children (especially daughters) to care for their younger siblings, often keeping them home from school to do so. Other children spent long hours unattended, basically fending for themselves, although neighbors did the best they could to look out for one another. African American families have historically been generous in informally adopting children and, while these contributions are not to be minimized, the addition of children often places severe strains on already-scarce family resources. Over time, however, many of these traditions were disrupted, at first by northward migration and later by the stresses of urban living.

During the 1920s, my father became the first in his family to migrate northward, and the boundaries of our household fluctuated continually as his mother and a succession of siblings moved in with us until they could establish themselves in the city. My paternal aunts, who left their children in Arkansas while getting settled, found work in a laundry or as domestic servants. They then sent for their children, but their long work hours curtailed the time and energy they were able to devote to mothering. Having large families did not always create a sufficient supply of child care help, and children were often pressed into accepting adultlike responsibilities to help out. I became a mother at age nineteen, and, especially since my own mother had died early (at age fifty-eight), I found no ready supply of grandmothers or relatives to assist me as I struggled to balance marriage, motherhood, and employment. Instead, in an era when adequate day care was even scarcer than it is today, I was often left with the frightening prospect of culling babysitters from ads in local newspapers. Today, racial integration, class diversity, and changing family patterns have further diminished patterns of shared mothering.

Of course, I do see multiple forms of child sharing among black women, especially in the (few) predominantly black arenas of my life. They range from minor events, such as someone relieving a mother of a fussy infant during church services, to organized instances of community mothering. Preceding a recent interview with a mother who lived in a public housing complex, I sat with a group of low-income mothers who had volunteered to run a summer lunch program for the children in the neighborhood. Lunches were delivered through a contract with the school district, and each day at noon these mothers set up a picnic table for the children, made sure all the children were fed, and spent a good portion of their afternoon supervising them, constantly referring to them as "our kids."

African American women do share a cultural tradition that supports a sense of efficacy in caring for children and an ideology that the work of mothering should be shared by communities and extended families. But like all cultural ideologies, it is class based, contested, and often touted more than lived. Many people are heavily invested in the "it takes a village" symbols but much less in its substance, and examples of significant child sharing have grown thinner. Deteriorating neighborhoods, greater class disparity, and changing social policies have led to divergent patterns of motherhood among black women.

The mothering practices and challenges of most middle-class black women pretty much parallel those found in the dominant society. Most are employed, many in professional jobs that impinge on family life and make it difficult for them to spend much time offering practical support to other mothers. As is the case for other mothers, balancing the demands of family and work, finding affordable day care, achieving gender equity in the distribution of housework and child care, and investing in multiple dimensions of their children's welfare consumes most of their time. Many make at least some contribution to supporting less advantaged mothers, either through their church affiliations or because these mothers are members of their own extended families. But it is also the case that class polarization has led others to abandon the poor both geographically and intellectually, by becoming more critical of their lifestyles and less willing to jeopardize their own resources to help. Thus, especially for the poor, multiple factors converge to make motherhood a perilous journey.

Confronting the Challenge of Voluntary and Equitable Motherhood

> How can we possibly confront racial injustice in America without tackling this assault on Black women's procreative freedom?
>
> —Dorothy Roberts[60]

In the United States and globally, the oppression of women translates into high rates of unwanted pregnancy, while patriarchy and the perception by women of few opportunities beyond childbearing diminish the effective use of birth control. Today, ensuring that motherhood is a choice, that health resources needed for safe childbirth and delivery are available, and that the rights of mothers are respected remain challenging, especially for economically disadvantaged and race-ethnic women. Females who are young, poor, and racial minorities have the least control over their bodies. For example, black adolescent girls are twice as likely as their white counterparts to be victimized by coercive, involuntary sex. Even in mutually consensual sexual encounters, black teenagers are less likely to use contraceptives at first intercourse or to use them regularly thereafter, partially because they lack the power to negotiate the use of birth control with their partners, but also because they see their sexuality as the only way to gain love, self-esteem, or a better life for themselves. Unwanted and unplanned pregnancy correlates with other important health risks, such as the transmission of sexual diseases and, in some cases, chronic illnesses to children. African Americans account for a significant majority of all cases of sexually transmitted diseases, and slightly more than half of the females over the age of thirteen with AIDS are black. Death rates from HIV infection among black women between twenty-five and forty-four are twelve times higher than for white women.[61]

Poor women still confront inadequate access to medical care, leading to serious prenatal and postnatal health care risks. Although all black women, regardless of class position, have higher rates of low-birth-weight infants and infant mortality, the risk is exacerbated among those who are poor. Black women receive prenatal health care later than white women and are less likely to be warned about the dangers of tobacco and alcohol use. Increasing rates of prenatal care in recent decades have not decreased the racial gap in the birth of premature or low-birth-weight babies, suggesting that quality of care may be as important as its availability.[62] Black women also have rates of maternal mortality that are four times higher than those of white women.[63]

While deprived of the benefits of early and adequate prenatal health care, poor women of color are much more likely to experience the oppressive aspects of biomedicine's reproductive technologies; for example, about 80 percent of court-ordered obstetrical interventions for pregnancy- and childbirth-related problems are for women of color.[64] Medical authorities show extravagant concern for the welfare of the unborn black children, especially when it means demanding prenatal surgeries against the will of pregnant women and participating in drug testing and sterilization efforts. The war against drugs has served as a convenient pretext for penalizing pregnant black women, and medicine often colludes with other organizations in implementing coercive fertility control problems. The use of crack cocaine became prevalent among poor black women during the 1980s, according to Dorothy Roberts, and the number of newborns affected by the drug grew (from 11 percent to 25 percent) between 1985 and 1990. Since then, black expectant mothers have been especially targeted for medical screening and prosecuted for maternal drug use. They are ten times more likely than white women to be reported to government authorities for substance abuse, and women of color comprise 75 percent of all prosecutions for fetal abuse. Roberts suggests these prosecutions reflect a growing hostility toward black mothers, who have been arrested, shackled, and taken to court or jail days and sometimes even hours after giving birth. "Thinking about an expectant Black mother chained to a belt around her swollen belly to protect her unborn children . . . [and] bound in shackles," writes Roberts, "is a modern-day reincarnation of the horrors of slavemaster's degrading treatment of their female chattel."[65]

In addition to these prosecutions, illicit drug use has been the impetus for other programs aimed at getting poor women sterilized. In her work on the reproductive rights movement among women of color, Jennifer Nelson points out that during the 1990s, programs emerged in several states targeting women with any history of drug abuse for sterilization. One such program, CRACK (Children Requiring a Caring Community), offers women who have had two children and who are addicted to or recovering from drugs $200 if they agree to sterilization or long-term contraceptives such as Depo-Provera or Norplant. Founded in 1997 in Anaheim, California, this program has now been expanded to other cities and recruited several hundred women. Black women, who are often recruited from bus stops, welfare offices, and medical settings, are the primary targets of the program.[66]

Poverty, the drug epidemic, and changes in welfare policies during the latter twentieth century have increased the number of African American children who are now living in "no-parent" families—left with relatives, friends, or foster families. In 1967, the federal government made illegitimacy an issue again by allowing states to move children from poor homes into foster care, with nonmarital childbearing, race, and poverty key factors disqualifying women from their parental rights.[67] The threat of taking children from mothers on welfare was revived in the 1980s by political conservatives such as Charles Murray, who argued that the government should "no longer try to help the innocent children by subsidizing the parents who made them victims" but instead should "spend lavishly on adoption services and lavishly on orphanages."[68] Children of color are more than twice as likely to be found among the five hundred thousand children living in foster care, and most were removed from families receiving some type of public assistance. Richard Wexler, the executive director for the National Coalition for Child Protection, argues that despite the "brutally abusive, hopelessly addicted parents who make headlines," most of these children are from homes where parents were simply unable to meet basic standards of living.[69]

Although having and raising children has been, especially for many poor black women, a major way to claim status and womanhood, it is also the case that they have tried to control their own childbearing. African American women have disproportionately sought abortions, for example, even when they had to resort to dangerous and illegal practices. Prior to the *Roe* decision legalizing abortion, medical abortions were most prevalent among economically affluent, urban, highly educated, younger, white women, while abortions for poor women "commonly meant a twisted coat hanger and two dozen quinine pills."[70] Indeed, 80 percent of deaths caused by illegal abortions involved black and Puerto Rican women.[71] Since *Roe*, black women have obtained a disproportionate share of all abortions, which has accounted for most of the decline in neonatal mortality among blacks between 1964 and 1977, including the reduction of unwanted births. The high rate of abortion among black women historically stood in contrast to their more moderated ideological support for it.

Today, attitudinal support for abortion among African Americans parallels that found among whites and rates of abortion among blacks are two to three times higher than among whites, despite Hyde Amendment restrictions on the use of federal funds for abortions.[72] Public insurance, however, has continued to reimburse up to 90 percent of the cost of sterilization, and by the mid-1990s, black women were slightly more likely than whites to be sterilized. For poor black women, sterilization is often done through hysterectomies; such operations are almost standard practice in some teaching hospitals although, compared to tubal ligations, they dramatically increase medical costs and the risk of maternal mortality.[73] Still, rates of sterilization are increasing: Among married couples in 2000, 37 percent of black wives (vs. 22 percent of white wives) had tubal ligations, and 4 percent of black husbands (vs. 18 percent of white husbands) had vasectomies.[74]

The greatest race and class barrier to reproductive rights may prove to be access to the growing number of reproductive technologies used among infertile women and men. The highest rates of infertility are among black and Latina females enrolled in Medicaid,[75] yet they are unlikely to be candidates for expensive procedures that create pregnancy. In her study of black female infertility, Rosario Ceballo points out that white middle-class women are more likely to receive sympathy and support as tragically unable to bear children, while black women continue to be stereotyped as "baby factories," Ceballo describes the loneliness many black women experience as a result of infertility, noting that the

> ethos of self-reliant isolation and silence is, in part, attributable to African American women's internalization of social stereotypes that typically

portray only white women as having difficulty conceiving. This self-imposed loneliness is magnified because many African American women believe that they are, in fact, alone—that there are not others who have similar experiences with infertility.[76]

Summary

In discussing the historic cross-cultural reproductive mandate and how motherhood was seen in the context of colonial America, I have sought to show that there were many parallels as well as differences in the mothering experiences of black and white women. Yet the differences that existed were amplified with the abolition of slavery and modernization of society, leading to the competing constructions of motherhood based on class and racial status. Confronting the policies of eugenicists, middle-class women advocated publicly for the right to control their own fertility, although this often meant that white women fought for the right to have fewer children and black women for the right to have any at all.

Research on black American families grew during the 1960s and 1970s, showing how their race and class position had fostered unique strategies of shared motherhood that allowed them to prevail against formidable odds while providing for their children. Thus, when white feminists of the 1970s proffered a critique of motherhood as being used to exclude women from the workforce and silence them in social and political arenas, women of color contested the idea of oppressive motherhood. Their articulation of a qualitatively different experience of mothering than that of white women gave rise to what I call a black cultural ethos of motherhood.

This chapter has examined the assumptions embodied in that ethos in light of growing class differences among African Americans and changing economic, structural, and familial forces. I have argued that in black churches, communities, and families, the "it takes a village" philosophy waxes stronger in rhetoric than in practice and that the black cultural ethos may ignore the perils of pregnancy and motherhood, assume that black women are ever-available to mother, and neglect the historic struggle by black women for their reproductive rights. These factors have made motherhood a high-risk venture for many black women. In the following chapter, I look at how this class diversity shaped the socialization of African American children.

Notes

1. T. McMillan (1987 :15–16).
2. C. W. Williams (1991:34).
3. S. A. Hill (1994).
4. B. Christain (1994:96).
5. B. Dickerson (1995).
6. C. Stack (1974); H. Gutman (1976).
7. B. T. Dill (1994); P. H. Collins (1990).
8. P. H. Collins (1990:118).
9. B. Hartmann (1987:241).
10. B. Hartmann (1987:43).
11. S. Kitzinger (1995).
12. B. Landry (2000).
13. D. C. Hine and K. Thompson (1998:84).
14. See A. Davis (1981), for example.
15. C. B. Booker (2000:7).
16. L. Ross (1993).
17. J. Rodrique (1990).
18. J. Rodrique (1990).
19. J. Rodrique (1990).
20. Quoted in A. Berg (2002).
21. P. Giddings (1984).
22. Quoted in A. Berg (2002:15).
23. W. Kline (2001).
24. F. Dikotter (1998); W. Kline (2001).
25. W. Kline, (2001).
26. E. Adler (2002:A8).
27. J. Litt (2000:27).
28. A. Berg (2002:27).
29. W. Kline (2001).
30. Cited in S. Coltrane (1998:79).
31. S. Firestone (1970:81).
32. M. Andersen (2000).
33. S. Kitzinger (1995).
34. T. Arendell (2000:1194).
35. J. Lasker and S. Borg (1987).
36. M. O'Brien (1981:91).
37. S. Ruddick (1997); R. P. Kahn (1995).
38. N. Wolf (2001).
39. C. Bobel (2002:47).
40. N. Wolf (2001:7).

41. B. K. Rothman (1989).
42. P. DiQuinzio (1999).
43. M. McMahon (1995).
44. A. Crittendon (2001).
45. M. C. Ward (1986:1).
46. M. McMahon (1995:178).
47. M. McMahon (1995:51).
48. R. Solinger (1998).
49. S. A. Hill (1999).
50. B. Dickerson (1995:xv).
51. M. Burns (1995).
52. C. W. Williams (1991).
53. C. B. Leggon (1983).
54. J. A. Ladner and R. M. Gourdine (1984:23).
55. E. B. Kaplan (1996).
56. "Children of Young Disadvantaged Women" (1998).
57. L. Haney and M. March (2003).
58. C. G. Ellison (1990).
59. L. J. Ross (1993:146).
60. D. Roberts (1997b:4)
61. C. F. Collins (1996).
62. D. B. Smith (1999).
63. A. Spake (1999).
64. L. Nsiash-Jefferson (1989).
65. D. Roberts (1997b).
66. J. Nelson (2003).
67. R. Solinger (2001).
68. R. Solinger (1998:203).
69. R. Wexler (2002:8).
70. K. Y. Scott (1991).
71. L. J. Ross (1993:155).
72. R. Solinger (2001).
73. B. Hartmann (1987).
74. E. L. Barbee and M. Little (1993:191).
75. R. Solinger (2001).
76. R. Ceballo (1999:11).

CHAPTER 6

Socializing Black Children

The Impact of Social Class

In terms of organizational purpose of the Black family, the family's reason for being can be considered childcenteredness. By this is meant that the purpose of the Black family focused on, if not required, the presence of children. The family unit exists for the growth and development of children, rather than for the self-actualization of the adult members of the unit.

—Wade W. Nobles[1]

Although the ethos of black motherhood (see chapter 5) and the work of family scholars often assert the importance of children and childbearing among African Americans, researchers have seldom devoted much attention to studying their child socialization processes or parenting practices. Consistent with the pathological perspective that once dominated studies of black families, the handful of studies conducted during the 1940s and 1950s emphasized the inability of poor black parents to raise successful, well-adjusted children.

For example, in a work intended to criticize racial oppression more than black families, Abram Kardiner and Lionel Ovesey's 1951 *The Mark of Oppression* nevertheless produced a dire portrayal of poor black parents as inconsistent, demanding, and lacking affection for their children. Mothers were often "loveless tyrants," according to Kardiner and Ovesey, while fathers tended to be "seclusive, taciturn, violent [and] punitive."[2] Other social psychological research, such as the classic doll studies by Kenneth and Mamie Clark, contended that racism and segregation had devastated black children's self-esteem, leading to self-hatred and internalized racism.

147

These stereotypical images were effectively challenged during the civil rights era by scholars who argued that racial differences in child socialization were related to social class,[3] justified the seemingly harsh disciplinary and child-rearing strategies of black parents as produced by ecological factors like living in poor, dangerous neighborhoods,[4] and rejected the idea of pervasive self-hatred or even diminished self-esteem among black children. Afrocentric theorists especially idealized the child-rearing work of black families by describing the typical child as being raised in "an atmosphere of family orientation and unconditional love which place a special emphasis on strong family ties, respect for the elders and see the child as possessing natural goodness."[5]

Despite this work, the social-problem focus on the lives of black children reemerged by the late 1980s, justified by evidence that the welfare of black children was being undermined by the epidemics of violence and illegal drug use in urban areas, and the demise of extended family support systems. The adaptiveness of mothers in poor families that had earlier been highlighted by work such as Carol Stack's *All Our Kin* gave way to research reporting an undeniable link between growing up in single-mother families and adverse childhood outcomes. Eventually, studies of adolescent childbearing, welfare-dependent families, children's exposure to and victimization by violence, and the unprecedented placement of black children in foster care eclipsed interest in other aspects of child socialization, such as their racial and gender socialization.

My interest in child socialization in African American families began with a study of the caregiving experiences of mothers who had children diagnosed with sickle cell disease, and this research led me to a broader exploration of the gender socialization of black children. My initial study of caregiving revealed that mothers of sons, in comparison to those with daughters, saw their children as sicker, were more concerned about their welfare, performed more elaborate caregiving work, and were more likely to say their caregiving work prevented them from being employed.[6] After exploring and rejecting alternative explanations for this gendered pattern of caregiving, I argued that the sex of the child influenced these mothers' perception of the severity and consequences of this chronic illness on their children, and thus the intensity of their caregiving work.[7] Mothers saw their daughters as more reliable and more capable of self-care; they imposed fewer restrictions on their behaviors to protect them from the debilitating pain crises that characterize the disease, and they did not see the illness as restricting their daughter's life chances. Typical of mothers of daughters were comments such as "We don't restrict her too much. Anything she thinks she can do, she goes ahead."[8] Mothers of sons, on the other hand, saw boys as naturally aggressive and inclined to participate in male-typed physical activities that would endanger their health. Speaking of how easy it was for her son to engage in behaviors that provoked pain crises and often led to hospitalization, one mother said, "He can go from my door down to the parking lot, maybe do a little running around that thing out there, the yard, and just like that start paining."[9] As their children grew older, mothers described daughters as increasingly able to cope effectively with the disease but saw their sons as growing more frustrated with the limitations imposed by the disease.

On the surface, the greater freedom and responsibility accorded black daughters seems to confirm conventional wisdom suggesting that African American daughters are taught to be strong and self-reliant—an observation that never seriously addresses exactly what black sons are being taught. An alternative explanation, however, was simply that mothers expected their daughters to engage in more "feminine" (or nonaggressive) behaviors than sons and thus worried less about their health. Their greater concern over the health of their sons could reflect an inclination to see boys as naturally aggressive and sickness as making that expression of masculinity more perilous.[10] Maternal protectiveness toward sons is already enhanced by the belief that being young, male, and black is a high-risk venture; for example, they are maligned as menaces to society and those living in poor neighborhoods are exposed to crime and a street culture demanding toughness. Moreover, the dominant cultural construction of black masculinity revolves around notions of physical prowess, making illness and fragility especially costly. The race and class disadvantage faced by poor black boys makes it unlikely they will be able achieve masculinity through more conventional avenues, such as career or economic success, so they rely more heavily on the physical activities—a route to masculinity restricted by sickle cell disease. Despite the notion that there is less emphasis on gender training among African Americans—an idea based mostly on the ability and necessity of black women to bend gender traditions—there is little evidence that young, black males, especially those in low-income families, have much flexibility when it comes to finding alternatives to aggressive forms of masculinity.

Thus, gender seemed to significantly influence the expectations that mothers had for their chronically ill children; yet, since most of the mothers were single and low-income, I began to consider whether this was the case for parents with healthy children or those in middle-class or two-parent families. African American feminists have often argued that the historic exploitation of their productive and reproductive work precluded their conformity to the gender images and behaviors defined as appropriate for white women, thus yielding a broader view of womanhood. Rather than portraying black women as fragile, submissive, and domestic, the social construction of black womanhood has emphasized strength and independence. But do these historic and even precolonial experiences inform the gender training of black children today? And how do race and class shape the gender socialization of black children? I eventually conducted a broader study of parenting and child socialization, based on survey and interview data collected from a race- and class-diverse group of parents of young children to explore these multiple dimensions of child socialization (see the appendix).

In this chapter, I use an intersectionality approach to examine research findings from that study, essentially analyzing how social class position affects the race and gender beliefs of blacks and their childrearing practices. Drawing on survey data I collected from a class-diverse sample of African American parents on their child-rearing strategies, I find some level of support for teaching children the value of gender equality regardless of the sex of the parent, the sex of the focus child, or the family's social class standing. More than 90 percent of the black parents I surveyed, for example, agree that it is equally important for girls and boys to get an education; moreover, most support equal opportunity for women in the labor market and have similar child-rearing goals and values for sons and daughters. The majority of these parents did not think that either gender or racial inequality would adversely affect their children's ability to get a good education or a good job. Fewer than one-fourth of these parents, for example, believed that being a woman made success more difficult, and fewer than half (41 percent) believed that race did. Yet the interview data proved especially insightful in showing that social class mattered a lot in terms of the strength and breadth of their support for gender equality, their perceptions of race, and the racial socialization of their children. Here I argue that the notion that the race and social class positions of black people have legitimized support for a broader conception of womanhood, diminished the gender training of children, and produced some level of gender equality in families has often ignored the fact that these same inequalities have also heightened support for patriarchal traditions, especially when it comes to families.

This chapter has three sections. The first uses an intersectionally perspective to examine and critique studies of the gender, race, and class socialization of African American children. For the most part, studies of the impact of class, defined narrowly in terms of being poor, have been most common, with the concept of class and race conflated and gender virtually ignored.

In the second section, I draw on interview data from my own research to construct a typology of these parents as either securely middle class, newly middle class, or economically disadvantaged, and then I show how class standing affects the attitudes about gender and race that are passed on to children. Class is examined in terms of educational level of these parents and, equally important, the class background of their family of origin. Both the securely and newly middle class have at least some college education and a professional/managerial job position, but their current middle-class status belies important differences between them. The securely middle class grew up in middle-class families and re-created that class position through their own career attainments; they were also more likely to be married and thus have a higher family income. For them, class predicts the strongest support for teaching their children the value of gender equality, and they are also more concerned that racial disadvantage may adversely affect their children's futures.

The newly middle class (those who grew up in poor families and, while having at least some college education, tend to be single) have the most conflicted attitudes about inequality, due largely to status anxiety and their views about religion and sexual orientation. They see gender-ordered families as consistent with their new class position and as a way to distance themselves from their own class origins. Moreover, their Christian beliefs, including the idea that homosexuality is a learned behavior and is sinful, leads them to support teaching boys traditional masculine behaviors.

Attitudinal support for gendered families and male authority in the home is highest among those who are economically disadvantaged, although by virtue of their class standing they are also less likely to have the resources to live such ideologies. These parents offer the greatest ideological support for patriarchal families; indeed, their performance of gender is vitally linked to their definitions of what it means to be a man or woman. The practical realities of daily survival, however, render them least capable of living their professed ideology. Moreover, the work of child rearing in poor families makes the issue of gender socialization almost irrelevant, as parents prioritize meeting the daily material needs of their families, controlling their children, and protecting them from the perils they face in their communities and schools.

The final section of the chapter, as a precursor to chapter 7's discussion of violence, discusses how class and race inequality places poor children in a position to grow up in a nexus of violence, fostered by parental disciplinary patterns, the neglect and stigma they face in schools, and a street culture where aggression is prized.

An Intersectionality Approach to Child Socialization

As young children, we were brother and sister, comrades, in it together. As adolescents, he was forced to become a boy and I was forced to become a girl. In our southern black Baptist patriarchal home, being a boy meant learning to be tough, to mask one's feelings, to stand one's ground and fight—being a girl meant learning to obey, to be quiet, to clean, to recognize that you had no ground to stand on. I was tough, he was not. I was strong-willed, he was easy going. We were both a disappointment.

—bell hooks[11]

Gender is socially constructed on the basis of economic factors, political ideologies, and patriarchal traditions and reproduced in a variety of institutions, most notably families. Barbara Risman, for example, has noted that families are often the linchpin of gender inequality, as they assign different rights and responsibilities to men and women and often incorporate those norms in their childrearing work. The premise of gender socialization is that children "observe, imitate, and eventually internalize the specific attitudes and behaviors that the culture defines as gender appropriate by using other males and females as role models."[12] The sex roles approach, especially, has emphasized the importance of families in this process; indeed, some studies have found that the family is the most important setting for the construction and perpetuation of gender.[13] The dominant pattern of gender role socialization, as summarized in a review essay by J. Block, shows that parents want their sons to be "independent, self-reliant, highly-educated, ambitious, hard-working, career-oriented, intelligent, and strong-willed" and their daughters to be "kind, unselfish, attractive, loving, well-mannered, and to have a good marriage and to be a good parent."[14] These behaviors are reinforced by social structures and interactions in the broader society, such as the media and schools; indeed, as C. West and D. Zimmerman have explained, we are continually "doing gender."[15] Feminists have criticized gender training as privileging boys and disadvantaging girls, yet the extent to which race and class influence gender training has rarely been the explicit topic of research.

Intersectionality theory asserts that race and class shape social definitions of gender, and it points out that the dominant stereotypes used to control black women and the work expected of them defied the tenets of white femininity. Many contend that black daughters are taught the values of strength and independence, and a few studies show girls are urged to get an education and prepare for careers rather than relying on marriage for economic security and to expect to share responsibility in their families and communities.[16] A related theme has been that gender matters little in the socialization of black children.[17] Diane Lewis claims that the gender socialization of girls or boys in black families was minimal, especially in the early years, as all children were taught the value of mothering, assertiveness, willfulness, and independence. According to a study by M. Peters, a child's age and competency shape the expectations of black parents much more than their sex.[18] Joseph W. Scott echoes a similar theme in explaining why raising black daughters can be difficult. He contends that black girls "are socialized to be at once independent and assertive as well as familistic and nurturant . . . to be sexually assertive . . . to be as authoritative, individualistic, and confident as African American sons are, and as economically self-sufficient and personally autonomous as sons are."[19] A recent observational study supports this claim by noting that young black children exhibited fewer gender stereotypical behaviors than white children.[20] Race inequality is seen as having diminished the emphasis on gender, since black women model less traditional roles and because the survival of families often demands more flexibility in the work roles of men and women. The evidence of gender neutrality in the socialization of black children is sparse, however, and has rarely been the topic of systematic research. In addition, it focuses more on women than men, highlights behaviors rather than beliefs, and ignores how race and class inequality shapes gender distinctions in socialization.

Racial oppression circumscribes the lives of black children in myriad ways, from limiting their ability to obtain a decent education to generating stereotypes that challenge their value, self-esteem, and identity. Dominant societal images of black children often portray them as prone to aggression, behaviorally disordered, unattractive, unintelligent, and sexually promiscuous. Racial socialization studies have focused on parental attempts to counter these negative stereotypes, and also "prepare their children for the realities of being Black in America."[21] The explicit objective of parents is to define blackness in a positive manner, thus strengthening the self-concept and confidence of children and teaching them how to respond to racial insults. In reality, racial socialization occurs formally and informally, as children learn a set of competing messages about being black from mainstream society, their families, and expressions of the black culture in their communities. Interestingly, some research has found that racial socialization messages are often gendered; P. J. Bowman and C. Howard discovered a tendency for parents to talk more to sons about the obstacles they will encounter as a black man, while spending more effort instilling values of pride and commitment in their daughters.[22] This may reflect the tendency to see daughters as having more opportunities for success, while reinforcing the view that black males are more likely to be adversely affected by racism.

While gender has received at least a nod of recognition in studying racial socialization, the conflation of race and class has rendered the impact of the latter especially oblique. Research on poverty, rather than social class, prevails, thus creating the impression that being black and poor are synonymous, or that studying the poor captures "the" black experience. The work of Janice E. Hale, while contributing immensely to understanding patterns of child socialization in black families and communities, describes an African-based pattern of socialization that is highly class based and gendered, yet she offers no critical reflections on the implications of either form of inequality. Boys, she points out, are released at an early age to the older children in the neighborhood, where they learn proficiency in several important areas, like developing their own distinctive walk (or "pimp"), athletic prowess, sexual competence, and generally becoming streetwise. In contrast, she describes black girls as developing their own identities around the duties they perform in the household—mothering younger children and performing domestic duties—and cultivating their own sense of beauty and style.[23] These descriptions of socialization clearly characterize the lifestyles of poor children more than those who are middle class; moreover, this distinctive gendering of their behavior is ignored. As is frequently the case, the behaviors of the poor are seen as reflective of the entire black population.

While middle-class African Americans have seldom received much attention in such studies, research does indicate that social class impacts child socialization strategies. In the 1950s, Melvin Kohn, expanding on earlier studies of how modernization was affecting child rearing, noted that lower- and working-class parents, compared to middle-class parents, were much more likely to expect obedience and conformity from their children, more likely to use physical punishment, and less likely to be verbally expressive with their children.[24] More recently, Annette Lareau reports that class continues to shape how parents socialize their children. She describes middle-class parents as engaging in "concerted cultivation" in raising their children; that is, they used reasoning as a discipline strategy, negotiated with their children, and invested heavily in structured leisure time activities and in fostering their children's talent and intellectual growth. Working-class and poor parents relied on "accomplishment through natural growth," in that they "viewed children's development as spontaneously unfolding, as long as they were provided with comfort, food, shelter, and other basic support."[25] Moreover, these parents emphasized the subordinate status of their children, relied more on directing rather than negotiating with their children, and tended to teach their children to resist or be distrustful of institutions and authorities outside of the family. Lareau's research included black and white parents, and it found social class a much stronger predictor of parenting behaviors than race, although she points out that race may become more important as the children grow older.

The following analysis offers a more nuanced portrait of how class shapes what parents say about the gender and racial socialization of their children, in that it takes into consideration the impact of recent class mobility on their ideologies. Moreover, it emphasizes the difficulties and struggles that economically disadvantaged parents and their children face in their families, schools, and communities.

The Securely Middle Class

No gender roles for me—my husband says I traumatize the kids by talking so much about what they're going to do when they get older. . . . We treat all able bodies the same: work is work, and anybody can do it. I plan to have [my son] help with anything that needs to be done. I wouldn't care if he did feminine things, like take dancing. He wanted to take dancing lessons a long time ago, and he loves to brush and fix hair, but lately he's turned toward male stuff, playing ball. But I tell him I'll love him regardless of what he does; be happy with his life, [and] I won't have a problem with it.

—Sharon Davis

Sharon Davis, a married, college-educated mother of two sons, didn't have to think twice when I asked her to tell me whether gender was influencing her expectations for her children. She emphatically rejected the idea that gender should govern parental expectations, noting that she had no reservations about her sons engaging in activities seen as feminine. She and her husband both hold full-time professional jobs, while doing their best to prioritize spending time with their children. I refer to Sharon and her husband as "securely" middle class because they grew up in middle-class families and re-created that class standing through their own educational and career achievements; thus, they evince a certain level of comfort and security about their status. Neither seems threatened by violating gender traditions, which was characteristic of most parents who were of their educational and class background. For example, another mother who grew up in a middle-class family, asked whether she ever found herself having different expectations for her daughters and son based on their sex, replied that gender at best played a small role in her practices. She described the expectations that she has for her twelve-year-old son but overall emphasized the importance of teaching both daughters and sons the value of independence:

I have the same expectations of him as I do from my daughters. . . . I tell my daughters that they should be able to take care of themselves, and he should be able to take care of himself, whether he's married or not. He should know how to wash his clothes, keep his house, take care of his books—he should be able to be independent, just like the girls should. . . . We talk about this all the time, and when I forget, my girls remind me!

Some mothers were especially proud of teaching their sons to become involved in domestic responsibilities, as one mother said: "My son, when he was three years old, was setting the table, and I [didn't expect] to have to tell him every day. He was taught where to put the plates and the silverware at age three."

Educated black fathers were equally supportive of gender equality, especially in wanting their daughters to pursue an education and a career. One forty-two-year-old respondent, a schoolteacher and the father of three children, including an adolescent daughter, said, "I'm teaching my daughter to have a career. If she then chooses to go back in the home, a decision between her and her future spouse, then that's fine. . . . My daughter wanted to be a doctor . . . if my daughter wants to be a doctor, we're going to find the money to pay for it."

All parents had high educational expectations for their children, and the sex of the child did not influence those aspirations. Although sons often aspired to become professional athletes, parents tried to steer their sons away from those aspirations. Speaking of a nine-year-old son, one mother said, "He wants to play basketball, but we try to stress right now that he's going to Harvard, and he's going to be a doctor. . . . It's a form of brainwashing, but they need that. And I had a brother who went to Harvard and became a doctor, so he has a good role model."

These parents emphasized education and expected their children to be successful in life, yet they also expressed more concern that race could adversely affect their children's future. This enhanced awareness of racial barriers probably reflects their own educational background, as well as the fact that they live and work in settings that require interaction with whites, and send their children to racially integrated schools where black students are the minority. As a result, nearly 22 percent of securely middle-class parents said their child had been victimized by racism, compared to only 13 percent of other parents. These parents were also more proactive in teaching their children about race, often exposing their children to black history and taking the initiative to discuss race. As one mother stated, "I want [my daughter] to be aware that they are black in a white world where there are people who may possibly treat you badly just because of that." They often took a great deal of care in trying to get their children to understand how dominant racial images could affect their thinking. In discussing his approach to teaching his seven-year-old son about race, one father noted, "He's just beginning to notice racial differences. We try to focus on the positive, point out black role models, blacks who are achieving. We did the test where you have two dolls, one black and one white, and ask the child which is the prettiest. He chose the white doll, so we talked about that."

Thus, the securely middle class expressed the broadest support for teaching children the value of gender equality and were most active in the racial socialization of children. A majority, however, did not believe that race and gender inequality would pose significant barriers to their children's success. Not surprisingly, parents were willing neither to believe nor to convey to their children a lack of faith in their ability to succeed.

The Newly Middle Class

I guess I'm trying to instill—quote/unquote—a lot of middle-class values in her. And to me that means you don't steal, don't destroy other people's property, you work for what you have, and you don't expect something for nothing. . . . Those are the kinds of things I consider middle-class values.

—Elisha Martin

Although she has a college education and a professional job as a contract compliance officer, Elisha Martin, a widowed mother of an eleven-year-old daughter, is still trying to distance herself from popular stereotypes of what it means to be poor and black. Her description of being middle class is largely behavioral—it means one does not steal, destroy other people's property, expect to get something for nothing. Engaging in such behaviors is clearly not characteristic of the majority of people in poor families, yet such images proliferate, often to the shame of those who grew up in low-income families. Thus, not surprisingly, those who have recently moved into the middle class are eager to disassociate themselves from their lower-class roots. Their quest for respectability often means offering ideological support for patriarchal families and endorsing at least some level of gender training for children. Overall the newly middle class—although they often have as much education as those in the securely middle class—are much more conflicted about what to teach children about gender and race, and these views are further mediated by their religious ideologies and understanding of homosexuality.

While they see gender equality as a good thing and have high expectations for their sons and daughters, a careful analysis of their interviews revealed a more tentative or contradictory stance on the issue. When Elisha was asked what she expected of her eleven-year-old daughter, she emphasized that she was teaching her to be a "warrior," carrying on "the struggle [for racial justice] by fighting every day of her life for the respect of Black people," and her own personal respect. While this reflects a strong and even nontraditional image of womanhood, this mother also emphasized that she was teaching the value of more traditionally feminine characteristics, such as being "ladylike":

> I tell her that she has to carry herself well, and she can't go around being loud and screaming and yelling because that is one thing she likes to do. I tell her she has to sit properly and is expected to act like a lady by carrying herself well—when you go somewhere, you have to sit properly . . . so I speak to that a lot, that she's a girl and these are the kinds of things girls should do, like being ladylike.

Being a "warrior" and a "lady" seemed like a contradictory stance on the issue of gender, and it led me to consider the sources of variation in support for gender equality among parents who were similarly educated and middle class in status. An analysis of background information on the interviewees revealed that first-generation middle-class parents were more tentative in their support for gender equality. Less secure in their middle-class status, these parents were more likely to aspire to the gender roles seen as proper in the dominant culture. I read their ambivalent support for gender equality as stemming from wanting their children to embrace the norms they see as consistent with middle-class "respectability," without sacrificing the cultural tradition of strength and activism as characteristic of a black woman. These parents emphasize more traditional gender roles in the home and equality in the workplace. Elisha, asked if she would teach her daughter that men and women should have equal rights and equal responsibilities, was quite equivocal in her response: "I will in one sense, but not in another. In terms of the family, I'm teaching her that a man is supposed to take care of her . . . but in the workplace, I'm teaching her that they are equal."

Support for equality in the workplace but not in the family reflects the tensions many upwardly mobile middle-class parents experience, as they try to merge norms of career success for women with gender traditionalism in families. Elisha's racial socialization strategy was also affected by her class position: She was skeptical of her daughter's accusation of being treated in a racist way by her teachers: "She's quick to do a thing and then say that the other person doesn't like her because she's black. So I have to get the whole story to know if she's telling the truth or if she's just using race to get out of trouble for mouthing off."

Gender and racial socialization messages often intersect in interesting ways. For example, a mother whose gender socialization message emphasized strength and independence for women also had a racial socialization message that urged her daughter to learn to deal with the realities of white power and privilege:

> I tell her that she has to learn . . . that white people are going to be here, wherever she goes, and they're *always* going to tell her what to do. No matter what, there is always going to be some white person telling you what to do, and nine times out of ten you're going to have to do it, and do it with the right attitude.

In her effort to prepare her daughter for racism and help her manage it, she stresses the need for submissiveness to and respect for white authority, which she takes as a given. In fact, accepting white authority and conformity to perceived middle-class values in families and at work are often ways to relieve status anxiety among those from lower-class backgrounds. By conforming, they distance themselves from the stereotypes associated with poor, black people and validate their own achievement and respectability.

Recent class mobility and striving toward more acceptable gender norms often intersect with religiosity to mediate parents' support for gender equality. Elisha emphasized that what she wants most for her daughter is "to present herself as a Christian lady," a value often mentioned by mothers in this study. Self-professed levels of religiosity were high among the black parents I interviewed, and, while religious people can have liberal and progressive beliefs, this view led most of the parents in this study to offer at least ideological support for male-headed families.

Fear of homosexuality intertwined with religious ideology to produce ambiguous support for gender equality in socialization. A few parents in this study, when asked if their child rearing was influenced by the sex of their children, immediately responded by talking about sexual orientation or homosexuality, expressing a concern that gender-neutral training (especially for boys) could lead to homosexuality. One mother of two sons and a daughter, asked if there should be differences in the way girls and boys are reared, rejected any biological/genetic explanation of homosexuality, implying that it could result from socialization:

> I watch my kids.... They say how kids are born homosexuals? I find that hard to believe, you know. . . . But I've watched my kids, and my boys are boys and my girl is a girl. But when [my son] liked to play with dolls, I caught myself saying "No, you don't need to play with that!". . . so I don't really encourage [boys playing with dolls]. But he only did that for a little while; it's not that he acts prissy or anything . . . it's just the fact that he had that doll that bothered me a little bit.

Most parents are especially interested in protecting their sons from engaging in female-typed activities, and they link such activities to homosexuality. Fathers were more likely than mothers to express this concern. One couple interviewed jointly talked about the father's fear that female-typed toys could affect their son's sexual orientation. They explained:

> [Mother] Our son wanted a stove and refrigerator for Christmas once, and I was going to get it, but he [the father] wouldn't let me, even though he's a cook.
> [Father] Well, today I know which way he's going, so I would.
> [Interviewer] You mean his sexuality?
> [Father] Yeah . . . if he wants to play with girl things now, it's OK, because I know which way he's going.

Concern over homosexuality also shapes their gender socialization practices. Research has emphasized that African Americans are especially intolerant of homosexuality;[26] however, other research reports that there is a tendency among parents of all races to be more supportive of their children when they engage in sex-typed behaviors rather than cross-sexed behaviors.[27] A study by D. R. McCreary, for example, explored the reasons why males are taught to avoid female-typed behaviors and punished more gender role transgressions than are females and concluded that the underlying concern was not social status but sexual orientation.[28]

Economically Disadvantaged Families

> I am very marriage minded! I believe in the cooking and the cleaning. . . . I'm an old-fashioned woman, right out of Proverbs 31. I believe in going to the sales and making sure I get the best for my family, fixing breakfast, and ironing clothes. I am not the modern woman!
>
> —Terry Carter

Terry Carter, a divorced mother of two children who works as a punch press operator, is a strong supporter of the traditional family and its gender hierarchy. Like most parents in the low and/or working class whom I interviewed, her support for gender equality is limited to the idea that women should be able to work outside the home and progress in the labor market. But male-headed families are advocated, and rarely is there support for fundamental changes in the family, especially when it comes to the socialization of boys. Marriage and male-headed families are often seen as the solution to the problems that ail black communities, and black women are sometimes even blamed for relieving men of this responsibility. For example, asked to explain why so many black mothers are single, one married mother implied that men had been displaced in families:

> I would imagine that men, black men, [aren't being] taught to take responsibility for the family. . . . The black man has seen, too much of the time, women being so responsible that he doesn't even feel responsible, nor is he taught that he's responsible. . . . Not just the teaching, but just seeing so many black women take responsibility, what's to encourage him to take on that role?

Thus, parents with a high school education or less had the narrowest perspective on gender equality: They wanted equality for daughters in the labor market, were supportive of high career aspirations for daughters, but were resistant to the idea of bending gender traditions in the home or having their sons engage in female-typed behaviors. In addition, they engaged in less explicit racial socialization and saw race as posing fewer barriers to their children's success. There was a strong tendency, especially among the parents of young children, to deny that either race, poverty, and academic challenges would diminish their children's success. Shawn Branson, a twenty-two-year-old, single, unemployed mother of four children, had high hopes for her six-year-old daughter, who had already been diagnosed as having a learning disability. Asked if she thought being black would affect her child's success, Shawn replied, "No, not really. You just have to be determined, have a goal in life. If you have a goal in life or what you want to do and what you want to become, you can do it. She shouldn't have any problem . . . you have to do well in school, and get a scholarship, or whatever."

Despite the absence of ideological support for egalitarian gender norms in economically disadvantaged families, these parents often experience the greatest gap between their stated ideologies and actual behaviors, thus validating the common notion of a diminished impact of gender in black families and in their socialization of children. For the most part, the issue of gender equality ranks low in significance among poor people, where the daily struggle for survival, safety, and control over their own lives consumes most of their energy. For them, race and class inequalities intersect in ways that result in being exposed to negative racial stereotypes, living in high-risk neighborhoods, and enduring the myriad distresses of poverty. In many such families, headed by poor, single mothers, gender traditionalism is scarcely an issue as they have no one with whom to negotiate the distribution of housework. The practical realities of life shape their performance of gender; indeed, single mothers of necessity expose their children to less traditional notions of gender, and some studies have shown that children who grow up in such families define themselves more in terms of self-reliance, independence, and aggressiveness.[29]

The issue in sex role training becomes whether it is what parents teach or what they do that has the greatest impact on the gender thinking they pass on to children. Stories like that of Jake Houser, who is now twenty-eight years old and a single father, suggest that it may be what parents do that has the greatest impact. Jake, who takes on much of the responsibility for raising his own children, explains that growing up in a single-mother household meant that he learned to accept adult responsibilities early in life, including helping out in the domestic arena as much as he could:

> I had to be more of an adult. I loved my mother a lot, and I didn't want to see her take all of the pressure. So I tried to make sure . . . that we

cleaned up the house I had to play two roles. I had to watch out for my sisters, had to watch out for my mother. I had to play that role, because we didn't have a father image.

Despite support for traditional gender ideologies in families, those who are economically disadvantaged are equally likely to want sons and daughters to get a college education. Yet it is often the case that poor black boys face more obstacles to academic success than do girls, from the perils of street life to the stigma and marginalization they encounter in schools. In addition, as M. A. Messner has pointed out, black girls are more likely to express a value in academic achievement, while boys hope to "show their stuff" in sports.[30] Therefore, parents often come to place their hopes for success in daughters rather than sons, often highlighting the inroads black women have already made. Terry Carter, for example, asked if gender might affect her children's opportunity for success, emphasized that being male would be more of an obstacle than being female:

> I think [my daughter] will have a better career than she would have had in the past, because there are so many black females entering the labor force in every area . . . pioneering the way for our children. I'm more concerned about my son than I am my daughter. Society has a tendency to lift up a black woman before they'll lift up a black man—it's easier for the black woman now to accelerate in the workforce.

Thus, parents who are economically disadvantaged have the narrowest views of gender and racial equality. They want their children—sons and daughters—to go to college but are less likely to see race as a barrier or acknowledge that their class background (especially the quality of education their children are receiving) makes success improbable. They accept labor market participation by women but idealize marriage and gender traditionalism as a way to strengthen black families. The realities of survival, however, generate behaviors that supercede these ideologies. Moreover, despite their idealization of patriarchal families, there is little to suggest that they will sacrifice the stability they have achieved to marry men who are inadequate wage earners or seen as untrustworthy (e.g., see chapters 2 and 3).

The Perils of Poverty

This chapter has thus far explored how parents' social class positions affect the racial and gender socialization of their children. As a precursor to the following chapter on violence, I conclude with a discussion of how class inequality—or, more specifically, poverty—can create a family–school–community nexus of abuse and violence that not only endangers the welfare of children but also may lay the foundation for violence in adult life. Here I contend that this family–school–community nexus in which poor black children are socialized tends to foster high levels of child abuse, aggression, and violence.

My own research coincides with other studies that have found poor and working-class parents more likely to rely on corporal punishment, or spanking, as a discipline strategy. General support for spanking children is high among African Americans regardless of social class position; black parents almost universally accept the use of corporal punishment as necessary, even if they do not rely on it much. Such beliefs are entrenched in black cultural traditions and frequently reinforced from the pulpits of black churches. Many African Americans attribute the high rates of disrespect, violence, and homicide among the younger generation to the failure of their parents to use corporal punishment. Yet despite high levels of ideological support for spanking, the tendency of parents to *actually use* this form of discipline diminishes with social class mobility. One economically disadvantaged mother I interviewed, asked about the disciplining of her eleven-year-old son, made it clear that spanking was seen as appropriate and was frequently used, even when she understood her son's offense to be inadvertent:

> Van is talked to the first time and then spanked five licks the second time. . . . Right now, with us having just moved, and we just got married in July, and he just started school, so he's going through a lot of transitions. And he's distracted from the things that are expected, and he's been getting spanked about once every two weeks.

More affluent black parents also advocate spanking children, although they find less reason to use it as a disciplinary strategy. The mother of two daughters, married to a physician, believed in the value of spanking but said, "For Kelly, if she understands what she's supposed to do and why, reason and logic work best for her. She rarely has to be spanked; I haven't spanked her for years. If she knows why it's important, it's not a problem."

Many newly middle-class parents, asked how their own child-rearing work differed from that of their parents, said they relied less on physical punishment. As one stated, "Well, we got more whippings. I don't whip him as much; that's the big difference. . . . Mostly, he doesn't do anything severe enough to call for a whipping. I just take away some privileges or something."

Spanking is not considered a form of child abuse in the United States; indeed, a majority of parents report hitting their children. Yet spanking is the most common context in which child abuse occurs, and the stresses of poverty, single-mother families, live-in male partners, and the tradition of teaching children "toughness" as a survival strategy enhance the risk that children will be abused by their parents. While the majority of poor mothers manage to raise children who successfully take hold of adult life, others find themselves overwhelmed by the demands of juggling child rearing with employment, the frustrations of making a living, the stress of dangerous neighborhoods, and the feeling that their own needs are not being met. These factors, coupled with the black cultural tradition that almost demands that black women take on the mantle of strong motherhood, lead some to become strict, tough disciplinarians who feel they must "get their bluff in early" if they are to control and protect their children, and their frustrations grow as they watch their children mature and become less compliant. Moreover, exposure to nonbiological parents, especially live-in male partners, enhances the risk of child abuse. As a case in point, in the span of a few short months, four toddlers in the greater Kansas City area where I live were beaten to death by their mothers' cohabiting male partners.[31]

Discussions of the abuse that black children experience in their families often generate a host of issues and dissenting voices, from those who contend that authorities are simply more likely to *report* suspected cases of child abuse among blacks to those who interrogate the very concept of child abuse by arguing that the black culture and adverse ecological factors necessitate the strict disciplinary practices of parents. Such defensiveness is rooted in the long history of stigmatizing and unduly penalizing poor black families when, in fact, the majority are functional units where parents do their best to love, protect, and properly discipline their children. Yet poverty remains the strongest predictor of child abuse, neglect, and violence, and African Americans are overrepresented among the poor. And while the unequivocal link between structural forces of inequality and violence makes it easy to attribute child abuse to macrolevel factors such as racism, social exclusion, and the absence of opportunity, as Marino Bruce has recently argued, it is also important to understand how culture and the microlevel social processes foster patterns of violence.[32]

Schools often offer children little respite from violence; in fact, many black children living in poor neighborhoods attend schools where they are maligned, mistreated, and expected to fail in life. For example, a high school science teacher in California recently sparked controversy by defying rules of political correctness to declare that the chronically bad behavior of black students had nothing to do with poverty, racism, or inadequate schools but rather the social deficiencies of students. Recent research by Ann Ferguson shows such attitudes are more the rule rather than the exception in many inner-city schools, where negative stereotypes of black children are reinforced. In her ethnography of fifth and sixth graders in a public elementary school, she found that teachers and school officials routinely judged the behaviors of black students, especially boys, out of social context. Rather than being seen as engaging in normal childhood antics, they saw black boys as essentially different from whites and easily stereotyped them as "hypersexual, shiftless, lazy, and of inferior intellect." According to Ferguson, the two broad representations of black masculinity were the endangered species and the criminal, leaving the former "marginalized to the point of oblivion," and the others callously labeled as destined for prison. Early in life, boys learn the value of aggression and fighting if they are to survive. Ferguson quotes one young student as saying:

> It's probably like dumb, but if somebody wants to fight me, I mean, I don't care even if I know I can't beat 'em, I won't stop if they don't stop. I mean I'm not scared to fight anybody. I'm not a coward. I don't let anybody punk me around. If you lets people punk you around, other peoples want to punk you around.[33]

Poor parents may reinforce these sentiments by insisting that children learn to defend themselves, as they can offer little protection from the street violence their children encounter away from home. As Elijah Anderson points out, parents commonly tell their sons, "Don't you come in here crying that somebody beat you up; you better get back out there and whup his ass. I didn't raise no punks."

The neighborhood socialization of poor black children often completes the nexus of violence. As many as half of all black children are growing up in poverty, often in communities where crime, substance abuse, and child neglect are common. These conditions reinforce high levels of stress, physical aggression, and crime, with children often the victims and/or perpetrators. For example, a spate of child deaths in Detroit, caused by gunfire, revenge, and gangs, led to the deaths of 15 children by mid-2002, leaving parents and community leaders fearful and recalling the fact that 365 children were shot (43 of them died) in 1986.[34]

A survey of junior high school girls living in a poor, racially segregated area of New York City found that more than one-third had recently been involved in fights, weapon carrying, or weapon use, and more than one-half had threatened others with violence.[35] While the arrest of adolescent girls for status offenses declined between 1985 and 1994, their arrest for violence offenses nearly doubled.[36] One study identified the key background characteristics for adolescent girls who are arrested for violence or criminal acts as living in single-mother families, having a drug-abusing parent, and experiencing sexual or physical abuse in their homes.[37]

While girls are by no means immune from the ravages of violence, boys are especially apt to embrace violence and aggression as a survival mechanism and a masculinity strategy. Growing up in a social context where men are scarce, unemployed, and frequently degraded as worthless by mothers who are struggling to raise their children alone, boys are left to establish their identity and independence in the streets, and doing so enhances their aggressiveness.[38]

Noted Journalist Michael Datcher, in *Raising Fences: A Black Man's Love Story*, speaks of his own experience growing up a single-mother family and a crime-ridden neighborhood, where the longing for fathering or male attention among young boys is almost palpable. Far from an indictment of their single mothers as inadequate or inept parents— indeed, these mothers are usually praised and appreciated—Datcher speaks of the yearning among poor boys to share activities with a father and to live in what society defines as a normal family. "Picket fence dreams," the aspiration to live in a middle-class, two-parent family, were prevalent among the young boys he grew up with, although few held much hope of ever having such a family. Their cultural adaptation to race and economic disadvantage demanded a brand of masculinity taught on the streets that disdains and preys on weakness, thus teaching boys to adopt a tough exterior:

Gang culture had a powerful impact on the neighborhood. It fascinated me. I liked to just sit in the cut and observe. Even the brothers who weren't gang-banging had to embrace a gangsta like hardness just to walk the streets. Any softness was immediately marked and recorded as weakness. . . . Exploiting targets was the easiest, fastest, and safest way to build a rep. Targets were in demand.[39]

Displays of power, control, and strength become vital for young men in search of respect and identity, and such displays often take the form of what R. Majors and J. M. Billson describe as "cool pose," or a form of masculinity where boys learn to be "calm, emotionless, fearless, aloof, and tough," regardless of the situation. This performance of masculinity is embraced by young boys as a way of empowering and making themselves visible, yet cool pose can have a devastating impact on their lives, personal growth, and interpersonal relationships, as it encourages not only violence but also the suppression and numbing of feelings. Majors and Billson contend that cool pose helps explain why black males die earlier and faster than white males from suicide, homicide, accidents, and stress-related illnesses, and their involvement in criminal activities. Research has linked the repression of emotions, especially the tendency to deny that emotions like fear even exist, with higher levels of domestic violence among men.[40]

An especially devastating rash of violence erupted in black communities during the latter decades of the twentieth century, attributed to joblessness, the rise of the hip-hop culture, and the deterioration of inner-city areas. A proliferation of gangs, drugs, and guns permeated black communities and homicide became the leading cause of death for young black men. In light of these statistics, efforts to save young black men mushroomed in communities and churches, from the creation of all-male academies to provide role models and boost their self-esteem, to the development of special rites of passage meant to institute a new, more positive sense of manhood. All too often, however, these laudable efforts to help young black men deal with their despair ignored the devastating consequences of violence in the lives of black women.

Notes

1. W. W. Nobles (1985:83).
2. S. A. Hill (1999:34).

3. H. P. McAdoo (1983).

4. B. G. Holliday (1985).

5. W. W. Nobles (1985:84).

6. S. A. Hill (1995).

7. S. A. Hill (1994); S. A. Hill and M. K. Zimmerman (1995).

8. S. A. Hill (1994:124).

9. S. A. Hill (1994:122).

10. S. A. Hill and M. K. Zimmerman (1995).

11. b. hooks (1992:87).

12. W. Ickes (1993:79).

13. A. C. Crouter, S. M. McHale, and W. T. Bartko (1993); C. West and D. Zimmerman (1987).

14. J. Block (1983:1341).

15. C. West and D. Zimmerman (1987).

16. E. Higginbotham (1981); E. Higginbotham and L. Weber (1992).

17. D. Lewis (1975).

18. M. Peters (1997).

19. J. W. Scott (1993:73).

20. P. T. Reid and K. H. Trotter (1993).

21. R. J. Taylor, L. M. Chatters, M. B. Tucker, and D. Lewis (1990).

22. P. J. Bowman and C. Howard (1985).

23. J. E. Hale (1986).

24. M. L. Kohn (1963).

25. A. Lareau (2002:773).

26. J. Battle and M. Bennett (2000).

27. C. Leaper, L. Leve, T. Strasser, and R. Schwartz (1995).

28. D. R. McCreary (1994).

29. M. Slavkin and A. D. Stright (2000).

30. M. A. Messner (1991:70).

31. E. Peterson (2002:1–2).

32. M. A. Bruce (2000, 2003).

33. A. A. Ferguson (2000:189).

34. A. Marks (2002a).

35. A. Stueve, L. O'Donnell, and B. Link (2001).

36. M. Chesney-Lind (1997).

37. M. Chesney-Lind (1997).

38. K. M. Roche et al. (2003).

39. M. Datcher (2001:87).

40. R. Majors and J. M. Billson (1992).

CHAPTER 7

Gendered Violence

Racial Oppression and the Assault on Black Women

For too many women, every day the violence takes the form of a purse
snatched, face beaten, body raped, a woman murdered. I know only a
handful of women, of any color, who have not been hit by a man. I do not
know any who have not been verbally abused, either by a loved one or
an anonymous man on the street. I know more than a few women who
have been raped, most often in their own homes, by some man they
thought they knew or wanted to know.

—Jill Nelson[1]

Black communities must begin facing up to the lethal consequences of
our own sexism. The time is over for expecting black women to be silent
about the sexual violence and personal suppression they experience in
ostensible fidelity to our common cause.

—Michael Eric Dyson[2]

Nothing disturbs notions of African Americans expressing cultural values
of community, interdependence, spirituality, extended family ties, female
strength, and relative gender equality more than the demoralizing violence that plagues their communities, families, and intimate partner relationships. Violence has always been a major social, political, and health
issue for black people, rooted in societal forces such as slavery, racism, patriarchy, poverty, and powerlessness. African Americans historically have
been victimized by personal, organized, and even legal violence, aimed at
exploiting their labor and thwarting their assimilation into mainstream
society. Racial oppression, negative stereotypes, economic inequality, and

171

the use of violence as a means of social control have diminished the value placed on the lives of black people in the dominant society—and, sadly, often in African American neighborhoods.

An undercurrent of disrespect and violence permeates the interpersonal interactions of many black people, especially those who are ensnared in poverty and most segregated from the mainstream society. It manifests itself in behaviors ranging from the hurtful turns that verbal bantering like "signifying" and "playing the dozens" can take to general support for toughness and physical aggression as survival strategies. For many young black men who fail to obtain an education or find a niche in the labor market, these survival strategies become the basis for engaging in violence, criminal acts, and antisocial behaviors. Although rates of violent crime have fallen in recent years, they remained two times higher among blacks than whites in 2002, and blacks accounted for nearly half (49 percent) of all homicide victims, with more than 90 percent of them murdered by other African Americans.[3] Moreover, the recent release of thousands of parolees, who return to their neighborhoods no better equipped to earn a living than when they were incarcerated, has led to a surge of homicides in some large cities.

In this chapter, I analyze the link between racial oppression, black subcultural behaviors, and the abuse and violence perpetrated against African American women at the hands of black men, including their spouses and intimate partners. Rejecting biological and cultural theories of violence has, in many ways, made race the "missing variable" in analyses of interpersonal and intimate partner violence. For example, studies often report that social class position is the strongest predictor of physical assault, violent crime, and murder; that is, those who are poor are most likely to engage in such behaviors. The corrosive impact of poverty also affects family life, leading to higher rates of intimate partner abuse and violence; indeed, statistics reveal that rates of domestic abuse are five times higher among the poor.[4] African Americans are more than twice as likely as whites to live in poverty, thus elevating the risk of domestic violence. Feminists, on the other hand, foreground the gender dimension of violence, pointing to the salient fact that in cases of severe intimate partner violence, women are usually the victims and men the perpetrators. Men are arrested for 90 percent or more of all rape, assault, and murder, and 80 percent of all intimate violence.[5] Patriarchal traditions of male dominance and female subordination, perpetuated by socializing boys in ways that define masculinity in terms of physical aggression and control, are seen as key factors in male violence against women.

For African American women, both their class and gender positions, and the fact that black men are especially apt to focus on physical aggression as an aspect of masculinity, heighten the risk that they will be victimized by violence in their communities and by men. Domestic abuse activist and scholar Beth Richie, working for an organization aimed at strengthening poor racial minority families, was among the first to report that so many "strong, culturally identified families . . . were dangerous places for some women to live."[6] Moreover, she found that it was difficult for these women to discuss the battering they experienced, since doing so seemed like a violation of racial loyalty that was likely to reinforce negative stereotypes about black families and increase public intervention in their lives—interventions that often prove more punitive than helpful.

Yet today, nearly all researchers report a higher rate of family violence among African Americans: For example, national figures from the Justice Department report that black females age twelve and over are 25 percent more likely to be assaulted by intimate partners than their white counterparts.[7]

Scholars have often unwittingly contributed to obfuscating the link between violence and racial oppression, as the racialization of black male violence is extremely risky. Many have worked hard to refute derogatory images of black people—their families, behaviors, sexuality—and have taken a vigilant stance against theories that invoke lingering notions that biology, or skin color, makes one prone to abuse, aggression, or assault. Generalizations about racial minorities are made all too easily and hastily, often with dire consequences, such as heightening suspicion of black men, instigating inappropriate aggressive interventions by police officers and other public authorities, or even justifying racial exclusion and discrimination. These risks have often led to downplaying race as a factor in intimate violence, or at least camouflaging it under the banner of class. Studies reporting higher rates of intimate and domestic violence in African American families are often criticized for including only a small sample of blacks or of ignoring class.[8] Some find the impacts of class and race impossible to untangle, while others dismiss reports of high rates of domestic violence among blacks as the result of racially biased reporting, greater scrutiny of their lives, or an insensitivity to black cultural norms. While these critiques clearly have some merit, they inadvertently shift attention away from frank discussions of violence among blacks or protecting victims of it to exposing the racist biases of researchers. In fact, efforts by scholars to avoid appearing racist or perpetuating stereotypes has led to a remarkable "deracialization" of studies of family and intimate violence.

Overview of the Chapter

In this chapter, I argue that there is a need to rethink the dynamic relationship between persistent racial oppression and the perpetuation of black cultural behaviors that foster violent behaviors. Racial oppression supports structures of social exclusion, discrimination, and segregation, all of which keep a disproportionate number of African Americans living at or near poverty and experiencing all of the stresses and frustrations that daily survival entails. Research frequently reports that African Americans face formidable barriers to decent housing due to both the loss of public housing subsidies and discrimination by bankers and realtors, and that they remain the most residentially segregated racial minority in the United States.[9] Douglas S. Massey's research shows that residential segregation significantly strengthens the correlation between poverty and crime, and he argues that it "*guarantees* that blacks will be exposed to a social and economic environment that is much harsher than anything experienced by whites" [emphasis in original].[10] Illicit underground economies based on drug sales and other illegal activities often thrive in poor neighborhoods, where commodities that bolster economic survival or at least a temporary escape from despair are in demand.

Racial oppression is also implicated in violence in that it devalues the worth of African Americans, generating stereotypes that associate them with aggression, sexual deviance, and dependency and portraying them as noncontributing members to society. The societal devaluation of black people, concentrated poverty, and second-class citizenship mean that violence among or directed toward black people is often normalized; indeed, as cultural critic Michael Dyson has pointed out, "black life is at a low premium, and to hurt, maim, or murder a black person [has] carried little punitive consequences or public concern."[11] Thus, noting the link between racial oppression and crime, B. D. Headley pointed out long ago:

"Crime is not the result of blackness . . . but rather of a complex of social and economic conditions—a negative situational matrix—brought on by the capitalist mode of production, in which both the black victim and the black victimizer are inextricably linked in a deadly game for survival."[12]

The cultural and intellectual responses of African Americans to racial oppression and the devaluation of their lives often inadvertently ignore, normalize, or even perpetuate violence. The demeaning of African American women as sexually promiscuous and matriarchal, for example, has been countered by black scholars highlighting their strength and independence. Yet the social construction of "the strong black woman" is incongruent with the dominant profile of "the battered woman," who is often characterized as trapped in an abusive relationship by learned helplessness or economic dependence. Some African American women buy into the notion that strength means enduring violence, defending themselves, and blaming racism for the violence they endure at the hands of black men. Moreover, while black women are seen as transgressing the boundaries of traditional femininity in the direction of greater liberation, black men are seen as perpetual victims of racial oppression. The call for strength, racial unity, and (often) silence on the part of women victimized by intimate partner violence and the reframing of that violence as an almost legitimate response to violations of manhood experienced by black men makes confronting battering difficult. Moreover, the societal denigration of black women leaves them little reason to believe that legal authorities have any interest in protecting their welfare.

Theorists such as Devon W. Carbado and Beth Richie have highlighted the theme of black male victimology in making African American women reluctant to hold men responsible for their violence. The historic victimization of black men and the "masculinity dilemma" they continue to face often overshadows and, for some, explains their violence toward women. Concern over further victimizing black men and the fear of tarnishing their images often weigh heavily in black women's response to gendered violence. Associating black men with crime clearly has been a central mechanism of social control, used to justify arbitrary surveillance, harassment, arrest, and criminal charges, and it resulted in the incarceration of a scandalous number of black men just during the latter twentieth century. Calling the police to manage black men can be especially risky; it not only reinforces stereotypes of them as dangerous and violent, but relying on aggressive policing jeopardizes their lives. Support for racial unity, reluctance to trust the intervention and protection of legal authorities, efforts to hold their families together, misguided perceptions of female strength, and the devaluation of the lives of black women all militate against effectively addressing male violence. However, as I will show in this chapter, even the theme of black male victimology may valorize the silence of women by depicting them as heroic protectors of their men. A broader view must consider the complexities of the multiple inequalities African American women face.

In this chapter, I try to inscribe race in the study of interpersonal and intimate partner violence, highlighting the role of racial oppression in the construction and perpetuation of black cultural patterns that promote gendered violence within and outside the context of intimate relationships. I begin by situating the experiences of black people in the accounts of family and domestic violence proffered by social historians, most of them in response to the implication of family violence as a new phenomenon. Instead, the denigration and abuse of vulnerable family members, especially women and children, has been as much the rule as the exception, and only with the emergence of the modern family did it come to be defined as a social problem.

The next section of the chapter analyzes sociocultural, class, and feminist perspectives on family violence. The sociocultural approach starts with the premise that intimate partner abuse and homicide can be understood within the broader societal context where violence is freely used and sanctioned. Violence has always been somewhat of an American tradition, used to extract land, labor, and deference from racial minorities, implement slavery, subjugate women, and quell social protest, and the pervasiveness of violence as a solution to trouble makes it likely also to occur at the interpersonal level. Class theory emphasizes poverty and economic inequality as the major predictors of domestic abuse, while feminists take a decidedly gender-centered approach that focuses on patriarchy. These perspectives, however, have deemphasized the experiences of race-ethnic women and the specific link between racial oppression and gender violence.

I conclude by looking at how racial oppression fosters stereotypes of black women and patterns of masculinity among black men that perpetuate gendered violence, using an interview with a victim of domestic violence for illustration. Still, efforts to confront and curtail assaults on black women are growing, and they often center on contesting the notion that the racial oppression experienced by African American men justifies their abuse of black women.

(Re)Discovering Family Violence

The study of family violence emerged with the discovery of the child abuse syndrome in the 1960s. As the so-called traditional family waned in light of white women's entry into the labor market and demand for greater equality, this scholarship gradually expanded to identify women and the elderly as frequent victims of abuse. This official recognition of family violence disrupted images of families as havens of love and harmony, highlighted family diversity, and spawned a genre of research proving that family violence was neither a new phenomenon nor restricted to a handful of pathological families. Indeed, the abuse of women and children dates back to antiquity; it was the result of their subordinate status and perceptions that they were less than human and/or property. In colonial America, parents could pretty much discipline their children as they saw fit, while patriarchal ideologies curtailed the rights of women in both the family and the public arena. While their labor was vital to the agricultural economy, women often lacked political and property rights, and, under the tenets of the traditional marriage contract, they were no longer separate, legal beings once they married. The bodies and (usually) property of white women belonged to husbands; they were expected to live under the patriarchal rule of their husbands, and could be whipped or fined for failing to do so.[13] Still, records from the colonial era show that wives did sometimes allege abuse at the hands of their husbands, although the concept of wife battering had not been fully articulated and the extent of such abuse is impossible to determine.[14]

Understanding the prevalence of domestic abuse and violence among African Americans, most of whom were enslaved during this era, is even more difficult. The overall context of slavery was permeated with beatings, mutilations, rape, and the devaluation of black life, making violence a normal, everyday aspect of life. Some research has described enslaved black parents as harsh and overly punitive in dealing with their children, although such parental behavior may well have been the dominant norm in colonial America. Black wives were also assaulted by their husbands—perhaps as much because slavery tended to attenuate rather than institutionalize patriarchal traditions, giving men little control over their wives and creating immense gender tension. As December Green has observed, cross-culturally "wife battery is most likely to occur in partnerships where the husband lacks personal power but lives in a society that expects him to be powerful."[15] The inability of black men to gain respect as the heads, providers, or protectors of their families, the common sexual assault by white men of black females, and the relentless emotional suppression required of all enslaved persons created high levels of frustration. Slavery enforced norms of dissimulation that forbid openly displaying sentiments in the presence of whites. As Tommy L. Bogger has argued, this may have enhanced tension in black families:

> The situation in the black household was more conducive to explosions, for both slaves and freed blacks were a subjected group of people living under the constant gaze of their oppressors. They could not freely indulge in strong expressions of frustration, disappointment, or hatred in the presence of whites. Blacks usually had to hold such emotions in check until they were back in their quarters.[16]

Being stripped of most economic resources and power and subjugated by white males may have made directing rage against wives easier for black men, although there was seemingly little to gain by doing so. Yet as historian Deborah Gray White has reported, there is evidence of family violence among slaves over issues such as sexual infidelity. Such behavior, however, tended to be "overshadowed by white male exploitation of black women, and . . . overlooked because it had no legal injunction against it."[17]

Industrialization redefined families and the roles of men, women, and children in the dominant society, and abusive behaviors that were once upheld by law and ideology were increasingly viewed as unacceptable and even illegal. The recasting of marriage in modern society emphasized romantic love and free choice in the selection of spouses, and intimacy and companionship in marriages—ideologies that highlighted the inappropriateness of hitting, punching, and neglecting family members. States rethought laws defending the right of husbands to "chastise" their wives,[18] usually ruling that the physical discipline of wives was a "relic of barbarism that has no place in an enlightened civilization." Despite these advances, however, the increasing privacy and sacredness of families made states reluctant to intervene in their affairs. As Nancy Cott has pointed out, many agreed with a North Carolina court decision that it was "better to draw the curtain, shut out the public gaze, and leave the parties to forget and forgive" than to intervene in family life.[19] While modernization led to an ideology that scorned the battering of women, it failed to challenge the gender hierarchy in marriage and fostered family structures that may well have heightened spousal abuse. The privatized family of modern society was no longer seen as part of the larger community; it was more shielded from the public, and the increasing social isolation of middle-class women in nuclear families and the emphasis on men as economic providers may well have increased gender tensions. In any case, the evolving family ideology was clearly embraced more readily by affluent whites than by those left out of the opportunity system—those in poor and/or racial minority families.

African American families in the late nineteenth century were still grappling with how to reconstruct their lives in the aftermath of slavery. Especially frustrating for men during the late 1800s was the realization that emancipation offered little by way of extending to them the dignity of manhood. Fox Butterfield, for example, offers numerous examples of the assaults on black men in South Carolina that continued long after slavery had ended, from the tradition supported by law of giving black sharecroppers a few lashes with a whip at the start of each day to the ability of white men to literally take the wives of black men, whether through physical force or seduction. A new generation of black men, however, soon emerged, leaving many southerners lamenting the demise of the "old-time darkey"—the black man who had grown up in slavery and knew his place—and the rise of the "New Negro"—who defiantly demanded respect and protected his reputation, even if it led to his own death. In his historic account of the Bosket family, Butterfield documents an intergenerational pattern of black male violence and crime that spanned from slavery to the urban ghettos of the twentieth century.

Efforts by the newly freed black men to protect their dignity and claim masculinity in the public arena also extended to the family. As Donna Franklin has pointed out, wife battering increased among African Americans after emancipation, as men sought to establish themselves as the heads of their own families.[20] Research has shown that black women frequently reported domestic abuse to the Freedmen's Bureau, often complaining that black men thought being free meant having the right to beat their wives.[21] The extent of gendered violence in the intimate relationships of African Americans left to the vagaries and uncertainties of emancipation has only recently begun to get scholarly attention, specifically by a handful of scholars who have noted that it played a part in black women's migration to the north. Yet novelists such as Alice Walker, in *The Third Life of Grange Copeland*, have graphically documented the dynamics of black men's violence toward black women during the early to mid–nineteenth century. Walker's novel is a disturbing picture of intimate violence under a sharecropping system where racial oppression had deprived black men of the resources to support their families and stripped them of their very sense of humanity, and she bases it on a real historic event in the town where she grew up. It was not until the 1970s, however, that domestic violence became a major national issue and theories were sought to understand its causes and consequences.

Theorizing Intimate Partner Violence

The broadest understanding of spousal and intimate partner battering places it within the larger sociohistorical and cultural context where violence is common. The United States ranks first among advanced industrialized societies in rates of violence, which remains a highly touted strategy for reaching economic and political goals. Violence played a key role in the founding of the country, the repression of racial minorities and acquisition of land, and even today coercive tactics by law enforcement officials are accepted, gun control efforts fail, and the popularity of politicians soars when military troops are activated. Baca Zinn and Eitzen describe families as microcosms of mainstream society, where violence is pervasive and glorified in the media, music, and even children's literature, and note that families can scarcely expect to be exempt from its impact. Most parents hit their children and believe that doing so is acceptable, and the concept of common couple violence even normalizes battering between intimate adults. Michael J. Johnson describes common couple violence as "occasional outbursts of violence" that occur in relationships, noting that they are instigated by women and men and involve minor incidents of battering that almost never escalate into severe abuse.[22] Women in heterosexual relationships initiate about half of all violence, and, although research is sparse and frequently based on small samples, it suggests that one-third to more than 50 percent of lesbian relationships are characterized by battering.[23]

The concept of common couple violence reveals that not all violence is motivated by an effort to control one's partner (especially the male control of women), nor does it necessarily lead to a cycle of violence. A recent national study found that 73 percent of those physically assaulted by intimate partners did not report it to the police, most often because they did not think it would do any good[24] but probably also because such confrontations are common. Yet the ease with which intimate partners resort to hitting, slapping, and pushing to express their frustrations or resolve conflict is problematic, and it speaks to the extent to which the battering of intimate partners is condoned. Moreover, it lends credence to the common notion that violence is "found in every walk of life"—a fact that can obscure how it is shaped by social inequality.

The Class Dimension of Domestic Violence

Although domestic violence is found among all social classes, research especially points to the corrosive impact that poverty and economic hardship have on families and relationships. Class inequality, especially linked to stressful events such as unemployment, hunger, unpaid bills, poor health, and living in high-crime communities, curtails the ability of many people to create nurturing, supportive relationships and heightens the risk of violence. When poverty definitions were developed during the 1950s, more than one-half of all African Americans were found to be living below the poverty line, with others only marginally above it. Today, poverty is at a historic low among black people (i.e., 25 percent), yet their rates of poverty and unemployment are twice as high as those for whites. Numerous studies show that high rates of domestic and intimate abuse correlate with male unemployment, inadequate income, low educational attainment, and high levels of stress. The link between poverty and domestic violence is also highlighted by the fact that, according to Ellen K. Scott and her colleagues, as many as 60 percent of welfare recipients have a history of abuse. Lower rates of marriage and having alternative living options have led to a decline in rates of intimate partner homicide; however, lower welfare benefits—which presumably lead women to stay in unsatisfactory relationships—has actually been correlated with an increased number of *men* murdered by their intimate partners.[25]

The Gender Dimension of Domestic Violence

The feminist perspective on intimate partner violence focuses specifically on gender, since in cases of severe abuse women are usually the victims and men the perpetrators. Research on the violence and assault women

experience at the hands of men, including their intimate partners, has proliferated since the 1970s, accompanied by extensive documentation of its
consequences and efforts to press the legal authorities into providing
more protection for women. Nearly one-third of all couples have at least
one incident of physical abuse, with the partner who is the least powerful
and most dependent usually the victim, and 10 to 14 percent of married
women report that they have been raped by their husbands—often multiple times.[26] Feminist analyses have focused on severe forms of violence
such as that recently defined as patriarchal terrorism, the "terroristic control of wives by their husbands that involves the systematic use of not
only violence, but economic subordination, threats, isolation, and other
control tactics."[27] Lenore Walker's cycle of violence concept, for example,
was based on the experiences of women in battered shelters, who are especially likely to have been victimized by patriarchal terrorism: One
study found that women in shelters experience, on average, sixty acts of
husband violence per year, and more than half were threatened or at-
tacked with weapons.[28]

Scholarship on domestic violence revolutionized our thinking about
the victimization of women by noting that they are more likely to be physically assaulted and raped by intimates, relatives, and acquaintances than
by strangers and that rape also occurs in marriage. The physical damage to
women from intimate violence ranges from bruises to broken bones to permanent bodily injury and death; indeed, Bureau of Justice figures reveal
that between 1976 and 1997, 30 percent of all female murder victims (compared to 6 percent of all male murder victims) were by an intimate partner.
Some research reports that nearly one-third of all women seen in emergency rooms have been battered by their intimate partners,[29] and a 1998 national study noted that nonlethal intimate partner violence costs nearly
$150 million a year in medical expenses, lost and destroyed property, and
lost pay by victims.[30] Suicide among women has also been related to battering: One study found that a majority (81 percent) of women who committed suicide or had a history of suicide attempts were victims of male
partner abuse, with African American women hospitalized for suicide attempts having experienced considerably more abuse from their partners.[31]

Feminist scholars explain the violence by men against women in
terms of patriarchal ideologies that support domination by men and subordination of women and, in many cases, denigrate women and objectify
the female body as instruments of male pleasure. Catharine MacKinnon
has theorized the link between the sexual assault of women and the use

of pornography that "eroticizes hierarchy [and] sexualizes inequality" by constructing acts like rape, battery, sexual harassment, and prostitution as what women want.[32]

Theorizing violence, promoting greater community awareness of female victimization at the hands of their intimate partners, and creating crisis hotlines, shelters for battered women, and legal advocacy programs all helped place the issue of domestic violence on the national agenda. The activism of women led to the passage of the 1994 Violence against Women Act and the Family Violence Option, which exempts victims of domestic violence from the requirements of the new welfare program. Rates of severe intimate partner violence and murder declined during the 1990s due to such activism, although the decline in intimate homicide is significantly the result of delayed marriages, no-fault divorce, and the growing economic independence of women.[33] However, the fact that the Bush administration in 2003 recognized October as Domestic Violence Awareness Month and created Family Justice Centers to assist its victims makes it clear that the issue is far from being resolved.

Despite substantial success in enhancing awareness of intimate partner and domestic violence, race-ethnic minority women have often claimed that their experiences and voices have been ignored. While class and gender inequality does explain much of the violence between black men and women, racism interacts with those inequalities to create a broader social context where gendered violence is often frighteningly pervasive but silenced. Beth Richie maintains that the antiviolence movement, and its central "rhetoric paradigm" that claims domestic violence "can happen to anyone," has meant that "those who mattered most in a society got the most visibility and the most public sympathy," even to the point of passing antiviolence policies, such as arrest laws, that further endangered black women. She sees the experiences of black women as having been "de-gendered" and placed in a special category.[34] I contend, however, that it has been the deracialization of these experiences that have diminished their visibility.

Racial Oppression and Black Masculinity

She knew that she didn't deserve her abuser's repeated blows. She knew he had no right to physically abuse her. [But] she wanted to raise the issue of whether locking up Black men was such a good idea. She asked whether prison would simply make them angrier, so that they would just find some other Black woman to abuse.

—D. Carbado[35]

Racial oppression is a structural force that fosters a pervasive devaluation of black life and in the process perpetuates social exclusion, poverty, and, ultimately, black cultural adaptations to these forces that are infused with violence. For example, racist exclusion has made it difficult for black men to gain authority and legitimacy in their families through economic dominance, leaving them to endure both stigma in the public arena and the private scorn of black women for failing to contribute adequately to their families. As feminist scholars have noted, hegemonic ideals of masculinity include authority, strength, and material possession by men,[36] and these socially acceptable expressions of manhood are easier to achieve in the context of white, middle-class society. Men from racially and economically disadvantaged backgrounds often focus inordinately on physical aggression, sports, and violence as routes to manhood, along with control over and exploitation of women. Poor, young African American males are especially apt to embrace such expressions of masculinity, placing their female counterparts at a high risk for violent victimization. They learn early in life that they will never be able to deliver to females what Michael Datcher calls the "picket fences" dream of stable, middle-class families, and they engage in a campaign for respect that endorses physical aggression, violence, and control over women.[37] Haki R. Madhubuti describes black male socialization as basically "antifemale, antiwomanist/feminist, and antireason," with boys commonly taught to characterize women outside their own family in derogatory ways.[38] For many, the first step in their claim for manhood is to put black women "in their place"—a theme that dates back to emancipation but was revived by black nationalism and the hip-hop culture.

The Hip-Hop Route to Masculinity

Controlling and denigrating women became a major theme in the hip-hop music that emerged during the past few decades, much of which assumes that the state and black women are almost equally responsible for the oppression and powerlessness experienced by black men.[39] Much has been written in defense and condemnation of the lyrics found in gangsta rap music, especially its tendency to direct black male rage disparagingly toward women by describing them as "ho's" and "bitches." Engaging in that debate is beyond the scope of this chapter, but suffice it to say that lyrics chillingly supportive of rape and violence, such as these sung by the Geto Boys, glorify terrifying images of violence against women:

> Her body so beautiful so I'm thinking rape
> Shouldn't have had her curtains open so that's her fate. . . .
> Slit her throat and watched her shake.

Rap music, of course, is diverse in content and theme, and a few rap artists today have even agreed to tone down the violence. Yet the case remains that its misogynist themes reflect and promote versions of manhood that include callousness and contempt for women, and a code of behavior that normalizes violence. The values expressed in rap music are often contested by parents and community leaders in African American neighborhoods, but all too often neither can effectively intervene to strengthen the moral development of black male adolescents or offer an appealing alternative route to respectable manhood. While the loss of jobs and economic opportunity may lie at the root of "cool pose," casual violence, and a pervasive disregard for human life, many young men today are beyond struggling through educational/vocational courses or accepting low-wage jobs that do not even enable them to achieve economic independence. One young man I interviewed spoke of learning to hate school and the world of low-wage work but, as a drug dealer, loving "to be the man" and enjoying the "cat and mouse" aspect of evading law enforcement officials. Similarly, rap music offers images of instant masculinity, esteem, and respectability, and the perils involved in achieving this brand of manhood through flouting laws and socially acceptable values adds to the drama.

Even if such music does not inspire actual acts of physical violence against women, it reinforces negative racial stereotypes and exploits both black men and women for profit. Hip-hop music is often mainstreamed in low-budget films that gross as much as 80 percent in profit.[40] As Jean Pierre Campbell has noted:

> As long as such notions of Black manhood are profitable—in film, music, news, the prison-expansion industry—America will prostitute the "bad

nigger" image until there are no real brothers left. It's an image predicated on being "hard," not on building community, protecting our children, or preparing ourselves for adult life in the twenty-first century.

Black female rap artists have also been lured by money and fame to produce denigrating music that resurrects and reinforces stereotypes of black female sexuality, illustrating what Tricia Rose calls the "profitability of racially distinct sexism."[41]

Racial Stereotypes and the Sexual Denigration of Black Women

The dominant societal devaluation of African American women centers on stereotypes that denigrate their physical attractiveness, malign their sexuality and reproductive behaviors, and imply they deserve little control over their bodies. The images of African American women propagated in hip-hop music and other forms of media reinforce a long tradition that denies their worth and control over their bodies. Sexist ideas controlled white women by depicting them as morally superior to men and even asexual yet characterized black women as sexual deviants and continually violated the sanctity and privacy of their bodies. The demeaning of black women during slavery by lewd stripping, fondling, and sexual assault is now evident in efforts to portray them as sexually promiscuous and to control their reproductive behaviors. Medical authorities are still sometimes empowered to subject African American women suspected of substance abuse to nonconsensual drug testing, arrest, and even sterilization.[42] A similar disregard for the privacy of black women's bodies is found in a General Accounting Office study of more than one hundred thousand people who were searched in airports on suspicion of drug smuggling. African American female citizens were almost twice as likely as white men or women to be strip searched and three times more likely than black men.[43]

Racial characterizations of African American women are intricately connected to their victimization by rape. As Paula Giddings has pointed out, the frequently overlooked corollary of the black male rapist has been the "lascivious character" of black women, whose own failure to report rape proves they are "morally obtuse."[44] Such devaluation of black women is seen in the testimony of black men who have found that they can rape them without impunity. Black power advocate Eldridge Cleaver, claiming rape was an "insurrectionary act," spoke freely of honing his "rapist skills" on poor, black girls.[45] In *Makes Me Wanna Holler*, Nathan McCall describes the "trains" (e.g., gang rapes) he and his friends often pulled on young, unsuspecting black girls. Even today, young black men in poor communities boast that "pussy is a penny a pound,"[46] and movies like *Baby Boy* and *She's Gotta Have It* suggest that sassy black women can be tamed by coercive sex and even rape by their intimate partners.

The historic denigration of African American women has made it difficult for them to talk much about their sexual lives, but, given an opportunity to do so, scholars such as Tricia Rose in *Longing to Tell* report finding their stories replete with accounts of sexual abuse and assault. Rape and sexual assault at the hands of black men inflict tremendous emotional harm on black women, as it often reinforces dominant images that challenge their worth. As one woman interviewed by Beth Richie pointed out:

> As a black woman, there is nothing more awful than being used by my man for sex. Such disrespect! It is like they say women were treated on the plantation: to have our bodies used and abused, to have our hearts broken, and then to be forced into sex with the very person who stole our dignity. Of all the things that I couldn't stand, having him all over me after beating me up was the worst. It made me feel like I was a true "nigger," and he, of all people, was my master.[47]

Accusations of rape by black women are viewed with suspicion, and in those handful of cases where their claims garner public attention, they draw the ire of the black community. As Jill Nelson points out, "Black women are seldom figures who elicit sympathy or support, much less become cause célèbres, whatever their status."[48] Moreover, African American men are seen as having endured the brunt of racial oppression and injustice, and the notion of "the black male rapist" is an especially sensitive issue. As scholars have frequently pointed out, during the first half of the twentieth century, black men accounted for 90 percent of those executed for rape, while virtually no white man has been executed for raping black women.[49] Episodes of intraracial rape and violence against black women rarely capture much media attention, and when they do, those in the black community are apt to come to the defense of black men. African American men are seen as facing formidable obstacles to success, and those who beat the odds by achieving wealth and public recognition are summarily heralded as role models, regardless of their personal character. Thus, when Mike Tyson, heavyweight boxing campaign, was accused and later convicted of raping a black woman (Desiree Washington), many black people (but especially men) were more concerned about Washington's betrayal of racial unity than her right to pursue justice.[50] Historically, social protest has often centered on issues such as ending the beating and lynching of black men, but seldom on ending the assault and rape of black women. Indeed, as Hazel Carby writes, "The institutionalized rape of black women has never been as powerful a symbol of black oppression as the spectacle of lynching. Rape has always involved patriarchal notions of women being, at best, not entirely unwilling accomplices, if not outwardly inviting a sexual attack."[51]

Black Male Victimology

The theme of racial unity colludes with the belief that black men have been the primary victims of racism in silencing many black women who are victimized by violence. Racial oppression is viewed as much more of a violation of masculinity, which connotes privilege, domination, and respect, than of the devalued status of femininity. Black men are often seen as needing protection because they are poor, marginalized, and likely to be victimized by the criminal justice system or because they are successful, high-profile and apt targets of racially inspired attacks on their character. Both are seen as being intimidating to white society, and African American women who accuse them of sexual misconduct are abetting societal efforts to destroy them. Community leaders and scholars rush to the defense of high-profile black men accused of sexual misconduct, as was the case when black lawyer Anita Hill accused Supreme Court nominee Clarence Thomas of such behavior. Thomas's behavior was defended as reflecting a different cultural code of sexuality that exists among African Americans—an idea that suggests that sharing crude sexual jokes and literature in the workplace is normative behavior for black people. Orlando Patterson claimed that Thomas simply had his "mainstream cultural guard down," arguing that Hill "perfectly understood the psychocultural context in which Judge Thomas allegedly regaled her with his Rebalaisian humor."[52] Thus, in addition to charges that they are being used by feminists and betraying racial loyalty, African American women who accuse black men of sexual misconduct may be made to question the reality and significance of their own victimization, since they are accused of being out of touch with racially specific sexual codes.

Racism is seen as having unduly penalized African American men while allowing black women to circumvent the generally subordinated status of woman. Patterson, for example, insists that "whereas the burdens of poor African American men have always been oppressive, dispiriting, demoralizing, and soul-killing, those of women have always been, at least partly, generating, empowering, and humanizing."[53] The overall status and educational advantage of African American women continue to be sources of gender tension. Black Muslim leader Louis Farrakhan admonishes African American women that their own educational success intimidates black men, furthers the assault of the white man on black manhood, and makes them "fair game for being the victim."[54] Accusing black women of playing a role in their own abuse by being successful borders on the ludicrous, yet a recent study by L. Dugan, R. Rosenfeld, and D. S. Nagin concluded that, at least for black women in nonmarital relationships, being educated elevated the risk of intimate homicide.[55] Casting black men as the key victims of racial oppression also suggests that their women should understand the frustrations they endure in the dominant society and be more patient and understanding. As one divorced man interviewed by Erma Jean Lawson and Aaron Thompson explained:

> [W]hen Black men are constantly battling racial myths that require a huge psychological expenditure of energy, they are tired and angry. Black men may be noncompromising because they just don't have the energy to do otherwise. . . . Much more is required of Black women, or of a woman who is involved with a Black man, since they are judged by their skin color with numerous stereotypes rather than by their educational attainment and job skills.[56]

African American men stand at the center of the discourse on racism, often as *the* central representatives of the black experience,[57] and their victimization and exclusion from social and legal justice—from historic lynching patterns to racial profiling and unprovoked beatings by police officers—is supported by volumes of research. The unjust treatment of African American men throughout the twentieth century, including being punished for numerous unsupported claims of rape and economically marginalized, makes their own violence seem almost like a defensible assertion of manhood. The growing criminalization of black men throughout the twentieth century has heightened the perception of racial injustice in the criminal justice system. Even the spate of trials and accusations in recent years that found prominent black men accused of sexual harassment, rape, and murder served to polarize the black community and strengthen the theme of black male victimization, while ignoring the plight of women.

Devon Carbado, commenting on a discussion of domestic abuse at the African American Women in Law Conference, noted that the consequences of violence for women often took a backseat to the issue of whether black men should be arrested or incarcerated for this crime. Explaining the dilemma, he quoted Professor Kristal Brent Zook:

> When the names Rodney King, O. J. Simpson, Mike Tyson, and Marion Barry and even Clarence Thomas become symbolic, like "Scottsboro," black women are left without a way to talk about how some of the Scottsboro "boys" (accused of raping two white women) actually did commit acts of violence and murder against their girlfriends and wives. Black women are left without a way to address Rodney King as anything other than a victim, even after his second arrest for domestic abuse. And we have no response to Tupac Shakur's nameless accuser, whose lonely plea—"I did not deserve to be gang raped"—paled in comparison to *Vibe* magazine's five-page cover story on Shakur as the "misunderstood" thug.[58]

The theme of black male victimization reinforces patriarchal ideologies by assuming that black men, simply by virtue of their maleness, ought to have more economic opportunity and power than women. Sadly, black male violence assumes that manhood can be claimed through the battering, rape, and exploitation of women, especially those who are poor and vulnerable. Fears of racial disloyalty, public intervention in their lives, and the feeling that black men behave as they do because they are victims of racism may make black women more tolerant of abuse. Beth Richie found that even groups that took on the issue of black male violence against women refused to see domestic violence (or any other social issue) as a problem in the black community. Rather, these women, most of them well educated and all victims of battering in their own homes, defined violence against black women as the result of the systematic deprivation and domination of African American men. Rejecting gender oppression or sexual inequality as underlying issues, they placed the blame for black male violence on white society and saw the only solution as racial liberation. According to Richie, these women imply that "the role of black women in our families is to receive regular whippings in order to alleviate black men's stress."[59]

Excusing black male violence as the result of racial oppression prioritizes the indignities they have suffered, while minimizing those of African American women and ignoring the dangerous ways that a new generation of black men are seeking status and power. The campaign for respect by black men, distorted images of masculinity based on control of women and physical aggression, and the historic denigration of black women's bodies set the stage for hostility in intimate partner relationships. Not surprisingly, the National Black Women's Health Project reports that husbands, boyfriends, and former lovers are responsible for the single largest category of injuries to women.[60]

Beyond Victimized Men: Class and Gender Subordination

At first I just stood there, and then I tried to push the gun out of his hand, and we really fought over that gun. And I got really beat up, just because he wanted to teach me that I was a woman, and I should learn to never fight a man . . . for any reason. So I got beat up for stepping out of a "woman's place," whatever that is. But later on that day he was sorry, he was so sorry, he didn't mean to beat me up, he was just trying to teach me a lesson.

—Mildred Harris

Mildred Harris is a forty-six-year-old African American single mother of three who was piecing together work and welfare to support her family when she met Ross more than twenty years ago. She describes Ross as the man of her dreams—he was a handsome, intelligent, personable college student working on a degree in sociology/criminology. Besides that, he was well known in the neighborhood and always had money—a fact that Mildred was initially reluctant to connect with the sale of drugs. In the early stages of their relationship, they spent nearly all their time together, but, as Mildred recalls, he soon began to "do his own thing," leaving her feeling alone and neglected. Her very first episode of violence with Ross occurred because she objected to this treatment, but over time periodic, unexplained beatings became a way of life, including an episode where Mildred found herself struggling over a gun Ross was wielding.

Asked if she was terrified by the abuse and the use of a weapon, Mildred said, "It kind of scared me, but he was very manipulative, and he just made me feel it was OK . . . that I had made him do something he didn't really mean to do. You know, when you're growing up they say that women have their place and men have their place. I didn't know where my place was supposed to be." Somehow, she accepted his somewhat contradictory explanations of the abuse as his efforts to help her become a "strong woman" and to teach her not to "step outside her place."

Trips to the emergency room had become so frequent that the medical staff knew Mildred "by sight and by name," and they urged her to make a police report, but she always refused:

> They would always say, "When are you going to get tired of this? Can we call anybody? Do you want to make a police report?" But I would always say no.
>
> [Interviewer] Why?
>
> Because I thought I was in love. I thought he loved me. I thought if I was a strong enough person, I could make this relationship work. I really thought it was all my fault.

In many ways, Mildred's story of physical violence parallels that of many women who have been victimized by violence, including the fact that she was made to feel she had brought the abuse on herself by stepping out of her place. Mildred's devotion to Ross was based on what she saw as the mutual love they had for each other, and her misguided notion that self-change—in this case becoming "a strong enough person"—could alter Ross's behavior. In the meantime, Mildred suffered serious physical violence and emotional abuse; for example, she lost many of her teeth in one violent episode and continues to have myriad health issues related to the violence she experienced. Just as devastating was the fact that Ross introduced her to crack cocaine, an addiction that took her nearly fifteen years to overcome and one that has been linked to severe and extreme cases of domestic violence.[61]

Class and gender inequality are important contexts for explaining the abuse Mildred suffered; for example, living in poor neighborhoods devoid of economic opportunity makes one more tolerant of aggression, violence, and illegal activities and more apt to pursue an escape from hopelessness through drugs. Racial oppression also matters: It elevates the risk of poverty, fosters black cultural behaviors conducive to violence, places little value on black life, and makes it less likely that those victimized by violence will either pursue or receive justice. While reported rates of intimate violence and homicide have fallen over the past two decades, the racial gap in female victimization remains an important issue. Nearly all studies find higher rates of domestic and intimate partner violence among African American couples.[62] Bureau of Justice Statistics report that rates of intimate homicide at the hands of a spouse or ex-spouse were three times higher among black than white women.[63] A comparative study by Janice Joseph found that battered white women were more likely than their black counterparts to have called the police, gone to court, or used the services of a family counselor. Black women also endured more episodes of violence before leaving their partners and were more likely to have been hospitalized as a result of the abuse.

African American women tolerate abusive relationships for the many reasons feminists have frequently articulated: low self-esteem, emotional/economic dependence, and feelings of helplessness. Yet women are usually far from passive receivers of abuse; as a recent longitudinal study by Neil S. Jacobson and John M. Gottman points out, they are usually heroic in defending themselves while actively seeking changes in their partners. A national study also refutes the idea that women offer no resistance to violence: The majority (77 percent) fight back, try to escape, get help, or confront their offender in some way,[64] and, of course, many eventually leave relationships that are persistently violent. Research has found that African American women are more likely to fight their abusers physically and even lethally. R. L. Hampton and R. J. Gelles reported that while the overall rate of violence by black husbands toward their wives was high but fairly constant between 1975 and 1985, the rate of violence by black women toward men increased 33 percent.[65] More recently, black wives have been found to be twice as likely as whites to engage in severe violence against their partners.[66] Those who fight back, however, are sometimes less likely to define the situation as one of abuse[67] and they face a less sympathetic criminal justice system.[68]

Class and race inequality shape perceptions and thus responses of abused women in other ways as well. Poor black women, for example, offer more ideological support for patriarchy, despite the fact that they are stereotyped as insufficiently subordinate to male authority. African American women, as previously discussed, often accept part of the blame for the frustrations black men experience. Compared to white women, black women reportedly sympathize more with black husbands accused of domestic abuse.[69] And while the number of men and women who believe battering of intimate partners is sometimes justified has fallen significant over the past two decades, research shows that nonwhites and men are more approving of this than others.[70] And, at least among those in the armed services, African American men are much more likely than whites to endorse these views, regardless of their social standing.[71] Racial considerations also color other perceptions of sexual misconduct: For example, one study found that black women tend to ignore and dismiss the significance of the sexual harassment of black men;[72] even more alarmingly, another study found those who experience completed rapes are less likely than white women to perceive themselves as victims of "real rape."[73]

The highly publicized shortage of black "marriageable" men may make women more tolerant of abusive relationships. The male numerical advantage contributes to an overall cheapening of intimate relationships, where women are often expected to accept infidelity, violence, and other indignities. The results of focus group research with young black females (ages sixteen to twenty-four), conducted at the University of Pennsylvania, found that "abuse ranging from hair pulling to being dumped out of a car and left stranded in the middle of nowhere to being threatened with weapons" was common; some of these young women even "talked about guys who made them prove their love by having sex with [his] friends or allowing his friends to watch them have sex."[74]

Economic factors also matter. The abusiveness of black male celebrities may be overlooked because of their money and fame. For example, when basketball star Allen Iverson kicked his seminude wife out of their home and later went on an armed pursuit of her, a close associate assured the media that the marriage would survive, despite the adverse publicity.

Socially constructed images of African American women as paragons of strength and black men as the primary victims of racial oppression, misguided efforts to prioritize racial unity over gender justice, and scholarly work aimed at debunking racial myths all inadvertently obfuscate analyses of gendered violence among African Americans. Black women have often been complicit in the silence surrounding intimate partner violence, in some cases because they accept the legitimacy of patriarchal traditions, but usually for the sake of protecting themselves, their partners, and their families and preserving racial unity. However, high-profile episodes of alleged black male misconduct, coupled with sexist attempts

in the black community to shield them from the consequences of such behavior, have now fueled the activism of black women.

Breaking the Silence and Fighting Back

> I taught these brothers to spit acid at the sisters. . . . I taught the brothers
> that the sisters were standing in their way; in the way of the Messenger,
> in the way of progress, in the way of God Himself. I did these things,
> brother. I must undo them.
>
> —Malcolm X[75]

Although Mildred Harris has never really given up on trying to become the "right kind of woman" for Ross, she shot him four times during
a prolonged episode of abuse. It started with Ross trying to provoke her
to fight with a female friend he had brought home:

> I'd had a long day at work; lots of things went wrong. . . . So that night,
> everything just went crazy. He got home with Judy, and I said I was go-
> ing to bed. And he said, "No, I want you to sit down and talk with me."
> So he started to manipulate us, saying Judy said she could whip me, and
> asking me how I felt about that. I said I felt I could whip her—that I'd be
> less than a woman if I didn't feel that way. He went on and on trying to
> provoke a fight between us. . . . I finally got my purse and tried to go to
> bed. He came in the room and started slapping me around, saying he
> wasn't through "driving" me yet, so get back in the living room. He kept
> smacking me around until I was finally crying, getting more and more
> hysterical. He said, "What kind of woman are you, sitting here crying?"
> This went on and on—me running around the house crying, trying to es-
> cape his blows. I was working as a security guard, and finally grabbed
> the gun I had left on the table. I told him and Judy to just get out of the
> house, and he said, "Alright, you done really stepped out of line. I'm go-
> ing to take that gun from you and show you how it feels to be shot." I
> don't know exactly when I started shooting. I don't know if he stood up
> first and started toward me, or if I shot him while he was sitting on the
> couch. . . . I shot him four times. I could have sworn that Judy was com-
> ing toward me, so I shot her, too.

Judy sustained a relatively minor injury, and Ross was critically in-
jured and expected to die; however, he survived. Mildred was charged

with attempted murder but was acquitted on the grounds of self-defense. She had no intention of killing Ross, but, like other women, she fought back to protect herself. In some cases, fighting back has led to the incarceration of black women, who now compose nearly half of all female inmates.[76] A study by Maura O'Keefe compared women incarcerated from killing their abusers to those incarcerated for other offenses and found the former were less likely to have a prior criminal record but had experienced a long duration of severe and frequent violence and felt their lives were in danger.[77] Such studies show that women convicted of killing their partners often were acting in self-defense.

Women also call the police, leave and divorce their violent partners, seek protective orders, and use shelters for battered women; indeed, one researcher has contended that learned helplessness was more a result of inadequate legal responses and protection for women than a psychological state.[78] African American women have begun to organize collectively to defend themselves against assault at the hands of their male partners; in fact, social activism against male violence has international dimensions among black women and is also a vital aspect of many community grassroots organizations. In doing so, they challenge the behaviors of men in their communities and the theme of black male victimization. Aaronette White, for example, points to efforts by an activist group in St. Louis to counter disparaging remarks made about African American women after Mike Tyson was convicted of rape.[79] Gender tension in black communities was high, as one radio talk show host lamented, "Why are black women compromising Black men's upward mobility and embarrassing the black community?" After the trial ended, some community groups launched fund-raising efforts and letter-writing petitions to have the guilty verdict overturned or at least have the sentence softened. Black female activists, however, countered these efforts with a full-page ad in a local black newspaper protesting racism and sexism, and with community efforts to educate poor and often illiterate women about rape. Similarly, African American Women in Defense of Ourselves, a group composed mostly of scholars, denounced the defamation of Anita Hill, a black lawyer who accused Supreme Court nominee Clarence Thomas of sexual harassment. Challenging the idea that her accusation had brought ridicule to the entire black community, they issued a statement that noted, "[T]hroughout U.S. history, black women have been stereotyped as immoral, insatiable, perverse; the initiators of all sexual contacts—abusive or otherwise . . .

[and] as Anita Hill's experience demonstrates, black women who speak of these matters are not likely to be believed."[80]

While racial oppression continues to foster patterns of disregard for and violence against black women, new initiatives are curtailing and challenging these long-standing problems. A recent study by Dugan, Rosenfeld, and Nagin found that declining rates of marriage have also resulted in less intimate homicide, especially for African American men, by lessening intimate partner exposure. Women's greater economic independence and delayed marriage, perhaps giving them a greater opportunity to make careful choices, was also important.[81]

The black media and community are also paying more attention to the issue of gender violence. A recent article in *Ebony* magazine described domestic violence as "Black America's worst-kept secret," noting that "thousands of Sisters are punched, slapped, pushed, beaten or threatened by the men in their lives."[82]

Still, as Beth Richie contends, African Americans are far too scarce among those who are leading the effort to end gendered violence, noting that the "lack of women of color in leadership roles in antiviolence programs is startling and contrasts sharply with the rhetoric of inclusion, diversity, and commitment to antioppression work."[83] As Richie insists: "We've paid our dues, and black men must be held responsible for every injury they cause."[84]

Notes

1. J. Nelson (1997 :154).
2. M. E. Dyson (1993:177–78).
3. The U.S. Department of Justice reports that violent crime per 1,000 persons age twelve and over was 6.6 for whites and 13.0 for blacks in 2002. See www.ojp .usdoj.gov/bjs/glance/tables/racetab.htm.
4. L. E. Beattie and M. A. Shaughnessy (2000); L. Greenfield (1998).
5. M. Kimmel (2000).
6. C. E. Rasche (2001).
7. L. Greenfield (1998).
8. R. L. Hampton and R. J. Gelles (1994).
9. J. R. Feagin and K. D. McKinney (2003); D. S. Massey (2001).
10. D. S. Massey (2001).
11. M. E. Dyson (1993:176).

12. Quoted in T. Rose (1994:141).
13. J. R. Aulette (2002).
14. M. B. Zinn and D. S. Eitzen (2002).
15. D. Green (1999:29).
16. T. L. Bogger (1997:118).
17. D. G. White (1999:152).
18. N. F. Cott (2000).
19. N. F. Cott (2000:162).
20. D. L. Franklin (1997).
21. L. A. Schwalm (1997).
22. M. P. Johnson (1995:285).
23. R. J. Gelles (1997).
24. L. Dugan, R. Rosenfeld, and D. S. Nagin (2003).
25. L. Dugan et al.(2003).
26. M. L. Andersen (2000).
27. M. P. Johnson (1995:284).
28. N. Stephens and R. McDonald (2000).
29. P. W. Sharpes and J. Campbell (1999).
30. L. Greenfield (1998).
31. N. Stephens and R. McDonald (2000).
32. C. MacKinnon (1997:402–3).
33. L. Dugan et al. (2003).
34. B. E. Richie (2000).
35. D. Carbado (1998:342).
36. R. Connell (1995).
37. See E. Anderson (1999) for an excellent discussion of the issue.
38. H. R. Madhubuti (1990).
39. T. Rose (1994:151).
40. S. Spruell (2002).
41. T. Rose (2003:398).
42. T. Rose (2003:395).
43. T. Rose (2003:394).
44. P. Giddings (1995).
45. C. B. Booker (2000:197).
46. H. R. Madhubuti (2001).
47. B. E. Richie (1995:90).
48. J. Nelson (1997:159).
49. M. Mauer (1999).
50. K. Brown (1999).
51. Quoted in O. P. Adisa (1997:197).
52. Quoted in J. N. Shelton and T. M. Chavous (1999:598).
53. O. Patterson (1993:92).

54. Quoted in D. W. Carbado (1998:339).
55. L. Dugan et al. (2003).
56. E. J. Lawson and A. Thompson (1999:86).
57. Also see D. Carbado (1998).
58. Quoted in D. Carbado (1998:337).
59. B. E. Richie (1995 :401).
60. S. L. Taylor (2002).
61. R. J. Gelles (1997).
62. See R. Caetano, J. Schafer, and C. B. Cunradi (2001).
63. The U.S. Department of Justice/Bureau of Justice Statistics for 1999 reports that 0.96 of every 100,000 white women are murdered by spouses or ex-spouses, and 3.03 of every 100,000 black women. See www.ojp.usdoj.gov/bjs/homicide/tables/intgreltab.htm.
64. L. Greenfield (1998).
65. R. L. Hampton and R. J. Gelles (1994).
66. R. L. Hampton and R. J. Gelles (1994).
67. V. Bush (2002).
68. L. E. Beattie and M. A. Shaughnessy (2000).
69. L. M. Locke and C. L. Richman (1999).
70. F. E. Markowitz (2001).
71. J. H. Newby et al. (2000).
72. J. N. Shelton and T. M. Chavous (1999).
73. G. E. Wyatt (1992).
74. V. Bush (2002:192).
75. Quoted in B. Ransby and T. Matthews (1995).
76. M. Chesney-Lind (1997).
77. M. O'Keefe (1997).
78. M. O'Keefe (1997).
79. A. White (1999).
80. P. Giddings (1995:424).
81. L. Dugan et al. (2003).
82. K. Davis (2003).
83. B. Ritchie (2000:1137).
84. Quoted in C. E. Rasche (2001).

CHAPTER 8

Resolutions

Broadening the Vision of Liberation

There has never been a time in this nation when the bonds of love
between black women and men have not been under siege. If slavery
was not an institution powerful enough to destroy the ties that unite and
bind us, we have every reason to hope that bonds of love, of union,
and reunion, will be possible between us.

—bell hooks[1]

The personal and political lives of African Americans have been significantly structured by gender, although the saliency of racial oppression has
always made its analysis secondary and contested. Slavery, racism, and
economic exclusion curtailed the ability and willingness of many African
Americans to conform to mainstream gender ideologies that call for economically dominant men, dependent/submissive women, and marriage-
centered families. African American families were stigmatized as deviant
and unstable throughout the twentieth century, although history shows
that many responded to racial oppression by creating more equitable and
innovative family relationships. For example, middle-class black women
virtually pioneered the trend of combining family and employment,[2] and,
as I argue in the postmodern perspective offered in chapter 3, lower-class
women often resisted patriarchal marriages altogether in favor of female-
centered family structures. As is the case for many poor women today, the
benefits of marriage to economically marginal men simply did not compensate for their loss of autonomy or the more reliable extended family resources. From their stories, we learn that racial oppression did not lead to
a monolithic black family experience; rather, the histories of African

Americans during centuries of slavery and afterward are continuing to emerge, and it is important that this diversity is not suppressed by the illusion of racial uniformity.

Intraracial diversity based on color, class, and political divisions is deeply rooted in the historic experiences of black people, and, although these differences were suppressed during the civil rights movement, they have now become even more pronounced. Progress by black people has been enormous, and their growing visibility in prominent, high-level positions belies the notion that they are trapped in the stranglehold of racism. In addition to class polarization, black diversity has also increased due to a growing number of African and Caribbean immigrants and interracial people, many of whom claim a multiracial background. Political disunity among black people has thus become more evident and the path to future progress more complicated. While significant disparities between whites and blacks in income, wealth, and health still exist, there is contentious debate over whether these inequalities are the result of racism, overall economic decline, or the cultural behaviors of disadvantaged African Americans. Asserting that racism is dead is simply implausible, as there is compelling evidence of personal bigotry and disrespect directed at black people, racial injustice in the criminal justice system, segregation in crucial areas such as housing and education, and discrimination and stereotyping in employment. Insisting on the vigorous enforcement of equal opportunity laws is imperative, but so are emphasizing job training and economic development and creating a culture of achievement among low-income black people.

Understanding how the racial hierarchy is perpetuated in the absence of explicit policies of racial segregation and in an era of greater opportunity for black Americans is also crucial. Middle-class blacks are not exempt from racism,[3] but sharper economic divisions do mean that racial inequality is increasingly experienced in class-based ways. For example, while middle-class blacks often complain of racially insensitive comments, oversurveillance in public places, and policies that hinder their educational and career mobility, economically disadvantaged African Americans struggle with essential survival issues. Many live in dangerous neighborhoods where they are unable to protect their children from violence and drug abuse and where their children's futures are marred by deficient schools and inadequate access to health care. Americans continue to tolerate high rates of childhood poverty and deprivation, despite the extraordinary economic and social costs (e.g., poor health, illiteracy, incarceration, inadequate job skills) associated with growing up poor. Thus, analyzing racism in class context has become imperative if we are to understand how an increasingly diverse black population continues to be affected by race and how to develop policies and initiatives to address the multifaceted consequences of racial oppression. Interracial coalitions are also crucial to accomplishing the mission of racial justice, and a key challenge is creating settings where race and racism can be openly and honestly discussed. I see practices such as using the label "racist" so widely that it becomes almost meaningless, re-creating the black victim/ white oppressor scenario where the hope for change implicitly lies exclusively in the hands of white people, and evading discussions of how the maladaptive behaviors of many economically disadvantaged blacks foster inequality as obstacles to this process. The racial attitudes of white people have changed, with a significant majority endorsing equal opportunity (in theory), and openly racist remarks have become verboten—at least in public and most interracial settings. And, while it is eye-opening to understand how white privilege and whiteness are naturalized, characterizing white or Western society as inherently racist and exploitative is alienating and will eventually become more contested. Conservative social critic David Horowitz decries the fact that academic programs devoted to studying racial minorities and women celebrate their achievements, while "white studies" are designed to denigrate white people.[4] Regardless of the merit of his argument, it will increasingly resonate with more white Americans, especially in an era where global economic forces are curtailing their wealth and opportunities. In addition to generating racial hostilities, it will also undercut the prospect of creating interracial coalitions.

I also see a need for much more introspection by African Americans on how their own behaviors and attitudes are shaped by classism and racism. Black people from diverse social class backgrounds have always been involved in doing antiracism work, especially since they recognized that their fates were intertwined but have rarely been able to work across class lines.[5] The tradition of racial uplift remains in communities and churches, but building coalitions that cross class boundaries has become even more difficult. Middle-class blacks are increasingly estranged from, critical of, and embarrassed by street-savvy, disrespectful, lower-class blacks, although often quick to claim that whites who stereotype them are racist. While ending white racist attitudes is a laudable goal, it is also the case that African Americans malign each other with similar racial stereotypes, as Debra Dickerson generously documents in her book *The End of Blackness*. Moreover, given that racial inequality and racism are so intricately connected, it is often unclear whether teaching people to think less poorly of African Americans deserves primary attention.

While racism remains a significant problem, there is also a need to rethink ideologies, family practices, and traditions that emerged out of racial oppression and are now enshrined as part of the "black culture." One legacy of revisionist scholarship has been its challenge to the deviancy discourse on black families, but another has been silencing almost any critical analysis of the harmful family patterns caused by poverty and oppression. Contesting racial stigma has often left us inadvertently romanticizing behaviors that once contributed to our survival but are now found disproportionately among the poor and are inimical to their well-being. The revisionist work of the civil rights era heralded the strengths of black families, including those headed by single mothers, as generations of black people have grown up in such families and gone on to live successful, productive lives. The fact that single-mother families are remarkably diverse in their resources, support networks, and the ability to rear children warrants rejecting the notion that they are inherently dysfunctional. But despite this diversity, most single black mothers are poor, increasingly socially isolated, and in many cases unable to protect their children from myriad threats to their safety, development, and well-being.

At a recent prayer vigil for my twenty-year-old great-nephew, who was shot to death in the neighborhood where he grew up, several speakers urged those present to "take back their communities." This has become a common theme in black communities plagued by high rates of violence, yet I doubted the efficacy of the strategies they offered for doing so (e.g., talking to the children in the neighborhood, calling the police on drug dealers). The problem seemed much more complex to me, such as why families, schools, and communities are individually and collectively unable to instill in so many young people a sense of hope, aspirations for success, or even respect for the sanctity of life. The violence often starts in families, where children are exposed to what bell hooks calls "poisonous parenting" practices such as being described as "bad" and liberally spanked.[6] Many claim that spanking is part of the black culture or necessary to teach children to survive in dangerous neighborhoods, creating a quandary for social workers who try to balance the protection of children with sensitivity to diverse cultural norms. The hitting and denigrating of black children in many families comprise one dimension of a nexus of violence that is reinforced in schools and communities.

There is also a need to draw out the implications of traditions such as the black cultural ethos of motherhood, which heralds black women's mothering work but often does not pay much attention to the sexual exploitation of adolescent girls or poor mothers' abysmal lack of reproductive rights, birth control, prenatal health care, and support in raising their children. Most single mothers would like the support of their male partners, and, despite the claim of there being an adequate supply of male role models in black communities, there is a palpable longing among African American children for their fathers. Too often, emphasizing strong black mothers and their ability to rear children either single-handedly or in conjunction with other females has eclipsed the importance of black fathers and ignored nonbiological "other fathers"[7] who do a lot to help single mothers raise their children. Many black fathers today are meeting the challenge of being involved and emotionally connected with their children, and studies show that children who grow up with families consisting of both of their biological parents fare better than those who do not.[8]

Revisioning Gender?

The matriarch concept, embracing the clichéd "female castrator," is, in the last instance, an open weapon of ideological warfare.

—Angela Davis[9]

Gender lies at the heart of the troubles encountered by black men and women in their relationships. Although African American scholars criticized the idea of matriarchal women and emasculated men advanced during the civil rights era, it remains the centerpiece of the gender dilemma now being debated in multiple forums. Many African Americans have formed strong, loving relationships despite the forces of racial oppression, but the general inability of others to conform to the dominant gender ideologies and societal codes of masculinity and femininity has left men and women stigmatized and disgruntled with each other. Black women have defined themselves as strong, sassy, independent women, and, while they have been applauded for these traits when it comes to employment and raising children, they have been criticized for them in their relationships with men. A key stereotype of black women has been that of "Sapphire," the dominant black woman recently described by a black therapist as being an "insecure, cynical, self-centered" woman who "only finds strength in tearing down her mate."[10] Thus, the misguided notion that weaker black women are needed to create stronger black men remains prevalent.

From the marriage campaign that followed emancipation to the welfare policies of the 1990s, African Americans have been urged to get and stay married, yet their resolve to do so seems to have eroded over the twentieth century. I have argued that the traditional marriage contract, with its emphasis on property, male headship, rigid gender roles, and legitimacy of children, has essentially been at odds with the race and class position of black people. While middle-class African Americans have a long tradition of marriage and of embracing enough flexibility in their gender expectations to enable women to combine family, work, and social activism,[11] marriage's gender bargain has always been less tenable to the poor. The notion of dominant husbands and deferent wives rests largely on the ability of men to gain power and authority in families based on their roles as providers, and holds little appeal for economically independent women. As is now seen in mainstream society, women will rarely tolerate such inequities when their own wage-earning abilities increase, especially when those of their male partners wane.

African Americans have historically lived this reality, and it has diminished both their incentive to marry and the success of their marriages. Lower- and working-class black women today highly idealize marriage and even patriarchal families, but most refuse to sacrifice their autonomy for marriage to marginally or unemployed men or ones they cannot trust.[12] They opt to raise their children alone or with the support of other family members, but they also often disparage black men for their meager earnings potential, unfaithfulness, and unwillingness to engage in family life. Black men have often responded to their tenuous grasp on masculinity and loss of respect in their families by embracing dysfunctional expressions of manhood, such as violence, cool pose, and oppositional identities, all of which reinforce stereotypes of them as dangerous.

Such behaviors not only make them ill suited for intimate relationships but all too often perpetrators of gendered violence. African American women have become much more vocal about the abuse they experience at the hands of black men, and national and community efforts to end such violence must continue.

But can African Americans resolve the gender tensions that beset them? In *Single Mom*, Omar Tyree shares a hopeful saga of healing in a story where love transcends class barriers. The black women in his novel are all single mothers but are neither valiantly strong nor the heads of weak, pathological families. Denise Stewart, the lead character, makes all the typical mistakes of young girls who grow up with few dreams beyond finding true love, and ends up the mother of two sons fathered by different men. Both fathers abandon her and their children—one is simply immature and has nothing to offer, while the other is in selfish pursuit of a better life. But Denise eventually lands on her feet: She gets a college education and becomes a highly paid financial expert. The storyline focuses on her budding romance with a gorgeous, sensitive, working-class man, Dennis Brockenborough, who is a truck driver by occupation. Dennis takes some ribbing from his pals for his involvement with a "corporate sista," but the story suggests that black women in search of good men might need to look beyond class factors. Yet "marrying down" is not as simple as it sounds. Money is important, but even more important to the success of relationships may be the educational, values, and lifestyle differences it connotes. Rather than suggesting black women should be less picky, a better solution is clearly removing the obstacles African American men face in obtaining a good education and career.

Tyree's book also focuses on the growing reflectiveness among African American men on their need to be there—economically, emotionally, and physically—for their families. One of the main characters in the novel drew his inspiration to become a better father from the 1995 Million Man March, spearheaded by the controversial African American Muslim leader, Minister Louis Farrakhan. Described as the only time in history a group has ever marched in protest of itself, male participants pledged never to abuse their wives and children and to eliminate words such as *bitch* from their vocabularies.[13] The attendance by thousands of people demonstrated how strongly the call for greater responsibility by African American men resonated with those in the black community. Yet black women were excluded from significant participation in the march, making it clear that this was about black men and reinforcing the notion that men have been the primary victims of racism. Cultural critic Michael Dyson, reflecting on the criticism he received from many black feminist friends for participating in the march, wrote of the tension that still faces black men and women this way:

> As I listened, I became painfully aware, for the umpteenth time, of how messy, how maddeningly complex, are the relations between black men and black women. Why is it so difficult for brothers to hear the suffering of black women, to acknowledge their hurts, to embrace them as co-sufferers in a world where black skin and black bodies have been under extraordinary attack? Why is it so difficult for brothers to heal, or at least help relieve, the bitter traumas of spirit and flesh that black women face, often at the end of a black man's hands or words? And why is it so difficult for sisters to see that because we live in a patriarchal society, black men represent a special challenge to white male power?[14]

In addition to excluding black women, the patriarchal terms of the renewed commitment were also glaring: The call for greater responsibility and leadership by black men was largely informed by religious views that endorse secondary roles for women. Farrakan, for example, explained: "Allah has given man a female whose duty by nature is to ease the burden of man, to console, to give peace, and quiet of mind."[15] Insisting on the literal interpretation and application of ancient Scriptures legitimates patriarchy, although it is often repackaged in benign wrappings. The Promise Keepers Movement, for example, has been especially adept at offering a compassionate brand of masculinity: They contend that there is complete equality between men and women—God simply ordained different positions for them in society. Racial healing has also been a focus of this movement. It has explicitly and successfully reached out to African American men, often sponsoring their attendance at conferences. Tony Evans, one of the most prominent African American members of the movement, recently instructed black men, "I'm not suggesting that you *ask* for your role back, I'm urging you to *take it back.* . . . There can be no compromise here. If you're going to lead, you must lead. Be sensitive, listen. Treat the lady gently and lovingly. But *lead.*"[16]

The call for greater black male leadership dates back to emancipation and was revived during the civil rights era—but even if they are willing to lead, will black women "follow"? The religiosity of African Americans makes compassionate patriarchy appealing to many, but it also resonates with their growing interest in strengthening families. Critiquing gender inequities such as the unequal distribution of housework seems like a luxury to those concerned about the absence of fathers in the lives of their children, and the struggles of many single mothers have taught them that being in charge is more exhausting than empowering. For many, the threat of being lonely and raising children without help looms larger than the fear of falling into the hands of a black "patriarch" especially one who is family and spiritually oriented. The truth is that while poor black women are wary of men who they believe will exploit them and contribute meagerly to the family, they are not adverse to the ideology of patriarchal families, which for most simply means having a responsible man in the house.

Espousing ideological support for patriarchy or gender equality in families probably matters less than how those in intimate relationships actually live their lives. Most committed couples are likely to pull together in performing domestic and labor market work, although there will undoubtedly be strains and negotiations. And no matter how attractive patriarchal families may appear to those who have never lived in them, it is unlikely that women of any class background will long endure marital unions in which they are silenced, overruled by male authority, unable to pursue their own interests, or abused. Expressing ideological acceptance of gender equality, as I have shown in chapter 6, usually comes with education and class mobility. Relatively egalitarian marital relationships are becoming the norm for middle-class (and especially young) black couples; fathers are quite involved in the lives of their children and strongly support teaching their children the value of equality between men and women. Blatant forms of male domination have always undercut the ability to create genuinely loving and supportive relationships, and they will increasingly give way to a variety of more equitable relationships.

Notes

1. b. hooks (2001:154).
2. B. Landry (2000).
3. J. R. Feagin and M. P. Sikes (1994); L. W. Myers (2002).
4. D. Fears (2003).
5. D. Gray White (1999); L. O. Graham (1999).

6. b. hooks (2004).
7. L. Haney and M. March (2003).
8. S. McLanahan and D. Schwartz (2002).
9. A. Davis (1995:216).
10. Ronn Elmore, quoted in Z. Hughes (2003:102).
11. B. Landry (2000).
12. L. Haney and M. March (2003).
13. For example, see C. B. Booker (2000).
14. M. E. Dyson (1997:199).
15. Quoted in C. B. Booker (2000:221).
16. Quoted in M. Messner (1997:32).

My basic orientation to research is grounded in the tradition of symbolic interactionism, which, in the words of Herbert Blumer, urges investigators to "get inside of the defining process of the actor in order to understand his action."[1] Closely associated are approaches referred to as interpretive and/or social constructionist, which seek to understand realities and meanings as socially created through human interaction, most often through the symbols of language. Thus, the material used in this book draws largely from qualitative and ethnographic data—mostly interviews and observations, but to a lesser extent biographies and themes from movies and novels.

Much of the interview data cited in this study were collected over the past fifteen years in the process of two previous studies I conducted, both of which reflect my interest in issues of family, gender, and child rearing. The first was a study of how mothers managed the care of children who had been diagnosed with sickle cell disease. In addition to wanting to explore family caregiving in African American families, I was also interested in the politics and racial myths surrounding what many understood as a "black disease" that had been largely ignored prior to the civil rights movement. I interviewed several health care and social service professionals associated with a regional health care clinic and thirty-two African American mothers who were providing care for their chronically ill children, discussing topics that ranged from how they managed medical emergencies to how the disease affected their reproductive decisions and their relationships with their male partners.

One of the interesting findings from this work, *Managing Sickle Disease in Low-Income Families*,[2] was that mothers of sons with sickle cell disease saw their children as sicker than those who had daughters, and they were more invested in elaborate, time-consuming care work. As I discuss briefly in chapter 5 of the current work, this observation peaked my interest in learning more about the gender socialization of African American children. Given the emphasis among liberal feminists and others endorsing the sex roles approach to understanding gender inequality, it was surprising that so few scholars had included black families in their research.

My interest in studying how the sex of the child influenced the child-rearing work of black parents led to a second project that culminated in the publication of *African American Children: Socialization and Development in Families.*[3] Although my initial focus was gender, the need to use an intersectionality approach that included race and class soon became evident. I sent surveys to elementary schools in the greater Kansas City area and received responses from 729 parents—525 were African American, and 204 were white. This sample allowed me to examine the impact of parents' race and class positions on a wide range of family and child-rearing issues (e.g., the values parents were teaching their children, their attitudes about how race and gender might affect their children's future, their views on teaching children gender equality, and how gender was organized in their own families). In addition, I conducted thirty-five in-depth interviews with black parents (twenty-five mothers and ten fathers), and some of that data has been used in the current study.

In addition to these two data sets, I conducted several additional interviews explicitly for the purpose of this study, including the interviews in chapter 4 (on intimacy) with Delia Williams and the one in chapter 6 (on violence) with Mildred Harris. My thinking on the history of African American families is also informed by my own genealogical interests, which have consisted of archival research and interviews with older members of my own and my husband's family. Most migrated northward from Arkansas or Kentucky during the turn of the twentieth century, and these interviews helped me understand the tremendous diversity of slaves, especially in terms of their marriage patterns.

Notes

1. H. Blumer (1969:16).
2. S. A. Hill (1994).
3. S. A. Hill (1999).

BIBLIOGRAPHY

Adisa, O. P. 1997. "Undeclared war: African-American women writers explicating rape." Pp. 194–208 in *Gender Violence: Interdisciplinary Perspectives*, ed. L. L. O'Toole and J. R. Schiffman. New York: New York University Press.

Adler, E. 2002. "Shame lingers decades after Missourian drove eugenics movement." *Kansas City Star*, April 27, pp. A1, A8.

Amato, P. R. 2000. "Diversity within single-parent families." In *Handbook of Family Diversity*, ed. D. H. Demo, K. R. Allen, and M. A. Fine. New York: Oxford University Press.

Amato, P. R., D. R. Johnson, A. Booth, and S. J. Rogers. 2003. "Continuity and change in marital quality between 1980 and 2000." *Journal of Marriage and the Family* 65:1–22.

Andersen, M. L. 2000. *Thinking about Women*. Boston: Allyn & Bacon.

Anderson, E. 1989. "Sex codes and family life among poor inner-city youths." *Annals of the American Association of Political and Social Sciences* 501:59–78.

———. 1990. *Streetwise: Race, Class, and Change in an Urban Community*. Chicago: University of Chicago Press.

———. 1999. *Code of the Street: Decency, Violence, and the Moral Life of the Inner City*. New York: Norton.

Arendell, T. 2000. "Conceiving and investigating motherhood: The decade's scholarship." *Journal of Marriage and the Family* 62:1192–1207.

Arriaga, X. B., and S. Oskamp. 1999. "Nature, correlates, and consequences of violence in intimate relationships." Pp. 1–16 in *Violence in Intimate Relationships*, ed. X. B. Arriaga and S. Oskamp. Thousand Oaks, Calif.: Sage.

Asante, M. K. 1987. *The Afrocentric Idea*. Philadelphia: Temple University Press.

———. 1981. "Black male–female relationships: An Afrocentric context." In *Black Men*, ed. L. E. Gary. Beverly Hills, Calif.: Sage.

Assensoh, A. B. 2000. "Conflict or cooperation? Africans and African Americans in multiracial America." Pp. 113–32 in *Black and Multiracial Politics in America*, ed. Y. Alex-Assensoh and L. J. Hanks. New York: New York University Press.

Attiyeh, J. 2002. "Black scholar renounces conservative 'crown.'" *Christian Science Monitor*, p. 18

Aulette, J. R. 2002. *Changing American Families*. Boston: Allyn & Bacon.

Austin, R. L., and H. H. Dodge. 1992. "Despair, distrust and dissatisfaction among blacks and women, 1973–1987." *Sociological Quarterly* 33:579–98.

Avellar, S., and P. J. Smock. 2003. "Has the price of motherhood declined over time? A cross-cohort comparison of the motherhood wage penalty." *Journal of Marriage and the Family* 65:597–607.

Axinn, W. G., J. S. Barber, and A. Thornton. 1998. "The long-term impact of parents' childbearing decisions on children's self-esteem." *Demography* 35:435–43.

Axtman, K. 2002. "A flood of parolees hits streets." *Christian Science Monitor*, December 2, pp. 1, 3.

Ball, R. E., and L. Robbins. 1986. "Marital status and life satisfaction among black Americans." *Journal of Marriage and the Family* 48:389–94.

Barbee, E. L., and M. Little. 1993. Health, social class and African American women. Pp. 182–202 in *Theorizing Black Feminisms: The Visionary Paradigm of Black Women*, ed. S. M. James and A. P. A. Busia. New York: Routledge.

Basu, A. (Ed.). 1995. *The Challenge of Local Feminisms: Women's Movements in Global Perspectives*. Boulder, Colo.: Westview.

Battle, J., and M. Bennett. 2000. "Research on lesbian and gay populations within the African American community: What we have learned." *African American Research Perspectives* 6:35–47.

Beale, F. 1970. "Double jeopardy: To be black and female." Pp. 90–100 in *The Black Woman: An Anthology*, ed. T. Cade. New York: Signet.

Beattie, L. E., and M. A. Shaughnessy. 2000. *Sisters in Pain: Battered Women Fight Back*. Lexington: University of Kentucky Press.

Belanger, K. 2002. "Examination of racial imbalance for children in foster care: Implications for training." *Journal of Health and Social Policy* 15:163–76.

Bell, D. 2001. "The sexual diversion: The black man/black woman debate in context." Pp. 168–76 in *Traps: African American Men on Gender and Sexuality*, ed. B. Guy-Sheftall and R. P. Byrd. Bloomington: Indiana University Press.

Berg, A. 2002. *Mothering the Race: Women's Narratives of Reproduction, 1890–1930*. Urbana: University of Illinois Press.

Berkeley, K. C. 1985. "'Colored ladies also contributed': Black women's activities from benevolence to social welfare, 1866–1896." Pp. 181–203 in *The Web of Southern Social Relations*, ed. W. Fraser, R. F. Saunders, and J. Wakelyn. Athens: University of Georgia Press.

Bernard, J. 1966. *Marriage and Family among Negroes*. Englewood Cliffs, N.J.: Prentice Hall.

Bernstein, N. 2002. "Side effect of welfare law: The no-parent family." *New York Times*, July 29.

Billingsley, A. 1968. *Black Families in White America*. Englewood Cliffs, N.J.: Prentice Hall.

———. 1992. *Climbing Jacob's Ladder: The Enduring Legacy of African-American Families*. New York: Simon & Schuster.

Blackwell, D. L., and D. T. Lichter. 2000. "Mate selection among married and cohabiting couples." *Journal of Family Issues* 21:275–302.

Blassingame, J. W. 1972. *The Slave Community: Plantation Life in the Antebellum South*. New York: Oxford University Press.

Blauner, B. 2001. *Still the Big News: Racial Oppression in America.* Philadelphia: Temple University Press.

Blee, K. M., and A. R. Tickamyer. 1995. "Racial differences in men's attitudes about women's gender roles." *Journal of Marriage and the Family* 57:21–30.

Block, J. H. 1983. "Differential premises arising from differential socialization of the sexes: Some conjectures." *Child Development* 54:1334–54.

Blumer, H. 1969. *Symbolic Interactionism: Perspective and Method.* Englewood Cliffs, N.J.: Prentice Hall.

Bobel, C. 2002. *The Paradox of Natural Mothering.* Philadelphia: Temple University Press.

Bobo, L., J. R. Kluegel, and R. A. Smith. 1997. "Laissez-faire racism: The crystallization of a kinder, gentler, antiblack ideology." Pp. 15–42 in *Racial Attitudes in the 1990s: Continuity and Change,* ed. S. A. Tuch and J. K. Martin. Westport, Conn.: Praeger.

Bobo, L. 2000. "Race and beliefs about affirmative action: Assessing the effects of interests, group threat, ideology, and racism." Pp. 137–64 in *Racialized Politics: The Debate about Racism in America,* ed. D. O. Sears, J. Sidanius, and L. Bobo. Chicago: University of Chicago Press.

Bogger, T. L. 1997. *Free Blacks in Norfolk, Virginia 1790–1860: The Darker Side of Freedom.* Charlottesville: University Press of Virginia.

Bograd, M. 1999. "Strengthening domestic violence theories: Intersections of race, class, sexual orientation, and gender." *Journal of Marital and Family Therapy* 25:275–89.

Bonilla-Silva, E. 2001. *White Supremacy and Racism in the Post–Civil Rights Era.* Boulder, Colo.: Lynne Rienner.

Booker, C. B. 2000. *"I Will Wear No Chain!" A Social History of African American Males.* Westport, Conn.: Praeger.

Bound, J., and L. Dresser. 1999. "Losing ground: The erosion of the relative earnings of African American women during the 1980s." Pp. 61–104 in *Latinas and African American Women at Work: Race, Gender, and Economic Inequality,* ed. Irene Browne. New York: Russell Sage Foundation.

Bowman, P. J., and C. Howard. 1985. "Race-related socialization, motivation, and academic achievement: A study of black youths in three-generation families." *Journal of the American Academy of Child Psychiatry* 24:134–41.

Boyd, J. A. 1997. *Embracing the Fire: Sisters Talk about Sex and Relationships.* New York: Plume.

Boykin, A. W., and F. D. Toms. 1985. "Black child socialization: A conceptual framework." Pp. 33–52 in *Black Children: Social, Educational and Parental Environments,* ed. H. P. McAdoo and J. L. McAdoo. Beverly Hills, Calif.: Sage.

Boykin, K. 2004. "Your blues ain't like mine: Blacks and gay marriage." *Crisis* 111:23–25.

Brewer, R. M. 1988. "Black women in poverty: Some comments on female-headed families." *Signs: Journal of Women in Culture and Society* 13:331–39.

——. 1993. "Theorizing race, class, and gender: The new scholarship of black feminist intellectuals and Black women's labor." Pp. 13–30 in *Theorizing Black Feminisms: The Visionary Pragmatism of Black Women*, ed. S. M. James and A. P. A. Busia. London: Routledge.

——. 1995. "Gender, poverty, culture, and economy: Theorizing female-led families." Pp. 164–78 in *African American Single Mothers: Understanding Their Lives and Families*, ed. B. J. Dickerson. Thousand Oaks, Calif.: Sage.

Brewster, K. L. 1994. "Race differences in sexual activity among adolescent women: The role of neighborhood characteristics." *American Sociological Review* 59:408–24.

Brewster, K. L., and I. Padavic. 2002. "No more kin care? Changes in black mothers' reliance on relatives for child care, 1977–1994." *Gender & Society* 16:546–63.

Bridges, J. S., and A. M. Orza. 1996. "Black and White employed mothers' role experience." *Sex Roles* 35:337–85.

Broman, C. 1988. "Satisfaction among blacks: The significance of marriage and parenthood." *Journal of Marriage and the Family* 50:45–51.

Brown, K. 1999. "The social construction of a rape victim." Pp. 147–58 in *Black Men on Race, Gender, and Sexuality: A Critical Reader*, ed. D. W. Carbado. New York: New York University Press.

Brown, K. M. 1996. *Good Wives, Nasty Wenches, and Anxious Patriarchs: Gender, Race, and Power in Colonial Virginia.* Chapel Hill: University of North Carolina Press.

Brown, M., M. Carnoy, E. Currie, T. Duster, D. B. Oppenheimer, M. Shultz, and D. Wellman. 2003. *Whitewashing Race: The Myth of a Color-Blind Society.* Berkeley: University of California Press.

Browne, I., and I. Kennelly. 1995. "Stereotypes and realities: Images of black women in the labor market." Chap. 9 in *Latinas and African American Women at Work: Race, Gender, and Economic Inequality*, ed. I. Browne. New York: Russell Sage Foundation.

Browne, I. 2000. "Opportunities lost? Race, industrial restructuring, and employment among young women heading households." *Social Forces* 78:907–29.

Bruce, M. A. 2000. "Inequality and delinquency: Sorting out some class and race effects." *Race & Society* 2:133–48.

——. 2003. "Contextual complexity and violent delinquency among black and white males." Discussion Paper No. 1273-03. Madison, Wisc.: Institute for Research on Poverty.

Bumpass, L., and S. McLanahan. 1989. "Unmarried motherhood: Recent trends, composition, and black–white differences." *Demography* 26:279–87.

Burgess, N. J. 1994. "Gender roles revisited: The development of the 'women's place' among African American women in the United States." *Journal of Black Studies* 24:391–401.

Burns, M. 1995. "A sexual time bomb: Declining fertility rate of the black middle class." *Ebony* 50:74–78.

Bush, V. 2002. "A thin line between love and hate." *Essence* 33:192–98.

Bush-Baskette, S. R. 1998. "The war on drugs as a war against black women." Pp. 113–29 in *Crime Control and Women: Feminist Implications of Criminal Justice Policy*, ed. S. L. Miller. Thousand Oaks, Calif.: Sage.

Butterfield, F. 1995. *All God's Children: The Bosket Family and the American Tradition of Violence*. New York: Knopf.

Caetano, R., J. Schafer, and C. B. Cunradi. 2001. "Alcohol-related intimate partner violence among white, black, and Hispanic couples in the United States." *Alcohol Research and Health* 25:58–65.

Campbell, K. 2002. "Can marriage be taught? The state of matrimony." *Christian Science Monitor*, pp. 1, 9.

Cancio, A. S., T. David Evans, and D. J. Maume Jr. 1996. "Reconsidering the declining significance of race: Racial differences in early career wages." *American Sociological Review* 61:541–56.

Carbado, D. W. 1998. "Black male racial victimhood." *Callaloo* 21:337–61.

———. 1999a. "The construction of O. J. Simpson as a racial victim." Pp. 159–93 in *Black Men on Race, Gender, and Sexuality: A Critical Reader*, ed. D. W. Carbado. New York: New York University Press.

———. 1999b. "Introduction: Where and when black men enter." In *Black Men on Race, Gender, and Sexuality: A Reader*, ed. D. W. Carbado. New York: New York University Press.

———. 2000. "Motherhood and work in cultural context: One woman's patriarchal bargain." Pp. 115–28 in *Global Critical Race Feminism: An International Reader*, ed. A. K. Wing. New York: New York University Press.

Carby, H. V. 1987. *Reconstructing Womanhood: The Emergence of the Afro-American Woman Novelist*. New York: Oxford University Press.

———. 1995. "Policing the black woman's body in an urban context." Pp. 115–32 in *Identities*, ed. K. A. Appiah and H. L. Gates. Chicago: University of Chicago Press.

Carolan, M. T., and K. R. Allen. 1999. "Commitments and constraints to intimacy for African American couples at midlife." *Journal of Family Issues* 20:3–24.

Carr, J. G., F. D. Gilroy, and M. F. Sherman. 1996. "Silencing the self and depression among women." *Psychology of Women Quarterly* 20:375–92.

Ceballo, R. 1999. "The only black woman walking the face of the earth who can't have a baby: Two women's stories." Pp. 3–19 in *Women's Untold Stories*, ed. M. Romero and A. Stewart. New York: Routledge.

Chesney-Lind, M. 1997. *The Female Offender: Girls, Women, and Crime*. Thousand Oaks, Calif.: Sage.

"Children of young disadvantaged women are unlikely to receive consistent support from their fathers." 1998. *Family Planning Perspectives* 30:291–92.

Chodorow, N. 1978. *The Reproduction of Mothering: Psychoanalysis and the Sociology of Gender*. Berkeley: University of California Press.

Christain, B. 1994. "An angle of seeing: Motherhood in Buchi Emecheta's *Joys of Motherhood* and Alice Walker's *Meridian*." Pp. 95–119 in *Mothering: Ideology, Experience, and Agency*, ed. E. N. Glenn, G. Chang, and L. R. Forcey. New York: Routledge.

Christopher, F. S., and S. Sprecher. 2000. "Sexuality in marriage, dating, and other relationships: A decade review." *Journal of Marriage and the Family* 62:999–1017.

Clark-Lewis, E. 1987. "'This work had a end': African-American domestic workers in Washington, D.C., 1910–1940." Pp. 196–212 in *"To Toil the Livelong Day": America's Women at Work, 1780–1980*, ed. C. Groneman and M. B. Norton. Ithaca, N.Y.: Cornell University Press.

Clinton, C. 1985. "Caught in the web of the big house: Women and slavery." Pp. 19–34 in *The Web of Southern Social Relations: Women, Family and Education*, ed. W. Fraser, R. F. Saunders, and J. Wakelyn. Athens: University of Georgia Press.

Collins, C. F. 1996. "Commentary on the health and social status of African-American women." Pp. 1–13 in *African-American Women's Health and Social Issues*, ed. C. F. Collins. Westport, Conn.: Auburn House.

Collins, P. H. 1990. *Black Feminist Thought: Knowledge, Consciousness, and the Politics of Empowerment*. Boston: Unwin Hyman.

———. 1994. "Shifting the center: Race, class, and feminist theorizing about motherhood." Pp. 45–66 in *Mothering: Ideology, Experience, and Agency*, ed. E. N. Glenn, G. Chang, and L. R. Forcey. New York: Routledge.

———. 1997. "Pornography and black women's bodies." Pp. 395–413 in *Gender Violence: Interdisciplinary Perspectives*, ed. L. L. O'Toole and J. R. Schiffman. New York: New York University Press.

———. 1998. *Fighting Words: Black Women and the Search for Justice*. Minneapolis: University of Minnesota Press.

———. 1999. "Moving beyond gender: Intersectionality and scientific knowledge." Pp. 261–84 in *Revisioning Gender*, ed. M. M. Ferree, J. Lorber, and B. B. Hess. Thousand Oaks, Calif.: Sage.

Collins, S. M. 1997. *Black Corporate Executives: The Making and Breaking of a Black Middle Class*. Philadelphia: Temple University Press.

Collins, L. 2002. "Critical race theory: Themes, perspectives, and directions." Pp. 154–68 in *Black Cultures and Race Relations*, ed. J. L. Conyers. Chicago: Burnham.

Coltrane, S. 1998. *Gender and Families*. Thousand Oaks, Calif.: Sage.

Connell, R. W. 1987. *Gender and Power*. Stanford, Calif.: Stanford University Press.

———. 1995. *Masculinities*. Berkeley, Calif.: University of California Press.

Connelly, C. D., R. R. Newton, J. Landsverk, and G. A. Aarons. 2000. "Assessment of intimate partner violence among high-risk postpartum mothers." *Women & Health* 31:21–37.

Connerly, W. 2001. "Republicans make a rotten peace with race preferences." *National Review* 53:42–44.

Cose, E. 1993. *The Rage of the Privileged Class.* New York: HarperCollins.

——. 1995. *A Man's World: How Real Is Male Privilege and How High Is Its Price.* New York: HarperCollins.

——. 2002. "Rethinking black leadership." *Newsweek*, January 28, pp. 42–49.

Cott, N. F. 2000. *Public Vows: A History of Marriage and the Nation.* Boston: Harvard University Press.

Crenshaw, K. W. 1997. "Beyond racism and misogyny: Black feminism and 2 Live Crew." Pp. 549–68 in *Women Transforming Politics: An Alternative Reader,* ed. C. J. Cohen, K. B. Jones, and J. C. Tronto. New York: New York University Press.

Crittendon, A. 2001. *The Price of Motherhood: Why the Most Important Job in the World Is Still the Least Valued.* New York: Metropolitan.

Cross, T., and R. B. Slater. 1998. Marshalling Black Voting Power to Increase African-American Opportunities in Higher Education. *Journal of Blacks in Higher Education* 21 (Autumn):94–99

Cross, W. E. Jr. 2003. "Tracing the historical origins of youth delinquency and violence: Myths and realities about black culture." *Journal of Social Issues* 59:67–82.

Crouter, A. C., S. M. McHale, and W. T. Bartko. 1993. "Gender as an organizing feature in parent–child relationships." *Journal of Social Issues* 49:161–74.

Dabel, J. E. 2002. "African American women and household composition in New York City, 1827–1877." Pp. 60–72 in *Black Cultures and Race Relations,* ed. J. L. Conyers Jr. Chicago: Burnham.

Daniels, S. 1996. "Reproductive rights: Who speaks for African-American women?" Pp. 187–97 in *African-American Women's Health and Social Issues,* ed. Catherine Fisher Collins. Westport, Conn.: Auburn House.

Datcher, M. 2001. *Raising Fences: A Black Man's Love Story.* New York: Riverhead Books.

Davidson, J. 1997. "Caged cargo." *Emerge* (October):36–46.

Davis, A. Y. 1981. *Women, Race, and Class.* New York: Random House.

——. 1993. "Outcast mothers and surrogates: Racism and reproductive politics in the nineties." Pp. 355–66 in *American Feminist Thought at Century's End: A Reader,* ed. L. S. Kauffman. Cambridge, Mass.: Blackwell.

——.1995. "Reflections on the black woman's role in the community of slaves." Pp. 200–18 in *Words of Fire: An Anthology of African-American Feminist Thought,* ed. B. Guy-Sheftall. New York: New Press.

——.1999. *Blues Legacies and Black Feminism.* New York: Vintage.

Davis, K. 2003. "Dying for love: The epidemic of domestic abuse cases." *Ebony* 58:150–53.

Dawson, M. 2000. "Slowly coming to grips with the effects of the American racial order on American policy preferences." Pp. 344–57 in *Racialized Politics: The Debate about Racism in America*, ed. J. Sidanius, D. O. Sears, and L. Bobo. Chicago: University of Chicago Press.

Deater-Deckard, K., K. A. Dodge, J. E. Bates, and G. S. Pettit. 1996. "Physical discipline among African American and European American mothers: Links to children's externalizing behaviors." *Developmental Psychology* 32:1065–72.

Delgado, R., and J. Stefancic. 2001. *Critical Race Theory: An Introduction*. New York: New York University Press.

"Desegregation levels are traveling backwards." 2004. *Kansas City Star*, January 18, p. A2.

Dickerson, B. J. (Ed.). 1995. *African American Single Mothers: Understanding Their Lives and Families*. Thousand Oaks, Calif.: Sage.

Dickerson, D. J. 2000. *An American Story*. New York: Anchor.

———. 2004. *The End of Blackness*. New York: Pantheon.

Dikotter, F. 1998. "Race culture: Recent perspectives on the history of eugenics." *American Historical Review* 103:467–78.

Dill, B. T. 1979. "The dialectic of black womanhood." *Signs: Journal of Women in Culture and Society* 4:545–55.

———. 1988a. "Our mothers' grief: Racial ethnic women and the maintenance of families." *Journal of Family History* 13:415–31.

———. 1988b. "'Making your job good yourself': Domestic service and the construction of personal dignity." Pp. 33–51 in *Women and the Politics of Empowerment*, ed. A. Bookman and S. Morgan. Philadelphia: Temple University Press.

———. 1994. "Fictive kin, paper sons, and compadrazgo: Women of color and the struggle for family survival." In *Women of Color in U.S. Society*, ed. M. B. Zinn and B. T. Dill. Philadelphia: Temple University Press.

DiQuinzio, P. 1999. *The Impossibility of Motherhood: Feminism, Individualism, and the Problem of Mothering*. New York: Routledge.

Diuguid, L. W. 2004. "Cloaked racism persists." *Kansas City Star*, February 13.

Dobash, R. E., and R. Dobash. 1979. *Violence against Wives*. New York: Free Press.

Downey, D. B., J. W. Ainsworth-Darnell, and M. Dufur. 1998. "Sex of parent and children's well-being in single-parent households." *Journal of Marriage and the Family* 60:878–93.

Du Bois, W. E. B. 1926. "Criteria for Negro art." *Crisis* 32 (October):296.

Dugan, L., R. Rosenfeld, and D. S. Nagin. 2003. "Exposure reduction or retaliation? The effects of domestic violence resources on intimate-partner homicide." *Law & Society* 37:169–98.

Dugger, K. 1991. "Race differences in the determinants of support for legalized abortion." *Social Science Quarterly* 72:570–87.

Dunaway, W. A. 2003. *The African-American Family in Slavery and Emancipation*. New York: Cambridge University Press.

Dyson, M. E. 1993. *Reflecting Black: African-American Cultural Criticism*. Minneapolis: University of Minnesota Press.

———. 1997. *Race Rules: Navigating the Color Line*. New York: Vintage.

East, P. L. 1998. "Racial and ethnic differences in girls' sexual, marital, and birth expectations." *Journal of Marriage and the Family* 60:150–62.

Edin, K. 2000. "What do low-income single mothers say about marriage?" *Social Problems* 47:112–13.

Edin, K., and K. M. Harris. 1999. "Getting off and staying off: Racial differences in the work route off welfare." Pp. 270–300 in *Latinas and African American Women at Work: Race, Gender, and Economic Inequality*, ed. I. Browne. New York: Russell Sage.

Edin, K., and L. Lein. 1997. *Making Ends Meet: How Single Mothers Survive Welfare and Low-Wage Work*. New York: Russell Sage.

Ellison, C. G. 1990. "Family ties, friendships, and subjective well-being among black Americans." *Journal of Marriage and the Family* 52:298–310.

Emerson, R. A. 2002. "'Where my girls at?' Negotiating black womanhood in music videos." *Gender & Society* 16:115–35.

England, P. 2000. "Marriage, the cost of children, and gender inequality." Pp. 320–42 in *The Ties That Bind: Perspectives on Marriage and Cohabitation*, ed. L. J. Waite, with C. Bachrach, M. Hindin, E. Thomson, and A. Thornton. Minneapolis: University of Minnesota Press.

Engsminger, M. E. 1995. "Welfare and psychological distress: A longitudinal study of African American Urban Mothers." *Journal of Health and Social Behavior* 36:346–59.

Farnham, C. 1987. "Sapphire? The issue of dominance in the slave family, 1830–1865." Pp. 68–83 in *"To Toil the Livelong Day": America's Women at Work, 1780–1980*, ed. C. Groneman and M. B. Norton. Ithaca, N.Y.: Cornell University Press.

Faryna, S., B. Stetson, and J. G. Conti (Eds.). 1997. *Black and Right: The Bold New Voice of Black Conservatives in America*. Westport, Conn.: Praeger.

Favor, J. M. 1999. *Authentic Blackness: The Folk in the New Negro Renaissance*. Durham, N.C.: Duke University Press.

Feagin, J. R., and M. P. Sikes. 1994. *Living with Racism: The Black Middle-Class Experience*. Boston: Beacon.

Feagin, J. R., and K. D. McKinney. 2003. *The Many Costs of Racism*. Lanham, Md.: Rowman & Littlefield.

Fears, D. 2003. "Different paths: African Americans trail black immigrants in education and income, a report says." *Washington Post Weekly Edition*, March 17–23, p. 39.

Ferguson, A. A. 2000. *Bad Boys: Public Schools in the Making of Black Masculinity*. Ann Arbor: University of Michigan Press.

Ferree, M. M., and B. B. Hess. 1994. *Controversy and Coalition: The New Feminist Movement across Three Decades of Change*. New York: Twayne.

Firestone, S. 1970. *The Dialectic of Sex*. New York: Morrow.

Fitch, C. A., and S. Ruggles. 2000. "Historical trends in marriage formation: The United States 1850–1990." In *The Ties That Bind: Perspectives on Marriage and Cohabitation*, ed. L. J. Waite, with C. Bachrach, M. Hindin, E. Thomson, A. Thornton. New York: Aldine de Gruyter.

Foston, N. A. 2004. "Is celibacy the new virginity?" *Ebony* (January):120–24.

Fox, G. L., and V. McBridge Murry. 2000. "Gender and families: Feminist perspectives and family research." *Journal of Marriage and the Family* 62:1160–72.

Francis, D. R. 2003. "Social-cause crowd blasts Bush budget." *Christian Science Monitor*, March 3, p. 17.

Frankel, N. 1999. *Freedom's Women: Black Women and Families in Civil War Era Mississippi*. Bloomington: Indiana University Press.

Franklin, D. L. 1997. *Ensuring Inequality: The Structural Transformation of the African-American Family*. New York: Oxford University Press.

———. 2000. *What's Love Got to Do with It? Understanding and Healing the Rift between Black Men and Women*. New York: Touchstone.

Frazier, E. F. 1957. *Black Bourgeoisie*. New York: Free Press.

———. 1966. *The Negro Family in the United States*. Chicago: University of Chicago Press. (Original published in 1939.)

Friedman, D., M. Hechter, and S. Kanazawa. 1994. "A theory of the value of children." *Demography* 31:375–401.

Furstenberg, F. F. 1996. "The future of marriage." *American Demographics* (June), 34–40.

Ganong, L. H., M. Coleman, A. Thompson, and C. Goodwin-Watkins. 1996. "African American and European American college students expectations for self and for future partners." *Journal of Family Issues* 17:758–75.

Gaudin, J. M., Jr. 1999. "Child neglect: Short-term and long-term consequences." Pp. 89–108 in *Neglected Children: Research, Practice, and Policy*, ed. H. Dubowitz. Thousand Oaks, Calif.: Sage.

Gelles, R. J. 1997. *Intimate Violence in Families*. Thousand Oaks, Calif.: Sage.

Genovese, E. D. 1974. *Roll, Jordan, Roll: The World the Slaves Made*. New York: Pantheon.

Giddings, P. 1984. *When and Where I Enter: The Impact of Black Women on Race and Sex in America*. New York: Bantam.

———. 1995. "The last taboo." Pp. 413–28 in *Words of Fire: An Anthology of African-American Feminist Thought*, ed. B. Guy-Sheftall. New York: New Press.

Gilkes, C. T. 1994. "'If it wasn't for the women . . .': African American women, community work, and social change." Pp. 229–46 in *Women of Color in U.S. Society*, ed. M. B. Zinn and B. T. Dill. Philadelphia: Temple University Press.

Gilmore, G. E. 1996. *Gender and Jim Crow: Women and the Politics of White Supremacy in North Carolina 1896–1920*. Durham: University of North Carolina Press.

Girshick, L. B. 1999. *No Safe Haven: Stories of Women in Prison*. Boston: Northeastern University Press.

Glenn, E. N., G. Chang, and L. R. Forcey. 1994. *Mothering: Ideology, Experience, and Agency*. New York: Routledge.

Glenn, E. N. 1998. "The social construction and institutionalization of gender and race: An integrative framework." Pp. 3–43 in *Revisioning Gender*, ed. M. M. Ferree, J. Lorber, and B. B. Hess. Thousand Oaks, Calif.: Sage.

Goldstein, D. 2002. "Talent pursues black voters." *Kansas City Star*, pp. A1, A6.

Goodwin, P. Y. 2003. "African American and European American women's marital well-being." *Journal of Marriage and the Family* 65:550–60.

Gordon, A., and C. Newfield. 1994. "White philosophy." *Critical Inquiry* 20 (Summer):737–57.

Gordon, L. 1982. "Why nineteenth-century feminists did not support 'birth control' and twentieth-century feminists do: Feminism, reproduction, and the family." Pp. 40–53 in *Rethinking the Family: Some Feminist Questions*, ed. B. Thorne and M. Yalom. New York: Longman.

Graham, L. O. 1999. *Our Kind of People: Inside America's Black Upper Class*. New York: HarperCollins.

Gray, M. R., and L. Steinberg. 1999. "Unpacking authoritative parenting: Reassessing a multidimensional construct." *Journal of Marriage and the Family* 61:574–87.

Green, D. 1999. *Gender Violence in Africa: African Women's Responses*. New York: St. Martin's.

Greene, B. 2000. "African American lesbian and bisexual women." *Journal of Social Issues* 56:239–49.

Greenfield, L. 1998. *Violence by Intimates: Analysis of Data on Crimes by Current or Former Spouses, Boyfriends, and Girlfriends*. Washington, D.C.: United States Department of Justice.

Gutman, H. G. 1976. *The Black Family in Slavery and Freedom, 1750–1925*. New York: Pantheon.

Guy-Sheftall, B. 1995. "The evolution of feminist consciousness among African American women." Pp. 1–22 in *Words of Fire: An Anthology of African American Feminist Thought*, ed. B. Guy-Sheftall. New York: New Press.

Hackstaff, K. B. 1999. *Marriage in a Culture of Divorce*. Philadelphia: Temple University Press.

Hale, J. E. 1986. *Black Children: Their Roots, Cultures, and Learning Styles*. Baltimore: Johns Hopkins University Press.

Hall, R. 1995. "The bleaching syndrome: African Americans' response to cultural domination vis-à-vis skin color." *Journal of Black Studies* 26:172–84.

Hampton, R. L., and R. J. Gelles. 1994. "Violence toward Black women in a nationally representative sample of black families." *Journal of Comparative Family Studies* 25:105–19.

Haney, L., and M. March. 2003. "Married fathers and caring daddies: Welfare reform and the discursive politics of paternity." *Social Problems* 50:461–81.

Hao, L., and A. Cherlin. 2004. "Welfare reform and teenage pregnancy, childbirth, and school dropout." *Journal of Marriage and the Family* 66:179–94.

Hartmann, B. 1987. *Reproductive Rights and Wrongs: The Global Politics of Population Control.* Boston: South End.

Hartsock, N. C. M. 1998. *The Feminist Standpoint Revisited and Other Essays.* Boulder, Colo.: Westview.

Haynes, K. A. 1994. "To spank or not to spank?" *Ebony*, pp. 64–67.

Haynes, D. V. 1998. "Program pays drug-addicted parents to become sterilized." *Kansas City Star*, May 3, p. A11.

Hays, S. 1996. *The Cultural Contradictions of Motherhood.* New Haven, Conn.: Yale University Press.

———. 2003. *Flat Broke with Children: Women in the Age of Welfare Reform.* New York: Oxford University Press.

Hemmons, W. M. 1996. *Black Women in the New World Order: Social Justice and the African American Female.* Westport, Conn.: Praeger.

Herrnstein, R. J., and C. Murray. 1994. *The Bell Curve: Intelligence and Class Structure in American Life.* New York: Free Press.

Higginbotham, E. 1981. "Is marriage a priority? Class differences in marital options of educated black women." Pp. 133–76 in *Single Life: Unmarried Adults in Social Context*, ed. P. Stein. Ann Arbor, Mich.: Institute for Social Research.

Higginbotham, E., and L. Weber. 1992. "Moving up with kin and community: Upward social mobility for black and white women." *Gender & Society* 6:416–40.

Higginbotham, E. B. 1993. *Righteous Discontent: The Women's Movement in the Black Baptist Church 1880–1920.* Cambridge, Mass.: Harvard University Press.

Hill, M. E. 2000. "Color differences in the socioeconomic status of African American men: Results of a longitudinal study." *Social Forces* 78:1437–60.

———. 2002. "Skin color and the perception of attractiveness among African Americans: Does gender make a difference?" *Social Psychology Quarterly* 65:77–91.

Hill, S. A. 1994. "Motherhood and the obfuscation of medical knowledge: The case of sickle cell disease." *Gender & Society* 8:29–47.

———. 1999. *African American Children: Socialization and Development in Families.* Thousand Oaks, Calif.: Sage.

Hill, S. A., and M. K. Zimmerman. 1995. "Valiant girls and vulnerable boys: The impact of gender and race on mothers' caregiving for chronically ill children." *Journal of Marriage and the Family* 57:43–53.

Hine, D. C. 1995. "Rape and the inner lives of black women in the Middle West: Preliminary thoughts on the culture of dissemblance." Pp. 380–87 in *Words of Fire: An Anthology of African-American Feminist Thought*, ed. B. Guy-Sheftall. New York: New Press.

Hine, D. C., and K. Thompson. 1998. *A Shining Thread of Hope*. New York: Broadway.

Hofferth, S. 2002. "Did welfare reform work? Implications for 2002 and beyond." *Contexts* 1:45–49.

Holliday, B. G. 1985. "Developmental imperatives of social ecologies." Pp. 53–69 in *Black Children: Social, Educational, and Parental Environments*, ed. H. P. McAdoo and J. L. McAdoo. Beverly Hills, Calif.: Sage.

hooks, b. 1989. *Talking Back: Thinking Feminist, Thinking Black*. Boston: South End.

———. 1992. *Black Looks: Race and Representation*. Boston: South End Press.

———. 2001. *Salvation: Black People and Love*. New York: HarperCollins.

———. 2004. *We Real Cool: Black Men and Masculinity*. New York: Routledge.

Horsley, L. 1993. "Our little boys are in trouble." *Kansas City Star*, March 18, p. 4.

Hossain, Z., and J. L. Roopnarine. 1993. "Division of household labor and child care in dual-earner African-American families with infants." *Sex Roles* 29:571–83.

Hughes, M. 1997. "Symbolic racism, old-fashioned racism, and whites' opposition to affirmative action." Pp. 45–75 in *Racial Attitudes in the 1990s: Continuity and Change*, ed. S. A. Tuch and J. K. Martin. Westport, Conn.: Praeger.

Hughes, M., and M. E. Thomas. 1998. "The continuing significance of race revisited: A study of race, class and quality of life in America, 1972 to 1996." *American Sociological Review* 63:785–95.

Hughes, Z. 2003. "Black men/Black women: Who says sisters can't be nice in relationships?" *Ebony* (March):98.

Hunter, A. G. 2002. "(Re)Envisioning cohabitation: A commentary on race, history, and culture." Pp. 41–50 in *Just Living Together: Implications of Cohabitation on Families, Children, and Social Policy*, ed. A. Booth and A. C. Crouter. Mahwah, N.J.: Erlbaum.

Hunter, T. W. 1997. *To "Joy My Freedom": Southern Black Women's Lives and Labors after the Civil War*. Cambridge, Mass.: Harvard University Press.

Hurst, C. E. 2004. *Social Inequality: Forms, Causes, and Consequences*. Boston: Pearson Education.

Hurston, Z. N. 1979. "What White publishers won't print." Pp. 169–73 in *I Love Myself When I Am Laughing . . . and Then Again When I Am Looking Mean and Impressive*, ed. A. Walker. New York: Feminist Press.

Hutchinson, E. O. 2002a. "The Other Black America." *Christian Science Monitor*, April 29, p. 9.

———. 2002b. "Looking beyond the color line." *Christian Science Monitor*, December 9, p. 9.

Hutchinson, J. F. 1999. "The hip hop generation: African American male-female relationships in a nightclub setting." *Journal of Black Studies* 30:62–84.

Ickes, W. 1993. "Traditional gender roles: Do they make, and then break, our relationships?" *Journal of Social Issues* 49:71–85.

"Ideology trumps science, critics say." 2004. *Kansas City Star*, March 7, p. A8.

Jacobs, J. L. 1994. "Gender, race, class, and the trend toward early motherhood." *Journal of Contemporary Ethnography* 22:442–62.

Jacobson, N. S., and J. M. Gottman. 1998. *When Men Batter Women*. New York: Simon & Schuster.

Jagannathan, R., and M. J. Camasso. 2003. "Family cap and nonmarital fertility: The racial conditioning of policy effects." *Journal of Marriage and the Family* 65:52–71.

Jarrett, R. L. 1994. "Living poor: Family life among single parent, African-American women." *Social Problems* 41:30–50.

———. 1996. "Welfare stigma among low-income African American single mothers." *Family Relations* 45:368–74.

John, D., and B. A. Shelton. 1997. "The production of gender among black and white women and men: The case of household labor." *Sex Roles* 36:171–93.

Johnson, M. P. 1995. "Patriarchal terrorism and common couple violence: Two forms of violence against women." *Journal of Marriage and the Family* 57:283–94.

Johnston, D., and E. Lightblau. 2003. "Justice department censors its own report on diversity." *Kansas City Star*, November 2, p. A4.

Jones, J. 1985. *Labor of Love, Labor of Sorrow: Black Women, Work, and the Family from Slavery to the Present*. New York: Basic Books.

Joseph, J. 1997. "Woman battering: A comparative analysis of black and white women." Pp. 161–69 in *Out of Darkness: Contemporary Perspectives on Family Violence*, ed. G. K. Kantor and J. L. Jasinski. Thousand Oaks, Calif.: Sage.

Kahn, R. P. 1995. *Bearing Meaning: The Language of Birth*. Urbana: University of Illinois Press.

Kaplan, E. B. 1996. "Black teenage mothers and their mothers: The impact of adolescent childbearing on daughters relations with mothers." *Social Problems* 43:427–43.

———. 1997. *Not Our Kind of Girl: Unraveling the Myths of Black Teenage Motherhood*. Berkeley: University of California Press.

Kardiner, A., and L. Ovesey. 1951. *The Mark of Oppression: Explorations in the Personality of the American Negro*. Cleveland: Meridian.

Kelly, R. R. 1995. "Black–white differences in kin contact and exchange among never married adults." *Journal of Family Issues* 16:77–104.

Kenney, J. W., C. Reinholtz, and P. J. Angelini. 1997. "Ethnic differences in childhood and adolescent sexual abuse and teenage pregnancy." *Journal of Adolescent Health* 21:3–10.

Kerbo, H. R. 2003. *Social Stratification and Inequality: Class Conflict in Historical, Comparative and Global Perspective*. Boston: McGraw-Hill.

Kiefer, F. 2002. "Fight over putting more work in workfare." *Christian Science Monitor*, February 28, pp. 2, 3.

Kimmel, M. S. 2000. *The Gendered Society*. New York: Oxford University Press.

King, A. O. 1999. "African American females' attitudes toward marriage: An exploratory study." *Journal of Black Studies* 29:416–37.

King, D. 1988. "Multiple jeopardy, multiple consciousness: The context of black feminist ideology." *Signs: Journal of Women in Culture and Society* 14:42–72.

Kitzinger, S. 1995. *Ourselves as Mothers: The Universal Experience of Motherhood.* Reading, Mass.: Addison-Wesley.

Kline, W. 2001. *Building a Better Race: Gender, Sexuality, and Eugenics from the Turn of the Century to the Baby Boom.* Berkeley: University of California Press.

Koball, H. 1998. "Have African American men become less committed to marriage? Explaining the twentieth century racial cross-over in men's marriage timing." *Demography* 35:251–58.

Kohn, M. L. 1963. Social class and parent–child relationships. *American Journal of Sociology* 63:471–80.

Kolker, A., and B. M. Burke. 1998. *Prenatal Testing: A Sociological Perspective.* Westport, Conn.: Bergin & Garvey.

Ladner, J. A. 1972. *Tomorrow's Tomorrow.* New York: Anchor.

Ladner, J. A., and R. M. Gourdine. 1984. "Intergenerational teenage motherhood: Some preliminary findings." *Sage: A Scholarly Journal on Black Women* 1:22–24.

———. 1992. "Adolescent pregnancy in the African-American community." Pp. 206–21 in *Health Care Issues in the Black Community,* ed. R. L. Braithwaite and S. E. Taylor. San Francisco: Jossey-Bass.

Landry, B. 1987. *The New Black Middle Class.* Berkeley: University of California Press.

———. 2000. *Black Working Wives: Pioneers of the American Family Revolution.* Berkeley: University of California Press.

Lareau, A. 2002. "Invisible inequality: Social class and childrearing in black families and white families." *American Sociological Review* 67:747–76.

Lasker, J., and S. Borg. 1987. *In Search of Parenthood: Coping with Infertility and High-Tech Conception.* Boston: Beacon.

Lawson, E. J., and A. Thompson. 1999. *Black Men and Divorce.* Thousand Oaks, Calif.: Sage.

Leaper, C., L. Leve, T. Strasser, and R. Schwartz. 1995. "Mother–child communication and sequences: Play activity, child gender, and marital status effects." *Merrill-Palmer Quarterly* 41:307–27.

Lee, S. M. 1993. "Racial classifications in the U.S. census: 1890–1990." *Ethnic and Racial Studies* 16:75–94.

Leggon, C. B. 1983. "Career, marriage, and motherhood: 'Copping out' or coping?" Pp. 113–34 in *Black Marriage and Family Therapy,* ed. C. E. Obudho. Westport, Conn.: Greenwood.

Leland, J., and A. Samuels. 1997. "Generation gap." *Newsweek,* March 17, pp. 53–60.

Leonard, E. D. 2002. *Convicted Survivors: The Imprisonment of Battered Women Who Kill.* Albany: State University of New York Press.

Lewis, D. K. 1975. "The black family: Socialization and sex roles." *Phylon* 36:221–38.

Lewis, H. 2000. "Women (under) development: Poor women of color in the United States and the right to development." Pp. 95–111 in *Global Critical Race Feminism: An International Reader*, ed. A. K. Wing. New York: New York University Press.

Lichter, D. T., D. K. McLaughlin, G. Kephart, and D. J. Landry. 1992. "Race and the retreat from marriage: A shortage of marriageable men?" *American Sociological Review* 57:781–99.

Lichter, D. T., D. Roempke Graefe, and J. B. Brown. 2003. "Is marriage a panacea? Union formation among economically disadvantaged unwed mothers." *Social Problems* 50:60–86.

Litt, J. S. 2000. *Medicalized Motherhood: Perspectives from the Lives of African-American and Jewish Women*. New Brunswick, N.J.: Rutgers University Press.

Littlewood, T. B. 1977. *The Politics of Population Control*. Notre Dame, Ind.: University of Notre Dame Press.

Locke, L. M., and C. L. Richman. 1999. "Attitudes toward domestic violence: Race and gender issues." *Sex Roles* 40:227–47.

Loeb, P. R. 2002. "A thousand points of hype." *Christian Science Monitor*, April 25, p. 9.

Lokeman, R. C. 1994. "'Gangsta rappers' demean the human race." *Kansas City Star*, p. B6.

Loprest, P. 2002. "The next welfare reform: Counter boomerang effect." *Christian Science Monitor*, September 20, p. 11.

Lorber, J. 1998. *Gender Inequality: Feminist Theories and Politics*. Los Angeles: Roxbury.

Loue, S. 2001. *Intimate Partner Violence: Societal, Medical, Legal, and Individual Responses*. New York: Kluwer Academic/Plenum.

Loury, G. C. 2002. *The Anatomy of Racial Inequality*. Cambridge, Mass.: Harvard University Press.

Luker, K. 1996. *Dubious Conceptions: The Politics of Teenage Pregnancy*. Cambridge, Mass.: Harvard University Press.

Lynxwiler, J., and D. Gay. 1996. "The abortion attitudes of black women: 1972–1991." *Journal of Black Studies* 27:260–77.

Lyson, T. A. 1986. "Race and sex differences in sex role attitudes of southern college students." *Psychology of Women Quarterly* 10:421–28.

MacKinnon, C. 1997. "Pornography, civil rights, and silence." Pp. 400–13 in *Gender Violence: Interdisciplinary Perspectives*, ed. L. L. O'Toole and J. R. Schiffman. New York: New York University Press.

Madhubuti, H. R. 1990. *Black Men: Obsolete, Single, Dangerous? The Afrikan American Family in Transition*. Chicago: Third World Press.

———. 2001. "On becoming anti-rapist." Pp. 158–67 in *Traps: African American Men on Gender and Sexuality*, ed. R. P. Byrd and B. Guy-Sheftall. Bloomington: Indiana University Press.

Majors, R., and J. M. Billson. 1992. *Cool Pose: The Dilemmas of Black Manhood in America*. New York: Lexington.

Manning, W. D. 2001. "Childbearing in cohabiting unions: Racial and ethnic differences." *Family Planning Perspectives* 33:217–24.

Marable, M. 2000. "Groundings with my sisters: Patriarchy and the exploitation of black women." Pp. 119–52 in *Traps: African American Men on Gender and Sexuality*, ed. R. P. Byrd and B. Guy-Sheftall. Bloomington: Indiana University Press.

Markowitz, F. E. 2001. "Attitudes and family violence: Linking intergenerational and cultural theories." *Journal of Family Violence* 16:205–17.

Marks, A. 2002a. "In Detroit, a crusade to stop child killings." *Christian Science Monitor*, July 24, pp. 1, 4.

———. 2002b. "One neighborhood's quest to reclaim its streets." *Christian Science Monitor*, October 30, 3.

Marks, C. 1989. *Farewell—We're Good and Gone: The Great Black Migration*. Bloomington: Indiana University Press.

"Marriage dilemma of college-educated women." 1997. *Journal of Blacks in Higher Education* (Autumn):52–57.

Marshall, A. 1996. "From sexual denigration to self-respect: Resisting images of Black female sexuality." Pp. 3–35 in *Reconstructing Womanhood, Reconstructing Feminism*, ed. D. Jarrett-Macauley. New York: Routledge.

Marshall, S. 1995. "Ethnic socialization of African American children: Implications for parenting, identity development, and academic achievement." *Journal of Youth and Adolescence* 24:377–96.

Massey, D. S. 2001. "Segregation and Violent Crime in America." Pp. 317–44 in *Problem of the Century: Racial Stratification in the United States*, ed. E. Anderson and D. S. Massey. New York: Russell Sage Foundation.

Massey, D. S., and N. A. Denton. 1993. *American Apartheid: Segregation and the Making of the Underclass*. Cambridge, Mass.: Harvard University Press.

Mauer, M. 1999. *Race to Incarcerate: The Sentencing Project*. New York: New York Press.

McAdoo, H. P. 1983. "Parenting styles: Mother–child interactions and self-esteem in young black children." Pp. 135–50 in *Black Marriage and Family Therapy*, ed. C. E. Obudo. Westport, Conn.: Greenwood.

———. 1990. "A portrait of African American families in the United States." Pp. 71–93 in *The American Woman, 1990–1991*, ed. S. E. Rix. New York: Norton.

McCabe, K., and D. Barnett. 2000. "First comes work, then comes marriage: Future orientation among African American young adolescents." *Family Relations* 49:63–70.

McCreary, D. R. (1994). The male role and avoiding femininity. *Sex Roles* 31, nos. 9–10:517–31.

McElroy, J. 2002. *Trophy Man: The Surprising Secrets of Black Women Who Marry Well*. New York: Fireside.

McFarlane, D. R., and K. J. Meier. 2001. *The Politics of Fertility Control: Family Planning and Abortion Policies in the American States.* New York: Chatham House.

McGee, Z. T. 2000. "Patterns of violent behavior and victimization among African American youth." Pp. 47–64 in *Race, Ethnicity, Sexual Orientation, Violent Crime: The Realities and Myths,* ed. N. J. Pallone. Binghamton, N.Y.: Haworth.

McLanahan, S., and D. Schwartz. 2002. "Life without father: What happens to the children." *Contexts* 1:35–41.

McLoyd, V. C. 1990. "The impact of economic hardships on black families and children: Psychological distress, parenting, and socioemotional development." *Child Development* 61:311–46.

McMahon, M. 1995. *Engendering Motherhood: Identity and Self-Transformation in Women's Lives.* New York: Guilford.

McMillan, T. 1987. *Mama.* New York: Washington Square.

———. 1992. *Waiting to Exhale.* New York: Viking.

McWhorter, J. H. 2000. *Losing the Race: Self-sabotage in Black America.* New York: Free Press.

———. 2003. *Authentically Black: Essays for the Black Silent Majority.* New York: Gotham.

Messner, M. 1997. *Politics of Masculinities: Men in Movements.* Thousand Oaks, Calif.: Sage.

Messner, M. A. 1991. "Masculinities and athletic careers." Pp. 60–75 in *The Social Construction of Gender,* ed. J. Lorber and S. A. Farrell. Newbury Park, Calif.: Sage.

Milardo, R. M., and S. Duck (Eds.). 2000. *Families as Relationships.* New York: Wiley.

Milardo, R. M., and A. Graham. 2000. "Social networks and marital relationships." Chap. 3 in *Families as Relationships,* ed. R. M. Milardo and S. Duck. New York: Wiley.

Moffitt, R. A., and P. T. Gottschalk. 2001. "Ethnic and racial differences in welfare receipt in the United States." Pp. 152–71 in *America Becoming: Racial Trends and Their Consequences,* ed. N. J. Smelser, W. J. Wilson, and F. Mitchell. Washington, D.C.: National Academy Press.

Moffitt, R. A., R. Reville, and A. E. Winkler. 1998. "Beyond single mothers: Cohabitation and marriage in the AFDC program." *Demography* 35:259–78.

Moore, V. A. 2001. "'Doing' racialized and gendered age to organize peer relations: Observing kids in summer camp." *Gender & Society* 15:835–58.

Morgan, P. D. 1998. *Slave Counterpoint: Black Culture in the Eighteenth Century Chesapeake and Low Country.* Durham: University of North Carolina Press.

Moss, P., and C. Tilly. 1996. "'Soft' skills and race: An investigation of black men's employment problems." *Work and Occupations* 23:252–76.

Moynihan, D. P. 1965. *The Negro Family: The Case for National Action.* Washington, D.C.: Office of Policy Planning and Research.

Mullings, L. 1997. *On Our Own Terms: Race, Class, and Gender in the Lives of African American Women.* New York: Routledge.

Murray, C. 1984. *Losing Ground: American Social Policy 1950–1980.* New York: Basic Books.

Myers, K. A., and P. Williamson. 2001. "Race talk: The perception of racism through private discourse." *Race & Society* 4:3–26.

Myers, L. W. 2002. *A Broken Silence: Voices of African American Women in the Academy.* Westport, Conn.: Bergin & Garvey.

Nelson, J. 1997. *Straight, No Chaser.* New York: Putnam.

———. 2003. *Women of Color and the Reproductive Rights Movement.* New York: New York University Press.

Neubeck, K. J., and N. A Cazenave. 2001. *Welfare Racism: Playing the Race Card against America's Poor.* New York: Routledge.

Newby, J. H., J. E. McCarroll, L. E. Thayer, A. E. Norwood, C. S. Fullerton, and R. J. Ursano. 2000. "Spouse abuse by black and white offenders in the U.S. Army." *Journal of Family Violence* 15:199–208.

Nobes, G., and M. Smith. 2002. "Family structure and the physical punishment of children." *Journal of Family Issues* 23:349–73.

Nobles, M. 2000. *Shades of Citizenship: Race and the Census in Modern Politics.* Stanford, Calif.: Stanford University Press.

Nobles, W. W. 1974. "Africanity: Its role in black families." *Black Scholar* 5:10–17.

———. 1985. *Africanity and the Black Family.* Oakland, Calif.: Institute for the Advanced Study of Black Family Life and Culture.

Nsiah-Jefferson, L. 1989. "Reproductive laws, women of color, and low-income women." Pp. 23–67 in *Reproductive Laws for the 1990s,* ed. S. Cohen and N. Taub. Clifton, N.J.: Humana.

O'Brien, M. 1981. *The Politics of Reproduction.* Boston: Routledge & Kegan Paul.

O'Keefe, M. 1997. "Incarcerated battered women: A comparison of battered women who killed their abusers and those incarcerated for other offenses." *Journal of Family Violence* 12:1–19.

Oliver, M. L., and T. M. Shapiro. 1995. *Black Wealth/White Wealth: A New Perspective on Racial Inequality.* New York: Routledge.

Oliver, M. L. 2004. "American dream? How government initiatives made blacks house poor." *Crisis* (September/October):17–20.

Olson, L. 2001. *Freedom's Daughters: The Unsung Heroines of the Civil Rights Movement from 1830 to 1970.* New York: Scribner.

Omolade, B. 1994. *The Rising Song of African American Women.* New York: Routledge.

———. 1995. "Hearts of darkness." Pp. 362–77 in *Words of Fire: An Anthology of African-American Feminist Thought,* ed. B. Guy-Sheftall. New York: New Press.

Orbuch, T. L., and L. Custer. 1995. "The social context of married women's work and its impact on black husbands and white husbands." *Journal of Marriage and the Family* 57:333–45.

Oropesa, R. S., and B. K. Gorman. 2000. "Ethnicity, immigrations, and beliefs about marriages as a 'tie that binds.'" Pp. 188–211 in *The Ties That Bind: Perspectives on Marriage and Cohabitation*, ed. L. J. Waite, with C. Bachrach, M. Hindin, E. Thomson, and A. Thornton. New York: Walter de Gruyter.

Page, C. 2004. "Black Americans could use some immigrant optimism." *Kansas City Star*, July 8, p. B9.

Pallas, A. M., D. R. Entwisle, K. L. Alexander, and P. Weinstein. 1990. "Social structure and the development of self-esteem in young children." *Social Psychology Quarterly* 53:302–15.

Parcel, T. L., and E. G. Menaghan. 1993. "Family social capital and children's behavior problems." *Social Psychology Quarterly* 56:120–35.

Parker, K. D., and T. Calhoun. 1996. "Gender differences in global life satisfaction among African Americans." *National Journal of Sociology* 10:1–13.

Parker, K. F., P. L. McCall, and J. Lane. 2002. "Exploring the racial discrimination and competitive processes of race-specific violence in the urban context." *Critical Sociology* 28:235–46.

Parvez, Z. F. 2002. "Women, poverty, and welfare reform." Pp. 1–5. Distributed by Sociologists for Women in Society; available online: www.socwomen.org; accessed August 15.

Patterson, O. 1993. "Blacklash." *Transition* 62:4–26.

———. 1997. *The Ordeal of Integration: Progress and Resentment in America's "Racial" Crisis*. Washington, D.C.: Civitas/Counterpoint.

Payne, B. K., and R. R. Gainey. 2002. *Family Violence and Criminal Justice: A Life-Course Perspective*. Cincinnati: Anderson.

Peters, M. F. 1997. "Parenting of young children in black families." Pp. 167–82 in *Black Families*, ed. H. P. McAdoo. Thousand Oaks, Calif.: Sage.

Peterson, E. 2002. Autopsy reveals extent of abuse. *Kansas City Star*, July 19, pp. 1–2.

Peterson, G. W., D. A. Bodman, K. R. Rush, and D. Madden-Derdich. 2000. "Gender and parent–child relationships." Pp. 82–104 in *Handbook of Family Diversity*, ed. D. H. Demo, K. R. Allen, and M. A. Fine. New York: Oxford University Press.

Phinney, J. S., and V. Chavira. 1995. "Parental ethnic socialization and adolescent coping with problems related to ethnicity." *Journal of Research on Adolescence* 5:31–53.

Pinkney, A. 2000. *Black Americans*. Upper Saddle River, N.J.: Prentice Hall.

Platt, A. 1991. *E. Franklin Frazier Reconsidered*. New Brunswick, N.J.: Rutgers University Press.

Pleck, J. H., F. L. Sonenstein, and L. C. Ku. 1993. "Masculinity ideology: Its impact on adolescent males heterosexual relationships." *Journal of Social Issues* 49:11–29.

Plotnick, R. D. 1992. "The effects of attitudes on teenage premarital pregnancy and its resolution." *American Sociological Review* 57:800–11.

Pohlmann, M. D. 1999. *Black Politics in Conservative America*. New York: Longman.

Polatnick, M. R. 1996. "Diversity in women's liberation ideology: How a black and a white group of the 1960s viewed motherhood." *Signs: Journal of Women in Culture and Society* 21:679–706.

Queen, S. A., and R. W. Habenstein. 1967. *The Family in Various Cultures*. Philadelphia: Lippincott.

Rainwater, L., and W. L. Yancey. 1967. *The Moynihan Report and the Politics of Controversy*. Cambridge, Mass.: MIT Press.

Raley, R. K., and E. Wildsmith. 2004. "Cohabitation and children's family instability." *Journal of Marriage and the Family* 66:210–19.

Rank, M. R. 2000. "Poverty and economic hardship in families." Pp. 293–315 in *Handbook of Family Diversity*, ed. D. H. Demo, K. R. Allen, and M. A. Fine. New York: Oxford University Press.

Ransby, B., and T. Matthews. 1995. "Black popular culture and the transcendence of patriarchal illusions." Pp. 526–35 in *Words of Fire: An Anthology of African-American Feminist Thought*, ed. B. Guy-Sheftall. New York: New York Press.

Rapp, R. 1982. "Family and class in contemporary America: Notes toward an understanding of ideology." Pp. 168–87 in *Rethinking the Family: Some Feminist Questions*, ed. B. Thorne and M. Yalom. New York: Longman.

Rapp, R., E. Ross, and R. Bridenthal. 1979. "Examining family history." *Feminist Studies* 5:174–200.

Rasche, C. E. 2001. "Minority women and domestic violence: The unique dilemmas of women of color." Pp. 86–102 in *Women Battering in the United States: Till Death Do Us Part*, ed. H. M. Eigenberg. Prospect Heights, Ill.: Waveland.

Reid, P. T., and K. H. Trotter. 1993. "Children's self-presentation with infants: Gender and ethnic comparisons." *Sex Roles* 29:171–81.

Rich, A. C. 1976. *Of Woman Born: Motherhood as Experience and Institution*. New York: Norton.

Richie, B. E. 1995. "Battered black women: A challenge for the black community." Pp. 398–404 in *Words of Fire: An Anthology of African-American Feminist Thought*, ed. B. Guy-Sheftall. New York: New York Press.

———. 1996. *Compelled to Crime: The Gender Entrapment of Battered Black Women*. New York: Routledge.

———. 2000. "A black feminist reflection on the antiviolence movement." *Signs: Journal of Women in Culture and Society* 25:1133–37.

Rickey, W. 2002. "One strike and out, in public housing." *Christian Science Monitor*, February 19, p. 2.

Ringle, K. 2002. "A different kind of roots planted at Melrose Plantation." *Kansas City Star*, August 18, p. H6.

Risman, B. 1998. *Gender Vertigo: American Families in Transition.* New Haven, Conn.: Yale University Press.

Risman, B., and P. Schwartz. 2002. "After the sexual revolution: Gender politics in teen dating." *Contexts* 1:16–24.

Roberts, D. E. 1995. "Race, gender, and the value of mothers' work." *Social Politics* (Summer):195–207.

———. 1997a. *Killing the Black Body: Race, Reproduction, and the Meaning of Liberty.* New York: Pantheon.

———. 1997b. "Unshackling Black motherhood." *Michigan Law Review* 95:938–65.

Robinson, T. L., and J. V. Ward. 1995. "African American adolescents and skin color." *Journal of Black Psychology* 21:256–74.

Roche, K., M. E. Ensminger, H. Chilcoat, and C. Storr. 2003. "Establishing independence in low-income urban areas: The relationship to adolescent aggressive behavior." *Journal of Marriage and the Family* 65:668–80.

Rockquemore, K., and D. L. Brunsma. 2002. *Beyond Black: Biracial Identity in America.* Thousand Oaks, Calif.: Sage.

Rodrique, J. M. 1990. "The black community and the birth control movement." Pp. 333–42 in *Unequal Sisters: A Multicultural Reader in U.S. Women's History,* ed. E. C. DuBois and V. L. Ruiz. New York: Routledge.

Rogers, R. 2000. "Afro-Caribbean immigrants, African Americans, and the politics of group identity." Pp. 15–59 in *Black and Multiracial Politics in American,* ed. Y. Alex-Assensoh and L. J. Hanks. New York: New York University Press.

Romano, R. C. 2003. *Race Mixing: Black-White Marriage in Postwar America.* Cambridge, Mass.: Harvard University Press.

Romero, M. and A. Stewart (Ed.). 1999. *Women's Untold Stories: Breaking Silence, Talking Back, Voicing Complexity.* New York: Routledge.

Roschelle, A. R. 1999. "Gender, family structure, and social structure: Racial ethnic families in the United States." Pp. 311–40 in *Revisioning Gender,* ed. M. Marx Ferree, J. Lorber, and B. B. Hess. Thousand Oaks, Calif.: Sage.

Rose, T. 1994. *Black Noise: Rap Music and Black Culture in Contemporary America.* Hanover, N.H.: Wesleyan University Press.

———. 2003. *Longing to Tell: Black Women Talk about Sexuality and Intimacy.* New York: Farrar, Straus & Giroux.

Rose, W. 2002. "Don't hurt welfare's successes." *Christian Science Monitor,* April 24, p. 9.

Ross, L. E. 1996. "Black-white college student attitudes and expectations in paying for dates." *Sex Roles* 35:43–56.

———. 1997. "Male selection preferences among African American college students." *Journal of Black Studies* 27:554–69.

Ross, L. J. 1993. "African American women and abortion: 1800–1970." Pp. 141–59 in *Theorizing Black Feminisms: The Visionary Pragmatism of Black Women,* ed. S. M. James and A. P. A. Busia. New York: Routledge.

Rothman, B. K. 1989. *Recreating Motherhood: Ideology and Technology in a Patriarchal Society.* New York: Norton.

Ruddick, S. 1997. "The idea of fatherhood." Pp. 205–20 in *Feminism and Families,* ed. H. Lindemann Nelson. New York: Routledge.

Ruggles, S. 1994. "The origins of African-American family structure." *American Sociological Review* 59:136–51.

Russell, D. E. H. 1983. *Rape in Marriage.* New York: Macmillan.

Russo, A. 2001. *Taking Back Our Lives: A Call to Action for the Feminist Movement.* New York: Routledge.

Savin-Williams, R. C., and K. G. Esterberg. 2000. "Lesbian, gay, and bisexual families." Pp. 197–215 in *Handbook of Family Diversity,* ed. D. H. Demo, K. R. Allen, and M. A. Fine. New York: Oxford University Press.

Schram, S. F. 2000. *After Welfare: The Culture of Postindustrial Social Policy.* New York: New York University Press.

Schwalm, L. A. 1997. *A Hard Fight for We: Women's Transition from Slavery to Freedom in South Carolina.* Urbana: University of Illinois Press.

Scott, C. F., and S. Sprecher. 2000. "Sexuality in marriage, dating, and other relationships: A decade review." *Journal of Marriage and the Family* 62:999–1017.

Scott, E. K., A. S. London, and N. A. Myers. 2002. "Dangerous dependencies: The intersection of welfare reform and domestic violence." *Gender & Society* 16:878–97.

Scott, J. W. 1993. "African American daughter–mother relations and teenage pregnancy? Two faces of premarital teenage pregnancy." *Western Journal of Black Studies* 17:73–81.

Scott, K. Y. 1991. *The Habit of Surviving: Black Women's Strategies for Life.* New Brunswick, N.J.: Rutgers University Press.

Scott, R. J. 1985. "The battle over the child: Child apprenticeship and the Freedmen's Bureau in North Carolina." Pp. 193–207 in *Growing Up in America: Children in Historical Perspective,* ed. N. R. Hiner and J. M. Hawes. Chicago: University of Chicago Press.

Seltzer, J. A. 2000. "Families formed outside of marriage." *Journal of Marriage and the Family* 62:1247–68.

Sharpes, P. W., and J. Campbell. 1999. "Health consequences for victims of violence in intimate relationships." In *Violence in Intimate Relationships,* ed. X. B. Arriaga and S. Oskamp. Thousands Oaks, Calif.: Sage.

Shaw, S. J. 1997. "Mothering under slavery in the Antebellum South." Pp. 297–318 in *Mothers and Motherhood: Readings in American History,* ed. R. D. Apple and J. Golden. Columbus: Ohio State University Press.

Shelton, J. N., and T. M. Chavous. 1999. "Black and white college women's perceptions of sexual harassment." *Sex Roles* 40:593–616.

Shende, S. 1997. "Fighting the violence against our sisters: Prosecution of pregnant women and the coercive use of Norplant." Pp. 123–35 in *Women Transforming*

Politics: An Alternative Reader, ed. C. J. Cohen, K. B. Jones, and J. C. Tronto. New York: New York University Press.

Sidbury, J. 1997. *Ploughshares into Swords: Race, Rebellion, and Identity in Gabriel's Virginia, 1730–1810*. Cambridge: Cambridge University Press.

Simpson, A. Y. 1998. *The Tie That Binds: Identity and Political Attitudes in the Post–Civil Rights Generation*. New York: New York University Press.

Slavkin, M., and A. D. Stright. 2000. "Gender role differences in college students from one- and two-parent families." *Sex Roles* 42:23–30.

Smith, D. B. 1999. *Health Care Divided: Race and Healing a Nation*. Ann Arbor: University of Michigan Press.

Smith, S. L. 1995. *Sick and Tired of Being Sick and Tired: Black Women's Health Activism in America, 1890–1950*. Philadelphia: University of Pennsylvania Press.

Smith, S. S., and M. R. Moore. 2000. "Intraracial diversity and relations among African-Americans: Closeness among black students at a predominantly white university." *American Journal of Sociology* 106:1–39.

Sobel, M. 1987. *The World They Made Together: Black and White Values in Eighteenth-Century Virginia*. Princeton, N.J.: Princeton University Press.

Solinger, R. 1994. "Race and 'value': Black and white illegitimate babies in the U.S., 1945–65." Pp. 463–78 in *Unequal Sisters: A Multi-Cultural Reader in U.S. Women's History*, ed. V. L. Ruiz and E. C. DuBois. New York: Routledge.

———. 1998. "Poisonous Choices." Pp. 381–402 in *"Bad" Mothers: The Politics of Blame in Twentieth-Century America*, ed. M. Ladd-Taylor and L. Umansky. New York: New York University Press.

———. 2001. *Beggars and Choosers: How the Politics of Choice Shapes Adoption, Abortion, and Welfare in the United States*. New York: Hill & Wang.

Sorensen, A. 1994. "Women, family, and class." *Annual Review of Sociology* 20:27–47.

South, S. J., and E. P. Baumer. 2000. "Deciphering community and race effects on adolescent premarital childbearing." *Social Forces* 78:1379–1408.

Spake, A. 1999. "The perils of motherhood." *U.S. News & World Report*, June 28, p. 60.

Springer, K. (Ed.). 1999. *Still Lifting, Still Climbing: Contemporary African American Women's Activism*. New York: New York University Press.

Spruell, S. 2002. "Hip-hop music." *Black Entertainment* (July):62, 66.

St. Jean, Y., and J. R. Feagin. 1997. *Double Burden: Black Women and Everyday Racism*. Armonk, N.Y.: Sharpe.

St. Lawrence, J. S., et al. 1998. "Factors influencing condom use among African American women: Implications for risk reduction interventions." *American Journal of Community Psychology* 26:7–27.

Stack, C. 1974. *All Our Kin: Strategies for Survival in a Black Community*. New York: Harper & Row.

Staples, R. 1978. "Race, liberalism-conservatism and premarital sexual permissiveness: A bi-racial comparison." *Journal of Marriage and the Family* 40:733–42.

———. (Ed.). 1994. *The Black Family: Essays and Studies*. Belmont, Calif.: Wadsworth.

Staples, R., and L. B. Johnson. 1993. *Black Families at the Crossroads: Challenges and Prospects*. San Francisco: Jossey-Bass.

Stearns, M. 2002. "Ashcroft is putting his stamp on agency." *Kansas City Star*, November 29, pp. 1A, 6A.

Stephens, R. J., and E. Wright. 2000. "Beyond bitches, niggers, and ho's: Some suggestions for including rap music as a qualitative data source." *Race & Society* 2:2340.

Stephens, N., and R. McDonald. 2000. "Assessment of women who see shelter from abusing partners." Pp. 78–101 in *Domestic Violence: Guidelines for Research-Informed Practices*, ed. J. P. Vincent and E. N. Jouriles. Philadelphia: Kingsley.

Stolberg, S. G. 1999. "Black mothers' mortality rate is under scrutiny." *New York Times*, August 8.

Straus, M. A., R. J. Gelles, and S. K. Steinmetz. 1980. *Behind Closed Doors: Violence in the American Family*. New York: Doubleday.

Straus, M. A., with D. Donnelly. 1994. *Beating the Devil Out of Them: Corporal Punishment in American Families*. San Francisco: Jossey-Bass.

Stueve, A., L. O'Donnell, and B. Link. 2001. "Gender differences in risk factors for violent behavior among economically disadvantaged African American and Hispanic young adolescents." *International Journal of Law and Psychiatry* 24:539–57.

Sudarkasa, N. 1996. *The Strength of Our Mothers: African and African American Women and Families: Essays and Speeches*. Trenton, N.J.: Africa World.

Summers, R. W., and A. M. Hoffman. 2002. "United States." Pp. 169–84 in *Domestic Violence: A Global View*, ed. R. W. Summers and A. M. Hoffman. Westport, Conn.: Greenwood.

Swidler, A. 1986. "Culture in action: Symbols and strategies." *American Sociological Review* 51:273–86.

Tamedy. L. 2001. *Cane River*. New York: Warner.

Tangri, S. S., and J. M. Browne. 1999. "Climbing out of the pit: From the Black middle class to homeless and (almost) back again." Pp. 125–41 in *Women's Untold Stories: Breaking Silence, Talking Back, Voicing Complexity*, ed. M. Romero and A. J. Stewart. New York: Routledge.

Taylor, R. J., L. M. Chatters, M. B. Tucker, and D. Lewis. 1990. "Developments in research on black families: A decade review." *Journal of Marriage and the Family* 52:993–1014.

Taylor, S. L. 1994. "Reflections on motherhood." *Essence* 25:69.

———. 2002. "Action, not silence." *Essence* 33:5.

Taylor, M. 1998. "How white attitudes vary with the racial composition of local populations: Numbers count." *American Sociological Review* 63:512–35.

Taylor, R. L. 2000. "Diversity within African American families." Pp. 232–51 in *Handbook of Family Diversity*, ed. D. H. Demo, K. R. Allen, and M. A. Fine. New York: Oxford University Press.

Terborg-Penn, R. 1986. "Women and slavery in the African diaspora: A cross-cultural approach to historical analysis." *Sage: A Scholarly Journal on Black Women* 3:11–15.

Terrelonge, P. 1995. "Feminist consciousness and black women." Pp. 490–501 in *Words of Fire: An Anthology of African American Feminist Thought*, ed. B. Guy-Sheftall. New York: New Press.

Thomas, G., M. P. Farrell, and G.M. Barnes. 1996. "The effects of single-mother families and nonresident fathers on delinquency and substance abuse in black and white adolescents." *Journal of Marriage and the Family* 58:884–94.

Thomson, E. 1997. "Couple childbearing desires, intentions and births." *Demography* 34:343–54.

Thorne, B. 1982. "Feminist rethinking of the family: An overview." Pp. 1–24 in *Rethinking the Family: Some Feminist Questions*, ed. B. Thorne and M. Yalom. New York: Longman.

Tilly, L., and J. W. Scott. 1978. *Women, Work, and the Family.* New York: Holt.

Tomaskovic-Devey, D., and V. J. Roscigno. 1996. "Racial economic subordination and white gain in the U.S. South." *American Sociological Review* 61:565–89.

Tower, C. C. 1996. *Understanding Child Abuse and Neglect.* Boston: Allyn & Bacon.

"Trickle down economics: The progress of black men who have not gone to college." 1999. *Journal of Blacks in Higher Education* 25:68–69.

Tuch, S. A., L. Sigelman, and J. K. Martin. 1997. "Fifty years after Myrdal: Blacks' racial policy attitudes in the 1990s." Pp. 221–37 in *Racial Attitudes in the 1990s: Continuity and Change*, ed. S. A. Tuch and J. K. Martin. Westport, Conn.: Praeger.

Tucker, M. B. 2000. "Marital values and expectations in context: Results from a 21-city survey." Pp. 166–87 in *The Ties That Bind: Perspectives on Marriage and Cohabitation*, ed. L. J. Waite, with C. Bachrach, M. Hindin, E. Thomson, and A. Thornton. New York: Walter de Gruyter.

Turell, S. C. 2000. "A descriptive analysis of same-sex relationship violence for a diverse sample." *Journal of Family Violence* 15:281–93.

Tyree, O. 1998. *Single Mom.* New York: Scribner.

Tzeng, O. C. S., J. W. Jackson, and H. C. Karlson. 1991. *Theories of Child Abuse and Neglect: Differential Perspectives, Summaries, and Evaluations.* New York: Praeger.

Umberson, D., K. L. Anderson, K. Williams, and M. D. Chen. 2003. "Relationship dynamics, emotion state, and domestic violence: A stress and masculinities perspective." *Journal of Marriage and the Family* 65:233–47.

U.S. Bureau of Census. 2003. Available online: www.census.gov/population/socdemo/race/black; accessed in April.

U.S. Bureau of Justice. 2001. *Homicide Trends in the U.S.* Washington, D.C.: U.S. Government Printing Office.

Valdes, F., J. M. Culp, and A. P. Harris. 2002. *Crossroads, Directions, and a New Critical Race Theory.* Philadelphia: Temple University Press.

Veroff, J., A. Young, and H. Coon. 2000. "The early years of marriage." Chap. 2 in *Families as Relationships*, ed. R. M. Milardo and S. Duck. New York: Wiley.

Vincent, J. P., and E. N. Jouriles (Eds.). 2000. *Domestic Violence: Guidelines for Research-Informed Practices*. Philadelphia: Kingsley.

Waite, L. J., with C. Bachrach, M. Hindin, E. Thomson, and A. Thornton (Eds.). 2000. *The Ties That Bind: Perspectives on Marriage and Cohabitation*. New York: Aldine de Gruyter.

Walker, A. (Ed.). 1979. *I Love Myself When I'm Laughing . . . and Then Again When I'm Looking Mean and Impressive*. New York: Feminist.

Walker, L. E. A. 2000. *The Battered Woman Syndrome*. New York: Springer.

Walsh, L. 1985. "The experiences and status of women in the Chesapeake." Pp. 1–18 in *The Web of Southern Social Relations: Women, Family and Education*, ed. W. Fraser, R. F. Saunders, and J. Wakelyn. Athens: University of Georgia Press.

Walsh, W. 2002. "Spankers and nonspankers: Where they get information on spanking." *Family Relations* 51:81–88.

Wang, C. T. 1999. *Current Trends in Child Abuse Report and Fatalities: The Results of the 1997 Annual Fifty State Survey*. Working Paper No. 808. Chicago: Center on Child Abuse Prevention Research, Prevent Child Abuse America.

Ward, M. C. 1986. *Poor Women, Powerful Men: America's Great Experiment in Family Planning*. Boulder, Colo.: Westview.

Watson, E. 1998. "Guess what came to American politics? Contemporary black conservatism." *Journal of Black Studies* 29:73–92.

Wattleton, F. 1992. "Reproductive rights and the challenge for African Americans." Pp. 301–14 in *Health Care Issues in the Black Community*, ed. R. L. Braithwaite and S. E. Taylor. San Francisco: Jossey-Bass.

Welter, B. 1973. "The cult of true womanhood: 1820–1860." Pp. 224–50 in *The American Family in Social-Historical Perspective*, ed. M. Gordon. New York: St. Martin's.

West, C., and D. Zimmerman. 1987. "Doing gender." *Gender & Society* 1:125–51.

West, T. C. 1999. *Wounds of the Spirit: Black Women, Violence, and Resistance Ethics*. New York: New York University Press.

Western, B., and K. Beckett. 1999. "How unregulated is the U.S. labor market? The penal system as a labor market institution." *American Journal of Sociology* 104:1030–60.

Wexler, R. 2002. "States unfairly take children from poor parents." *Christian Science Monitor*, July 31, p. 8.

White, A. M. 1999. "Talking black, talking feminist: Gendered micromobilization processes in a collective protest against rape." Pp. 189–218 in *Still Lifting, Still Climbing: Contemporary African American Women's Activism*, ed. K. Springer. New York: New York University Press.

White, D. G. 1985. *Ar'nt I a Woman? Female Slaves in the Plantation South*. New York: Norton.

———. 1994. "Female slaves: Sex roles and status in the antebellum plantation south." Pp. 20–31 in *Unequal Sisters: A Multi-Cultural Reader in U.S. Women's History*, ed. V. L. Ruiz and E. C. DuBois. New York: Routledge.

———. 1999. *Too Heavy a Load: Black Women in Defense of Themselves, 1894–1994*. New York: Norton.

White, E. C. 1985. *Chain, Chain, Change: For Black Women Dealing with Physical and Emotional Abuse*. Seattle: Seal.

Whitman, D. 1998. "Despite tough talk, states avoid workfare." *U.S. News & World Report*, January 12, pp. 26–27.

Wilcox, C. 1990. "Racial differences in abortion attitudes: Some additional evidence." *Public Opinion Quarterly* 54:248–55.

Williams, A. 2004. "Will economic need usurp racial diversity on campuses?" *Crisis* 111, 3:12.

Williams, C. W. 1991. *Black Teenage Mothers: Pregnancy and Child Rearing from Their Perspective*. Lexington, Mass.: Lexington.

Williams, O. J. 1998. "Healing and confronting the African American male who batters." Pp. 74–94 in *Family Violence and Men of Color*, ed. R. Carrillo and J. Tello. New York: Springer.

Wilson, W. J. 1987. *The Truly Disadvantaged*. Chicago: University of Chicago Press.

Winfrey, O. 2002. "Oprah talks to Condoleezza Rice." *O Magazine* (February):118–21.

Wolf, N. 2001. *Misconceptions: Truth, Lies, and the Unexpected on the Journey to Motherhood*. New York: Doubleday.

Wong, S. 1994. "Diverted mothering: Representations of caregivers of color in the age of 'multiculturalism.'" Pp. 67–94 in *Mothering: Ideology, Experience, and Agency*, ed. E. N. Glenn, G. Chang, and L. R. Forcey. New York: Routledge.

Wood, D. B. 2002. "L.A.'s troubling murder surge: A barbershop view." *Christian Science Monitor*, December 5, pp. 1, 3.

Wyatt, G. E. 1992. "The sociocultural context of African American and white American women's rape." *Journal of Social Issues* 48:77–92.

Young, A. A. 2004. *The Minds of Marginalized Black Men: Making Sense of Mobility, Opportunity, and Future Life Chances*. Princeton, N.J.: Princeton University Press.

Zinn, M. B., and B. T. Dill. 1996. "Theorizing difference from multiracial feminism." *Feminist Studies* 22:321–31.

Zinn, M. B., and D. S. Eitzen. 2002. *Diversity in Families*. Boston: Allyn & Bacon.

Shirley A. Hill is a professor of sociology at the University of Kansas whose work focuses on social inequality, families, and health care issues. She is the author of *Managing Sickle Cell Disease in Low-Income Families* (Temple University Press, 1994) and *African American Children: Socialization and Development in Families* (Sage, 1999).